Welcon

THE
EVERYTHING
DOG BREED GUIDES ®

AS THE OWNER of a particular type of dog—or someone who is thinking about adopting one—you probably have some questions about that dog breed that can't be answered anywhere else. In particular, you want to know what breed-specific health issues and behavioral traits might arise as you plan for the future with your beloved canine family member.

THE EVERYTHING® DOG BREED GUIDES give you clear-cut answers to all your pressing questions. These authoritative books give you all you need to know about identifying common characteristics; choosing the right puppy or adult dog; coping with personality quirks; instilling obedience; and raising your pet in a healthy, positive environment.

THE EVERYTHING® DOG BREED GUIDES are an extension of the bestselling EVERYTHING® series in the pets category, which include *The Everything® Dog Book* and *The Everything® Dog Training and Tricks Book*. These authoritative, family-friendly books are specially designed to be one-stop guides for anyone looking to explore a specific breed in depth.

Visit the entire Everything® series at www.everything.com

THE EVERYTHING

Chihuahua Book

Dear Reader,

Thinking about purchasing a Chihuahua puppy? Adopting a rescued adult Chihuahua? Or just interested in more information on the Chihuahua you already own and treasure? I wrote this book with you in mind.

For the soon-to-be owner, I've included lots of good, solid Chihuahua information. You'll find everything from how to find a healthy, sound Chihuahua to how to care for him throughout all the stages of his life. From birth to geriatrics, the information is here.

If you are adopting a rescued Chihuahua, I've included special information that applies specifically to integrating the previously owned dog into your home successfully. These Chis are terrific dogs, but if you adopt one that needs a little work, you'll know exactly what to do and where to find the help you need.

And not to leave out the seasoned Chihuahua owner, I hope I've unearthed some new and unique tidbits about the breed and also given you some food for thought when it comes to adding another Chihuahua to your life.

I hope you find reading this book as entertaining and enlightening as owning your Chihuahua will be!

¡Hasta luego!

Joan H. Wal

THE
EVERYTHING
CHIHUAHUA
BOOK

A complete guide to raising, training,
and caring for your Chihuahua

Joan Hustace Walker

Adams Media
Avon, Massachusetts

To my scrappy little guy with a big heart, r.w.

....

Publishing Director: Gary M. Krebs
Associate Managing Editor: Laura Daly
Associate Copy Chief: Brett Palana-Shanahan
Acquisitions Editor: Kate Burgo
Associate Development Editor: Jessica LaPointe
Production Editor: Casey Ebert

Director of Manufacturing: Susan Beale
Associate Director of Production: Michelle Roy Kelly
Cover Design: Paul Beatrice, Erick DaCosta, Matt LeBlanc
Layout and Graphics: Colleen Cunningham, Holly Curtis, Sorae Lee

An Everything® Series Book.
Everything® and everything.com® are registered trademarks of F+W Publications, Inc.

Published by Adams Media, an F+W Publications Company
57 Littlefield Street, Avon, MA 02322 U.S.A.
www.adamsmedia.com

ISBN 10: 1-59337-527-1
ISBN 13: 978-1-59337-527-0
Printed in Canada.

J I H G F E D C B

Library of Congress Cataloging-in-Publication Data

Walker, Joan Hustace
The everything chihuahua book : a complete guide to raising, training,
and caring for your chihuahua / Joan Hustace Walker.
p. cm.
Includes index.
ISBN 1-59337-527-1
1. Chihuahua (Dog breed) I. Title.

SF429.C45W35 2006
636.76--dc22

2005034600

This publication is designed to provide accurate and authoritative information with regard to the subject matter covered. It is sold with the understanding that the publisher is not engaged in rendering legal, accounting, or other professional advice. If legal advice or other expert assistance is required, the services of a competent professional person should be sought.

—From a Declaration of Principles jointly adopted by a Committee of the American Bar Association and a Committee of Publishers and Associations

Many of the designations used by manufacturers and sellers to distinguish their products are claimed as trademarks. Where those designations appear in this book and Adams Media was aware of a trademark claim, the designations have been printed with initial capital letters.

Interior Photography: Jean Fogle, *www.jeanfogle.com*

This book is available at quantity discounts for bulk purchases.
For information, call 1-800-289-0963.

- **Height:** Small and compact, usually between six and nine inches at the shoulder

- **Weight:** Average weight is four to six pounds; however, very small dogs may mature at two pounds, larger dogs may weigh as much as ten pounds

- **Head:** A well-rounded, domed head with large, wide-set, luminous eyes

- **Ears:** Large ears that are erect when alert

- **Feet:** Small and petite

- **Tail:** Somewhat long, carried up, out, or curled over the back

- **Coat:** Short and long coats; all colors in any combination of markings

- **Topline:** Level

- **Movement:** Swift, strong with head carried proudly

- **Temperament:** Loving, devoted, cheerful; bonds strongly with one person but will love an entire family, can be overly protective or fearful if not socialized early on in life

Acknowledgments

This book is only possible through the kindness and expertise of many knowledgeable Chihuahua fanciers, including Barb Pendergrass (Rafina Chihauhuas), Nick De Pompa (Chihuahua Toy Breed Rescue and Retirement), Lynn George (Poco Hacienda Chihuahuas), Robin Colley (Animal Haus Chihuahuas), Lynnie Bunten (National Rescue Chairperson for the Chihuahua Club of America and owner of Kachina Chihuahuas), and Michele Giroux (Proux Chihuahuas). I realize it was a lot of material to go through, but I so appreciate your help and dedication to this wonderful breed. And, of course, thanks go to Christine Neering, D.V.M., for making sure all my veterinary medical advice is sound, accurate, and up-to-date.

Contents

Chapter 12: Working with Multiple Dogs 163

Chapter 13: A New Way of Training 175

Chapter 14: A Few Basic Commands 187

Introduction

The Chihuahua has skyrocketed in popularity within the past decade. Television commercials featuring the breed as spokes-canine, movies starring this toy breed, and public appearances of the Chi in the arms (or fashionable handbags) of well-known television stars, singers, musicians, and movie stars have all helped to make the Chihuahua the dog of the moment, the dog everyone wants to be seen with and own.

Even without this celebrity status, the Chihuahua has been a favored breed almost since its introduction in this country. The reasons for this are many. The Chihuahua—in both short and long coats—is a very attractive dog. With the breed's wide variations in color, patterns, and markings, Chis offer a certain degree of uniqueness (no two are ever alike) to their owners. And, of course, what really makes this breed is the Chi's temperament. These dogs are loving, devoted, playful, a bit feisty (think terrier), and brave. (Chis have died trying to protect their owners.)

Dogs of this breed will make you laugh out loud at their crazy antics; gasp as they ricochet off your furniture and walls in wild, exuberant play; sigh with contentment when they curl up to sleep in your lap or softly kiss your cheeks; and groan as you discover the *latest* trouble your little mischief-maker has gotten into. The Chihuahua will take you through a whole range of emotions and experiences during her lifetime. And it's virtually a guarantee that when the time comes for her to leave this world that you, too, will shed a tear and agree that even a long-lived breed never lives long enough. The Chihuahua, without a doubt, will be the pet you remember forever.

Of course, your enjoyment and richness of experience with a Chihuahua rests heavily on two factors. First is the Chihuahua's breeding, which not only affects how she looks but more importantly how healthy she will be in her lifetime, and what sort of temperament she is hard-wired to have. Second is you, the owner. Even the best-bred Chihuahua with tremendous potential to succeed as a wonderful pet can fail if you cannot give the dog the care, attention, and upbringing she needs.

Unfortunately, thousands of Chihuahuas wind up in shelters, pounds, and rescues across the country or are euthanized because of poor breeding practices or poor ownership. Sickly Chihuahua puppies are not unusual, nor are adult Chis with rotten temperaments and/or expensive, chronic health issues. It's a heartbreaking situation when a family does all the right things (provides good nutrition, preventive veterinary care, exercise, socialization, and training) and the Chihuahua is still unhealthy or has an overly aggressive or fearful temperament.

On the other hand, just as many Chihuahuas wind up unwanted because their owners couldn't or wouldn't make the effort to meet the Chi's most basic needs. These are usually owners who purchased the Chihuahua on a whim and never really considered the fact that this was a dog and not a cute, cuddly toy that was pre-programmed to behave perfectly. When this owner discovers that raising and caring for a Chihuahua entails a lot more than simply providing the dog with a designer purse to ride around in—that is, that the Chihuahua eats, chews things up, relieves itself and requires housetraining, and is one of the more expensive breeds to maintain—then the dog becomes bothersome and annoying. For those who didn't think twice about purchasing a Chi, it's usually not too difficult a choice to drop the dog off and be rid of her.

The moral to this story is that the Chihuahua can make an incredible pet. It is, after all, an incredible dog. But most people are attracted to most breeds based primarily on what they've seen, or what the dog looks like. There's nothing wrong with this! But to make this highly adaptable breed a success in your home, you have to dig deeper. Learn what this dog is all about. Find out what makes this canine tick.

As you read *The Everything® Chihuahua Book*, hopefully you'll get a very good feel for this breed's distinctive needs, the problems you might encounter raising a Chi if you choose to purchase a puppy or adopt a rescued adult, and how you might have to adapt your lifestyle to make this breed work in your home and life.

Where there's a will, there's always a way to succeed with the Chihuahua. As long as you know what you're getting into and appreciate the level of commitment you will need to make for this loving dog, the Chihuahua will repay your kindness and care with a life as full of excitement and love as she is possible of giving. And for a Chihuahua, that's a whole lotta love.

A Dog Without Borders

The Chihuahua is one of the most popular breeds in the world—and for good reason. The breed's portable size, plucky personality, two coat lengths, and wide variation in coloration and markings, combined with the Chihuahua's uncanny ability to totally charm her "humans," has made this breed a favored pet for centuries.

Ancient Beginnings

The Chihuahua is thought to have its origins date back to the ninth century—prior to the Mayan civilization. References to the Chihuahua's progenitors appear throughout the legends, artifacts, and artwork of Mexico and Central and South America's ancient civilizations. The pyramids of Cholula contain materials (predating 1530) showing a dog that strongly resembles the modern-day Chihuahua. Relics from the Mayan ruins of Chichen Itza on the Yucatan Peninsula reveal additional visual proof that a Chihuahua-like dog existed during the fifth century.

One of the ancient breeds believed to have played a significant part in the development of today's Chihuahua was the Techichi—a longhaired, small breed that was raised by the Toltecs, possibly as early as the ninth century, and that existed with the Aztecs into the fourteenth century. The Techichi was not as diminutive as today's Chihuahua; rather, it was sturdier and heavier boned.

 **fact**

Small companion dogs historically have been a luxury of royalty or those of high social standing who could afford to own a dog for companionship only. Working-class people may still have owned dogs as companions; however, their dogs also had to have a worthy skill (such as herding livestock or pulling produce-laden carts) in order to literally earn their keep.

A closer representative of today's Chihuahua may have occurred with the crossing of the Techichi with a much smaller, possibly hairless dog. The hairless dog's origination is under debate. Some historians feel that it came from Asia and crossed the land bridge (now the Bering Strait) into North America. Others point out that records and artifacts show small, hairless dogs that were sacrificed along with the Techichi by the Toltecs.

 **Question?**

Are Chihuahuas part fox?
The Chihuahua does have an uncanny resemblance to a tiny desert animal—*Fennecus zerda*, or the Fennec fox. Luminous eyes, large erect ears, small feet, and a preference for living in packs of ten to twelve, the Fennec fox shares many characteristics of the Chihuahua. In 1980, the Fennec fox was successfully bred to Chihuahuas—an interspecies cross previously thought impossible.

Another opinion is that the Techichi was crossed not with a hairless dog but rather with a small shorthaired dog. Small dogs such as these were evident in many Indian tribes, including those that lived in the Southwest United States, Mexico, and Central and South America. The Maltese may also have been involved. The most compelling evidence of this is the molera, a soft spot or cranial gap in the skull that does not close entirely as the dogs mature. This physical trait is shared by the Maltese and the Chihuahua, indicating a common ancestor.

Sacred Canine

Progenitors of the Chihuahua (whether the longhaired Techichi or the dog of earlier art that more closely resembles the tiny Chihuahua of today) served a dual function in the Toltec and Aztec cultures. Not only were these small dogs favored pets, they also held significant religious status.

Historically, the color yellow was associated with death to the Toltecs and, later, to the Aztecs. Little dogs with golden-fawn coats were greatly valued as they were thought to be of great help in assisting deceased owners. A little yellow dog would be sacrificed in order to be waiting for her master in the afterlife. Only the companionship of the yellow dog would enable the master to make the perilous journey, which included navigating across wide, dangerous rivers to the Toltec's and Aztec's visions of heaven.

 Fact

> Montezuma II, the last of the Aztec rulers, apparently didn't want to take any chances that he wouldn't make it to Mictlan, the realm of the dead, when he died. It is reported that the ruler owned hundreds of Chihuahuas at his palace. Presumably, many—if not all—were the yellow-fawn dogs with their special powers in the afterlife.

Yellow dogs were not the only revered color of dog, however. According to some historians, red Chihuahua-like dogs may also have played a significant role in religious ceremonies. Red represented temptation, and dogs of this color were thought to possess the ability to assume the sins of the dearly departed. Unfortunately for the dog, that meant that the animal would be burned in the deceased's funeral pyre.

Latin America's Pet

The spread of the popularity of the Chihuahua north to northern Mexico and south to South America is widely attributed to the arrival of the Spanish conquistadors in the early 1500s. According to this theory, the Spaniards not only took these dogs with them as they conquered and pillaged, they also brought back Chihuahua-like dogs to Europe.

Some dog historians contest this theory. These researchers claim that the more likely result of the Spaniards' exploration and presence was the near decimation of all domestic dogs existing at the time. Upon their arrival, conquistadors enslaved the Aztec people. Aztecs, along with many other older civilizations, raised dogs not only for religious reasons and as pets but also for food.

 Esseñtial

> Another theory is that Spaniards brought black-and-tan terrier-type dogs with them and that this dog interbred with the Tolchichi to develop into today's Chihuahua. Though one would think that only the bare essentials would have been onboard the Spanish galleons that were already loaded with men, horses, and supplies, a rat-killing terrier might have been of benefit onboard ships noted for rodent infestations.

Dogs raised for consumption, of course, were raised as live-stock—typically larger in size, neutered, and fattened up with corn. The Aztecs had no need to eat their smaller dogs, which wouldn't have made much of a meal anyway. Under the cruel servitude of the Spaniards, however, the Aztecs were no longer in a position to raise these smaller dogs strictly as a luxury and religious item. Faced with starvation, the Aztecs could have turned to their revered, smaller dogs for survival.

The Spanish conquistadors likely turned to dog as a common meal during food shortages, too. Armies of conquistadors (whose horses required grain and depleted this source of food) are attributed with not only wiping out entire native civilizations from Florida through Mexico and into Central America, but also with raiding Indian tribes' camps for thousands of domestic dogs, whether they were raised as working dogs, a source of food, or as religious and luxury items.

The Dog from Chihuahua

The history of the Chihuahua and its predecessors is a bit murky from the 1500s to the early 1800s, a time period in which very few artifacts exist to record the dog's presence. But then the little dogs begin showing up in northwestern Mexico, specifically in Chihuahua, Mexico—the country's largest state (occupying 12.5 percent of Mexico's land mass), bordering Texas and New Mexico.

During those years in which records of the little dog of Mexico are scanty, many other cultures and *their* dogs could have played a role in the development of the diminutive Chihuahua of today. In addition to the arrival of Spaniards (from the 1600s to the early 1800s), the area was home to more than 200 different Indian tribes (including Apaches, present in the 1500s and 1600s) as well as Chinese railroad workers and German settlers in the 1800s, when Mexico was briefly part of the Austro-Hungarian empire.

In the late 1800s, enterprising Mexicans began selling small dogs (longhaired, shorthaired, and no-haired) to American tourists at border markets. It was natural then for the popular dog to be given the name "Chihuahua," after the Mexican state in which it was sold. In fact, all varieties were at one point called Chihuahuas; however, the hairless variety was later determined to be a separate breed and has now become the Mexican hairless. As for the Chihuahua, canine historians eventually discovered how wide-spread Chihuahua-like dogs were throughout Mexico and further south—a discovery that came too late for anyone who wanted to make changes to the breed's name.

 **Fact**

Generalissimo Antonio Lopez de Santa Anna (1794–1896), the cruel five-time president of Mexico, reportedly owned large numbers of small golden-fawn dogs that went into battle with him. After the military defeat that gave Texas its independence in 1836, a pack of little yellow dogs were reputedly found in his camp. Perhaps the general, too, feared death and wanted the presence of these dogs to ensure safe passage into the afterlife.

Recognition in North America

The cute, feisty little dog of Chihuahua is one of the oldest registered breeds in the United States; however, it was slow to become a popular pet. The first Chihuahua, Midget, was registered in 1904 in the American Kennel Club (AKC) registry. Ten years later, registrations were up to thirty dogs a year. The Chihuahua reached its peak in popularity in 1964, earning a twelfth-most-popular breed ranking that year.

Of course, the Chihuahua has also come a long way since the days of Midget, and even since those Chihuahuas of the 1960s, not only in terms of popularity and numbers but in looks as well. Previously, the conformation of the Chihuahua was much leggier with a more pointed head and larger, erect ears than the Chi of today (think of the Taco Bell dog). Today, the breed is more compact, with a much shorter muzzle, a rounder head, and larger, rounder eyes.

◀ Chihuahuas are very friendly dogs that love people and attention!

It is possible to find both conformation styles in the Chihuahua world today. The leggier, older breed type is often referred to as a deer Chihuahua. The Chihuahua that more closely adheres to the Chihuahua Club of America's (CCA) breed standard is referred to as the apple- or dome-headed Chihuahua.

Chihuahua Breed Standard

The standard for any dog breed specifically outlines the qualities that the breed should ideally exhibit. These are the qualities that reputable breeders breed for, and they include temperament as well as appearance. Conformation refers to how closely the dogs approach the ideal. Dogs that conform very closely to the breed standard—in both appearance and temperament—might be considered "show quality." A fine dog with a pleasant temperament that does not conform as closely to the breed standard would be considered "pet quality." Pet quality dogs are not lesser dogs; they might only be a nonstandard color or have slightly too-large ears, for example. A pet quality Chihuahua might simply be one that weighs a little over 6 pounds—enough deviation from the breed standard to disqualify him from the show ring, but not enough to affect his status as a great companion.

The official breed standard for the Chihuahua, as published by the American Kennel Club (and made available on their Web site, at *www.akc.org*), is as follows:

 Breed Standard

General Appearance:
A graceful, alert, swift-moving little dog with saucy expression, compact, and with terrier-like qualities of temperament.

Size, Proportion, Substance:
Weight—A well balanced little dog not to exceed 6 pounds. Proportion—The body is off-square; hence, slightly longer when measured from point of shoulder to point of buttocks, than height at the withers. Somewhat shorter bodies are preferred in males. Disqualification—Any dog over 6 pounds in weight.

Head:
A well-rounded "apple-dome" skull, with or without molera. Expression—Saucy. Eyes—Full, but not protruding, balanced, set well apart, luminous dark or luminous ruby. (Light eyes in blond or white-colored dogs permissible.) Ears—Large, erect type ears, held more upright when alert, but flaring to the sides at a 45 degree angle when in repose, giving breadth between the ears. Muzzle—Moderately short, slightly pointed.

Cheeks and jaws lean. Nose—Self-colored in blond types, or black. In moles, blues, and chocolates, they are self-colored. In blond types, pink nose permissible. Bite—Level or scissors. Overshot or undershot bite, or any distortion of the bite or jaw, should be penalized as a serious fault. Disqualifications—Broken down or cropped ears.

Neck, Topline, Body:

Neck—Slightly arched, gracefully sloping into lean shoulders. Topline—Level. Body—Ribs rounded and well sprung (but not too much "barrel-shaped"). Tail—Moderately long, carried sickle either up or out, or in a loop over the back, with tip just touching the back (never tucked between legs). Disqualifications—Cropped tail, bobtail.

Forequarters:

Shoulders—Lean, sloping into a slightly broadening support above straight forelegs that set well under, giving a free play at the elbows. Shoulders should be well up, giving balance and soundness, sloping into a level back (never down or low). This gives a chestiness, and strength of forequarters, yet not of the "Bulldog" chest. Feet—A small, dainty foot with toes well split up but not spread, pads cushioned (neither the hare nor the cat foot). Pasterns—Fine.

Hindquarters:

Muscular, with hocks well apart, neither out nor in, well let down, firm and sturdy. The feet are as in front.

Coat:

In the Smooth Coats, the coat should be of soft texture, close and glossy. (Heavier coats with undercoats permissible.) Coat placed well over body with ruff on neck preferred, and more scanty on head and ears. Hair on tail preferred furry.

In Long Coats, the coat should be of a soft texture, either flat or slightly curly, with undercoat preferred. Ears—Fringed. (Heavily fringed ears may be tipped slightly if due to the fringes and not to weak ear leather, never down.) Tail—Full and long (as a plume). Feathering on feet and legs, pants on hind legs and large ruff on the neck desired and preferred. Disqualification—In Long Coats, too thin coat that resembles bareness.

Color:

Any color—Solid, marked or splashed.

Gait:

The Chihuahua should move swiftly with a firm, sturdy action, with good reach in front equal to the drive from the rear. From the rear, the hocks remain parallel to each other, and the footfall of the rear legs follows directly behind that of the forelegs. The legs, both front and rear, will tend to converge slightly toward a central line of gravity as speed increases. The side view shows good, strong drive in the rear and plenty of reach in the front, with head carried high. The topline should remain firm and the backline level as the dog moves.

Temperament:

Alert, with terrier-like qualities.

Disqualifications:

- Any dog over 6 pounds in weight.
- Broken down or cropped ears.
- Cropped tail, bobtail.
- In Long Coats, too thin coat that resembles bareness.

Approved September 11, 1990
Effective October 30, 1990
Reprinted with permission from the Chihuahua Club of America.

Being Famous Is Not Fortunate

The Chihuahua has had several distinct periods of popularity. The first such period was during the 1930s, when Latin American music saw a simultaneous surge—particularly that of Rumba Kings. Xavier Cugat, rumba bandleader and later host of his own television show, was noted for carrying his Chihuahuas in his shirt pockets. Movie stars also were attracted to the uniqueness of the breed. Latin American actress Lupe Velez owned a very small Chihuahua named King. Perhaps adoring the drama of it all, Velez fed her Chihuahua with an eyedropper.

The second period of great popularity came roughly thirty years later, in the 1960s, and lasted about a decade, into the 1970s. In fact, the Chihuahua reached its peak in AKC rankings (calculated using registrations) in 1964. At this time, the Chihuahua is the tenth most-popular breed in the United States. However, with the current appeal of the Chihuahua among celebrities and the breed's resulting widespread visibility, the Chihuahua could easily top this record and move up in the AKC's top-ten standings in the first decade of the twenty-first century.

 Question?

Which celebrities own Chihuahuas?

The Chihuahua's popularity among female stars seems to have reached the point at which the diminutive dog is very nearly considered a much-needed fashion accessory among the Beverly Hills crowd. Paris Hilton, Britney Spears, Hilary Duff, Madonna, Jennifer Lopez, and Christina Ricci are just a few female icons frequently photographed with their Chis.

The problem with being a popular breed is that good Chis are now hard to find. Reputable Chihuahua breeders who produce quality dogs (those that possess excellent temperaments, health, and conformation) simply cannot keep up with today's skyrocketing demand for Chihuahuas. Nor do they want to meet this demand. Many—if not most—Chi pups are bought on impulse without any real thought as to the needs of this breed. The result? Hundreds and hundreds of Chihuahuas are dropped off in shelters, picked up as strays by animal-control officers, and surrendered to breed rescues.

Alert!

The Chihuahua has attracted an ugly undercurrent of human beings, too. Rescues in certain areas of the country report horror stories of Chis being tortured, abused, and killed—sometimes in a ritualistic or sacrificial manner. In addition to being inhumane and cruel, these cases also indicate a potential surge in the numbers of criminally abusive individuals (as animal torture is well linked to violent criminal behavior).

With demand far outreaching supply, every unscrupulous person interested in cashing in on the excess demand has entered the Chi picture. The result is that there are Chihuahua puppies for sale everywhere; however, very few of these pups will meet the expectations of the discerning pet owner who seeks a healthy, well-balanced companion.

Chi Strengths and Challenges

Chihuahuas present a number of unique and wonderful attributes that make them the perfect pets for many people. However, they can also have qualities and characteristics that make them a challenge to properly train and care for. When you are deciding on a Chihuahua to add to your family, make sure you are both fully aware of the breed's strengths and potential problems and ready to deal with these issues.

Strengths

Chihuahuas didn't become popular just because of their looks. The breed is a favorite among dog owners for many excellent reasons, including these:

- Small size
- Variety in coat lengths
- Solid, brindle, and spotted colors
- Light weight and easy to carry
- Can travel in-cabin
- Long lifespan (fourteen to eighteen years)
- Adaptability
- Ease of exercise
- Watchdog abilities
- Playfulness

Challenges

As with any dog breed, the Chihuahua has its own unique challenges. Many of these challenges are related to poor breeding and can be avoided by finding a quality breeder (these are indicated in the following list by an asterisk). Others have the potential to be inherent to all members of the breed:

- Extremely poor health*
- Aggressive or nervous behavior*
- Hard to housetrain
- Independent/difficult to train
- Not good with small children
- Requires coat care (longhaired variety)
- Delicate/susceptible to injury
- Yappy

- Tiny amounts of poisonous plants, foods, or chemicals can be fatal
- Seen as prey by many animals

Is This the Dog for You?

The Chihuahua can be an excellent pet in the right home with the right owner. In fact, because of its small size, the Chi can adapt to many different lifestyles quite easily. This breed can be equally as comfortable living with a retired couple in a high-rise apartment as growing up with a large family in a sprawling home in the suburbs.

The key to success in owning a Chihuahua lies with the owner. Owners must realize that despite its toy-like size and appearance, the Chihuahua is all dog. The second key is to understand that as a dog, the Chihuahua has specific needs, including socialization, training, exercise, proper nutrition, preventive veterinary care, and companionship. If you are willing and able to meet the Chihuahua's simple but important needs, the Chihuahua can make a fine, long-lived companion.

¡Yo Quiero Chihuahuas!

Y ou understand the challenges of owning a Chihuahua, as well as the benefits. And after much serious consideration, you know in your heart that this little dog is the right choice for you. Within the world of Chihuahuas, there is a huge range of Chis—from two different conformation types and coat lengths to virtually every color and marking pattern known to canines. From this wide range of Chihuahuas, you'll need to select the puppy or adult that is to become your companion for the next twelve to fifteen years or more.

Narrowing Down Your Choices

Once people have decided to purchase or adopt a specific breed of dog, it is not uncommon for them to immediately start looking at litters of puppies. Often, however, this headlong jump into searching for a Chi winds up with the individual making an impulsive, emotional choice.

There's nothing necessarily wrong with choosing the puppy or adult that strikes your fancy *and* has won your heart over virtually upon sight. Appearance and an emotional connection are certainly two factors that are important when selecting a canine companion. But just as with personal relationships that are built on love at first sight, it's often only a matter of time before you realize that the person who's swept you off your feet (or, in this case, the Chihuahua that wriggled into your heart) is neither what you thought she was nor what you were really looking for in the first place.

 **Essential**

Develop a list specifying your must-have qualities, your don't-want-these-under-any-circumstances qualities, and those breed aspects with which you are more flexible. You'll find that writing down exactly what you're looking for will enable you to choose the best puppy for you and that you'll still get to experience that love-at-first-sight puppy emotion.

When choosing a Chihuahua, the more you can focus your search before you look at that first puppy or dog, the better your chances of getting what you want. For example, by simply deciding whether you want an apple-headed Chihuahua with correct conformation or the "can't-take-it-in-the-show-ring-but-they're-still-pretty-cute" deer-type Chihuahua, you will have narrowed your search substantially.

Then there are the issues of size, color, and markings, coat type, and sex (if it matters whether you get a boy or girl). Are you absolutely set on purchasing a puppy, or would you consider a slightly more mature model? Developing a good understanding of the personal preferences you have for your new dog makes you more likely to find precisely the Chi you are looking for and one that will meet (and exceed) all of your expectations.

Of Apples and Deer

When Chihuahuas began entering the United States, the dogs' size, weight, and physical makeup varied widely. Some were long-legged. Others were short-legged. Some had longer muzzles or bigger ears. Eye shapes ranged from round to almond-shaped, and eye colors ran the gamut from dark brown to paler, tawny shades. The lack of uniformity found in these imported Chihuahuas is typical of all breeds in their early developmental stages.

When the Chihuahua Club of America (CCA) was founded in 1904, club members did some fine-tuning and determined what physical attributes they felt were the most desirable in the breed. These early Chi fanciers developed the first Chihuahua breed standard—the ideal of perfection toward which Chihuahua fanciers should breed.

 **Alert!**

Do not expect to find a choice of both the apple-head and deer conformation types in the same litter. A quality Chihuahua breeder will breed for only one type of Chihuahua, and that will be one that follows the breed standard as closely as possible—the "apple-headed" Chi.

Slight changes have been made in the Chihuahua breed standard over the years and, as is true of any breed standard, people interpret the written standard in different ways. This is how the two breed "types" most commonly seen today came into play.

During the Chihuahua's first heyday (from the 1950s to the 1960s), it was fashionable to breed leggier Chihuahuas with longer muzzles, larger ears, and more widely set eyes. Since the most popular color in the United States was (and still is) fawn, the adult dogs truly resembled small deer—therefore the name reference. The Chihuahua featured in former Taco Bell advertising is a deer-type Chihuahua. This conformation style, though endearing to many pet owners, is passé. Today, the deer type is not bred by experienced breeders who are involved in conformation.

Today's Chihuahua is a much more elegant dog—perhaps more suitable in style to the breed's history of being a favored pet and an important religious icon. The apple-headed Chihuahua, which follows the current breed standard, has a more rounded head, smaller ears, and large—almost luminous—eyes that are set forward in the dog's face. The Chi's legs are also shorter in proportion to its body, giving the dog a very balanced, symmetrical look. The effect is a very sophisticated and beautiful dog that still retains all the feistiness of its ancestors.

▲ Because of the recent publicity Chihuahuas have gotten, especially from the Taco Bell commercials, they are becoming very popular among dog owners.

Is Itty-Bitty Better?

Just as Americans have a fascination with oversized meals and immense road-warrior vehicles, we also have a love of small dogs. Really small dogs. Not since the mid-1900s have toy breeds been so popular. In fact, since 2000, four of the top ten most-popular breeds registered with the AKC have been small dogs (under twenty pounds)—with the Chihuahua holding steady as one of those four.

From time to time, a breeder may have a runt, or an exceptionally small puppy, born to a litter. This small pup is not special. He is not more valuable than his larger littermates. He does not command a higher price for his so-called rarity. He's just small. In fact, a very small puppy can require more veterinary care early on and take longer to wean from his mother.

 **fact**

According to the breed standard, the Chihuahua is not to weigh more than six pounds. Those exceeding this weight can still make terrific pets; however, they would be disqualified in the show ring. The reputable breeder tries to breed dogs that conform to the standard, usually weighing between three and six pounds.

As you can probably surmise, enterprising entrepreneurs figured out that there was a market for people who wanted a dog so small she would fit in their breast pockets or ride in a petite purse. These folks even gave Chihuahuas (that would not weigh more than one to two pounds at full maturity) special names in order to market them as being something very extraordinary, rare and, of course, expensive: "teacup," "pocket-size," "miniature," "tiny toys," and "tiny teacup" are just a few of those names.

It's okay to want a very small Chihuahua; however, you might want to keep the following things in mind:

- While a quality breeder does not breed for extremely small sizes, a quality breeder may still have a tiny Chihuahua show up in a litter.
- It often takes longer for these very little guys to begin thriving, so an experienced breeder will hold the occasional tiny puppy longer (more than twelve weeks) to make sure she is healthy and flourishing.
- Very small Chihuahuas may be more susceptible to a variety of illnesses and conditions, including hypoglycemia.

- Surgery, medications, and anesthesia can be more complex and expensive with the tiny Chihuahua.
- The only differentiation the CCA makes within the breed is coat type; there is no division according to size (such as the size division of toy, miniature, and standard that apply to the poodle, for instance).
- Chihuahua pups are small as it is, and a very small puppy requires even more attention from the owner to ensure her safety.
- Tiny Chihuahuas tend to remain frail and prone to injury throughout their adult lives.

If you really want a very small Chihuahua, do not seek a puppy from someone who advertises or breeds exclusively for exceptionally small dogs. It is not considered healthy or wise to breed for size. Find a quality breeder, and then wait for him to produce a small one. You very well might find that while you're waiting, a healthy, robust average-sized Chihuahua is plenty small and just what you're really looking for.

Not Just Fawning over Fawn

Solid fawn is probably the most popular and commonly seen color for Chihuahuas in the United States. Other colors seen with some regularity are cream (solid or particolor), black with tan markings or a splash of white on the chest, and red, also often with white markings. Less commonly seen are solid black, blue (a dilution of black), or chocolate. Unique markings, such as white with splashes of color, brindle (darker stripes running through a coat color), sable (black hairs in another color, such as red or fawn), and merle.

Rare colors—such as merles and many of the dilutes (such as the blues and chocolates)—often command prices in the thousands of dollars. If you are dealing with a reputable breeder, however, he will charge the same amount for a rare color as he would for a more common color, such as fawn. The only time he might charge more for a certain puppy is if she is show quality rather than pet quality.

 **Question?**

What exactly is a merle coat?
Present but uncommon in Chihuahuas, the merle coat is typically blue-grayish in color (but can also be reddish) and has varying patches of black throughout. Merles usually have one or two blue eyes or a brown eye that is marked with a splash of blue. Double merles (the offspring of two merle parents) have a higher risk of deafness and eye disorders.

Be wary, too, of the breeder who breeds for a certain rare color. A quality breeder will breed for health, temperament, and conformation. To breed for color alone is to put the most important companion dog qualities on the back burner, which can be disastrous. If you must have a rare color, make sure that the breeder has tested for (and has proof that the dam and sire are free of) deafness and blindness, as well as luxating patella, heart disease, and other potentially debilitating conditions common to the breed.

The Long and Short of Coats

The Chihuahua comes in two coat lengths: short- or smooth-haired and longhaired. Short- and longhaired Chihuahuas are considered different varieties within the breed and are shown in separate classes. Chis with different coat lengths can and often are bred to each other, which means it is not uncommon to find both short-haired and longhaired puppies born to the same litter.

Shorthaired

If you want a very maintenance-free, wash-and-wear kind of dog, consider the shorthaired Chihuahua. Though she will enjoy brushing, daily grooming is not necessary to keep this coat looking nice. Because the shorthaired Chihuahua doesn't have much hair and is very small (with little body fat), she will need to wear a jacket or sweater (made to fit, of course) for outside walks in cooler weather.

 Fact

At one time, the CCA allowed shorthaired Chihuahuas to be bred to a variety of long-coated toy breeds to reintroduce the longhaired coat and to add substance and length to those longhaired Chis already in existence.

Longhaired

Longhaired coats are more of a commitment. The Chihuahua's long coat is soft and can be substantial, a combination that makes it susceptible to matting. This coat requires regular brushing (daily is best). Don't let the long hair fool you; this Chi will still require bundling up before trips outside on nippy days.

Additionally, bathing a longhaired Chi requires some diligence. All shampoo must be rinsed thoroughly out of the coat, and the entire coat must be blown dry, all the way down to the skin. If you are already pressed for time in your life, adding these essential grooming requirements may put you on overload. Also, if you have difficulties manipulating your hands or have arthritis, you might ask your physician if brushing will help or cause further injury to your condition.

Male Versus Female

Many dog owners tend to anthropomorphize, or attribute human characteristics to their dogs. For instance, it is a commonly held belief that girl dogs are sweet, gentle, nurturing, and loving, while boy dogs aren't very affectionate, are rough and tumble, and are more likely to be protective and/or act aggressively. Nothing could be further from the truth.

Males

Male dogs are often the more loving and tolerant of the two sexes, particularly if they are neutered, or altered. Altering a male dog accomplishes many things. First, the dog is not on the search for females in season, which makes it less likely that he will want to escape and roam the neighborhood. Second, the dog is not as likely to mark in your home. Third, if a dog has any propensity toward being aggressive, neutering can often significantly lessen this undesirable trait. And finally, neutering eliminates the risk of certain cancers.

 **Alert!**

The majority of stray dogs picked up by animal-control officers are unneutered males. Additionally, the majority of dogs hit by cars have not been neutered.

Females

Female canines are less likely to be tolerant of any human action they find annoying or threatening. In other words, a female may be quicker to snap for smaller infractions. (Think of it in terms of a mother dog feeling it's her obligation to correct her puppies.) Females can also be less tolerant than neutered males of other dogs. Though Chihuahuas love to be pack animals (particularly when the other dogs are Chis), when a female dog decides she needs to be the ruler of the pack, she can be quite obstinate about it.

Altering or spaying a female prevents many reproductive cancers, unwanted pregnancies, and the mess of a dog in season. Altering does *not* mellow a female in the same way that neutering an aggressive male can.

Which to Choose?

So, which sex is for you? Chihuahua breeders often recommend looking at the temperament and characteristics of each individual puppy rather than focusing on one sex. If, however, you already own a Chi and want to add another, the best choice (the one with the least likelihood of starting a long-term argument) is a Chi of the opposite sex—both altered, of course!

Activity Level

The bad news is that the Chihuahua has one of the highest energy levels of any purebred dog. The good news is that the exercise needs for the Chihuahua are easy to meet whether you live in the city or the suburbs. Remember, the Chi is not a very big dog, so short walks are often enough to do the trick.

Additionally, not all Chihuahuas have the same energy level. Some are over the top while others seem to be more content to just follow you around and hop into your lap from time to time. If you specifically want a Chi that is not dashing madly up and over furniture throughout your house, demanding regular walks, or constantly underfoot with a ball in her mouth asking for yet another game of fetch, you have one of two options.

First, you can make "lower activity level" a must-have attribute when looking at puppies. Breeders should be able to tell you how energetic individual puppies in a litter are, as well as show you what you can expect when the pups mature by looking at the parents' exercise needs. Another option is to adopt a mature Chihuahua, as discussed in Chapter 4. Adult dogs are always a bit less active than ricocheting puppies, and their present activity level and exercise needs are a known commodity.

 Essential

If you are not very mobile or live in an apartment where access to walking areas is limited, the Chihuahua's need for exercise can still be satisfied. Chihuahuas are very playful and most will enthusiastically chase a ball or favorite toy. With the Chi's small size, an enthusiastic, energetic game of fetch can easily be played in a room or in the hall.

Temperaments

Chihuahuas as a whole tend to be devoted to their owners, friendly with other dogs and house pets, and a little reserved but cordial when meeting and greeting nonthreatening strangers for the first time. With so many people breeding Chihuahuas (and often not seeking a good temperament), the Chihuahua's temperament can range from exceptionally timid and nervous to highly protective and overly bold, instigating fights with dogs, usually those at least twenty times the Chi's body weight.

Of course, each Chihuahua is a unique individual, and as such, her temperament hinges on the qualities she has inherited from her parents and the environment in which she is raised. Your best predictor of a puppy's potential temperament is to observe and meet her parents. Keep in mind that Chihuahuas *do* tend to be a bit reserved and cautious when meeting strangers; however, they should be curious and alert—not cowering and shaking in another room or barking, snapping, and lunging incessantly at you.

Keep in mind, too, that you will only have so much influence on your Chihuahua's temperament at maturity. Puppies are genetically prewired for a certain disposition, and your efforts will only go so far in improving on what the puppy already has. For example, you may never quite be able to transform a cowering Chi into an extrovert, no matter how much socialization and confidence building training you do (though these efforts will go very far in achieving this goal). Your best bet is to find a breeder who breeds with sound, friendly temperaments in mind and whose puppies are predisposed for this temperament.

 Question?

What is "pancaking," and does it mean the dog is shy?
Pancaking is the term used for when a Chihuahua is startled and literally flattens itself to the ground—like a pancake. This action is thought to be instinctive and a reflexive response to what the dog perceives as a predator or a threat to her survival. It is not indicative of a shy or timid dog.

Puppy or Adult?

Raising a puppy and adopting an adult dog can both be memorable and heartwarming experiences. Both come with challenges and benefits. Determine what aspects of dog ownership you are most interested in, as these can influence whether a puppy or a rescued adult would be best for your lifestyle and current situation.

Puppies

Chihuahua pups need the same training as any other dog. A lot of a puppy owner's time is spent in socializing and training the puppy in order that it can become a good companion and a good canine. Of course, raising a puppy means that you are the pup's greatest influence, and you will be able to shape your Chihuahua into the adult dog he will become.

Puppies need diligent housetraining; the owner must be able to have the time and make the effort to achieve success in this area. Chi pups are very small, so while the puppy is learning, the potential mess is not nearly that of an untrained adult dog. Additionally, puppies go through a teething period in which anything and everything is a potential chew item. And puppies aren't just energetic—they're *highly* energetic. This is most likely why Chi puppies are so adorable; they have to be in order to make it through the first twelve months!

Adults

Adult dogs offer the pet owner the ability to know precisely what she is adopting. The dog's temperament is fully formed at this time. She's finished growing, so there are no guesses as to final size and weight. An adult dog is still energetic; however, it's not the same extraordinary level of energy as a puppy. With an adult dog, you'll be aware of her good (and undesirable) behaviors, as well as having a good feel for the dog's health status since many diseases are detectable in an adult and not in a puppy.

A potential downside to adopting an adult dog is that you won't experience the adorable but fleeting puppy stage. On the flip side, you've also avoided the potential destruction that goes along with puppy teething and housetraining. A rescued Chihuahua's life may also not be as long as a puppy's (because you've missed the first few years) but even this is not a given. Who really knows how long any individual dog is going to live?

Puppy Love At Any Age

Both puppy and adult Chihuahuas are wonderful to own. Each age has its advantages and disadvantages to keep in mind. If you make sure that when you select your Chihuahua you've made your decision based on research and guided by love, your choice will surely meet your expectations in a companion. After all, this is the Chihuahua we are talking about, a breed that is renowned for its affection, loyalty, and longevity. With good choices and a little luck, you will be owned by a tremendous canine companion.

CHAPTER 3

Choosing a Pup

The Chihuahua is unique in that it is considered the smallest purebred in the world. Born weighing only an ounce or two, Chi puppies often weigh less than eleven ounces by the time they are weaned and ready to go to a new home. Fitting comfortably in the palms of your cupped hands, but every bit a dog with brains and moxie, the Chihuahua puppy is the pup with the biggest "Awww" factor.

Puppies, Puppies Everywhere and Not a One to Buy

With the current fascination with toy breeds and the continued media exposure that the Chihuahua receives, one thing is certain: The Chihuahua will remain a popular breed for many years. A problem that all popular breeds have is that really good breeders can't keep up (nor do they really want to) with the newest surge in demand for puppies.

Breeding for Profit

When this happens, no matter what the breed, you are going to find that it's human nature for people to try to cash in on this deficit. There will be people who begin breeding Chihuahuas strictly for profit, not because they are interested in improving the breed's conformation, health, and temperament. No, they simply want to make money. Herein lies the problem. Whenever folks get involved in breeding dogs for profit, the dogs are considered (and treated as) livestock.

 **Question?**

Who is a backyard breeder?
The term "backyard breeder" is typically given to folks who breed a family pet to another dog. Though their hearts may be in the right place, they don't have any experience with the breed. They rarely know to test for hereditary diseases and can't take a puppy back if things don't work out. The price may be low; however, it is a "buyer beware" situation.

Cash-crop breeders are concerned with increasing their profit margins, which they can do in many ways, including the following:

- Limiting or reducing routine veterinary care of breeding animals
- Refusing to test breeding animals for genetic or hereditary diseases that could be passed on to the puppies
- Breeding marginal animals (those that do not meet the breed standard or may even have disqualifying faults)
- Breeding more than one breed of dog to maximize their market
- Breeding their animals as often as possible
- Advertising puppies as inexpensively as possible or selling to a middleman who will do the same
- Marketing any potential buyer whose credit card or check clears
- Selling the puppies for as high a price as possible

The Cost to the Dogs

These sources for puppies, often known as puppy mills, are best avoided at all costs. Conditions are often deplorable, with breeding dogs kept in cramped and frequently filthy conditions. Chihuahuas in particular suffer in these circumstances. They need human companionship and aren't physically equipped to handle extremes in temperatures.

 Essential

One of the best ways to avoid purchasing a puppy from a cash-crop breeder is to never allow a puppy to be shipped to you. Always go to the breeder's home so you can see the surroundings yourself and ask questions in person. If everything checks out (see the reputable breeder checklist on page 32) then you can travel home together with your pup.

What this translates to is that puppies from these sources are poorly bred and raised in squalid conditions. This has a variety of effects, including these:

- Makes puppies more susceptible to canine viral infections
- Increases risk of inheriting genetic diseases
- Makes puppies more apt to suffer from heavy worm, tick, and flea infestations
- Increases likelihood of less-than-average conformation (with some pups not even looking like Chihuahuas or coming from mixed parentage)
- Creates unstable range of temperaments, from exceptionally timid around humans to horribly ill-tempered. (Buyers cannot know what the temperaments of the parents are or could be.)

The Best Breeders Care

Now that you know whom not to go to for a puppy, whom should you go to in order to find a quality Chihuahua puppy? As the saying goes, quality begets quality. In other words, find a quality breeder and you will find quality dogs. For those who have not been dog fanciers for a significant number of years, being able to differentiate between a truly experienced, honest breeder and a slick operator can be difficult—until you know what to look for and what questions to ask.

Here's a checklist that can help you determine who the reputable breeders are. A reputable, experienced and honest breeder will meet all the following criteria:

- ❏ Be a member of the Chihuahua Club of America, a regional or local Chihuahua club, and/or an all-breed dog club
- ❏ Be dedicated to improving the breed, putting health and temperament first in breeding, followed closely by conformation
- ❏ Test and certify dogs for genetic diseases prior to breeding
- ❏ Raise his dogs in the home as companions—not "out back" or in a barn
- ❏ Willingly provide names and phone numbers of his veterinarian, as well as past puppy buyers for you to contact
- ❏ Want to know everything about you, what you do for a living, how many hours you spend at home or can spend with a dog, where you live, what your home is like, who lives with you and their ages, your experience with dogs, and your reasons for wanting a Chihuahua
- ❏ Require you to personally pick up your puppy; he will not allow any puppy to be shipped to you sight unseen, no matter how far away you live
- ❏ Not specialize in ultra-tiny sizes or "rare" colors or make any claims that these sizes or colors are more valuable

❑ Provide a health guarantee and a detailed contract requiring pet puppies to be altered by a certain time in order to receive full registration

❑ Always take his own dogs back, no matter what the owner's reasons

❑ Support the efforts of breed rescue

Of course, a breeder can be the most experienced and respected individual in the dog world, but if you don't find him approachable, friendly, and willing to openly and enthusiastically discuss the breed with you (and answer all your questions as if not a one of them is "dumb"), then you'll never be able to tap into his great expertise. You'll be too afraid to come to him for help when you need it the most. You need to work with a quality breeder you both respect and find easy to talk to, a breeder you can rely on throughout your Chihuahua's life.

Finding a Reputable, Knowledgeable Breeder

Knowing what makes for a great breeder and actually finding one can be two different stories. A few reputable breeders do advertise litters in the newspaper from time to time, but most don't. Newspaper advertising tends to draw a wide range of potential puppy buyers, and many breeders frankly don't want to have to sift through all the inappropriate owners—and those who claim to be something they're not—in order to find the great pet owners.

Magazine Ads

If a quality breeder is going to advertise, he will often place an announcement in the CCA's magazine in order to attract serious Chihuahua fanciers. The advertisement usually includes the full names (including all titles) of the sire and dam as well as their accomplishments (such as certain Best of Breed or Best in Group wins), and a two- to three-generation pedigree. Contact information will be given to reserve a puppy in the litter, which will require a prepayment (usually a percentage of the price of the puppy).

Web Sites

A less expensive way to advertise current show ring successes and upcoming litters is through the Internet. Many top-notch breeders have entered the electronic age and use their Web sites to keep Chihuahua fanciers updated on their kennels' accomplishments. Unfortunately, an equal number of Web sites are fronts for puppy mills, farms, or puppy brokers. It can be very difficult for someone who is new to the breed to tell the difference.

 **Alert!**

If a Web site is run by someone who is not a quality breeder, you may find telltale terms such as "tiny" or "teacup." Credit cards will be accepted, and pups will be shipped anywhere—often without any contact between buyer and seller. The use of pet names (such as Sam or Pancho) and the absence of registered names and pedigrees is another clue.

The only way you can truly see through the smoke that some "breeders" put up for the public is to call and talk to these people. Ask them direct questions, and see what answers you get. Visit the breeder in his home. Some red flags are if the breeder wants to meet you somewhere other than his home, or if he allows you to come into his home but you aren't allowed to see any dogs. Ask for referrals, and take the time to call these people.

Also, before working with a breeder—contact the American Kennel Club and ask if the breeder with whom you are working has received any fines or penalties. Though the AKC cannot police every register of puppies, they do respond to complaints and will ban offending breeders from registering any dogs for periods up to ten years. It never hurts to check. In this case, no news is good news, but it's not a guarantee of excellence by any means.

▲ Remember to never leave your Chihuahua unattended outside; she could get into mischief!

Your Best Resources

Other than the CCA's club publication, your best bet in beginning a search for a quality breeder is by calling the CCA's breeder referral service. This will connect you with several breeders in the area. There's no guarantee that any of these breeders will have any puppies available or in the near future; however, these breeders will be able to refer you to other breeders whom they trust and respect. Eventually, you will be put in contact with someone you will enjoy working with and who has the quality puppies in which you are interested.

Dog Shows

And there are always dog shows. Besides being fun to attend and a real learning experience for those uninitiated to the realm of conformation, a dog show can be a terrific place to meet area breeders in person, as well as talk to Chihuahua fanciers and owners. You will be able to learn a lot about the breed and perhaps find a breeder whose dogs you like as well as you like the breeder.

 **Essential**

Be patient when searching for a good breeder, and resist the temptation to pick up a puppy at the flea market or to ask "How much is that puppy in the window?" Taking the time to find a quality breeder who breeds quality dogs will more than compensate for any lost time in your search.

One of the best places to talk to Chihuahua fanciers at a dog show is actually far away from the ring itself. People who spend a lot of their weekend time traveling to dog shows to handle or to watch their dogs being handled can be found in the "RV Camp"— an affectionate name given to the acres of parking lot or grassy fields in which dog-show exhibitors can park their vehicles. You'll find most people in this area are relaxed and more than willing to talk about their dogs.

Other Reliable Sources

Additional sources for Chihuahua contacts would include a local Chihuahua Club's referral person or a local all-breed kennel club. National, regional, and local Chihuahua rescues can also be a good source for referrals to quality breeders. These people know better than anyone else who stands behind the dogs they breed and those who don't. And don't overlook your own veterinarian. No one is in a better position to know about breeders who raise Chihuahuas and who really put the health of their dogs and their progeny in the forefront of their breeding programs.

 Question?

When is the best time to talk to people at a dog show?
The times not to talk to an owner at a dog show are: 1) right before the owner is preparing to enter the ring; 2) during a class in which the owner or breeder has a dog being handled; and 3) any time at which the individual is intensely focused on the goings-on in the ring. Wait until a more relaxed time to approach an owner.

Health Tests and Certifications

The Chihuahua is often considered a relatively healthy breed. This may have been true prior to the most recent surge in popularity, and it still may be true of many well-bred lines of Chihuahuas. However, today the average Chihuahua has at least as many genetic diseases and chronic disorders as most other breeds.

Conscientious breeders are working to lower the numbers of dogs suffering from disease—particularly those diseases that have been proven to be hereditary. They test for these diseases and only breed dogs that have been certified free of them. All other dogs are altered so they can't perpetuate serious health problems within the breed.

Diseases for which there are tests and for which the Chihuahua has a higher predisposition to be affected by than the general dog population include luxating patellas, elbow and hip dysplasia, multiple eye diseases, and heart disease. The Orthopedic Foundation for Animals (OFA) keeps records on tests results for luxating patellas, elbow and hip dysplasia, and heart disease. The Canine Eye Registry Foundation (CERF) maintains records for eye diseases. (Dogs need to be tested annually for CERF; only one test result is required for OFA if the dog is twenty-four months or older.)

 fact

Not all diseases have tests that can determine if a dog has a disease or is carrying it. For these diseases—and for those that affect the Chihuahua but there is no proof that it is genetic in nature—a dedicated breeder will track the occurrence in his lines. Diseases or conditions that fall into this category would include epilepsy and collapsed trachea.

Contracts and Health Guarantees

Almost all breeders—with the exception of backyard breeders—have some sort of contract for their puppy buyers, which contains a health guarantee. If you're working with a reputable breeder and are buying a pet-quality dog or one that is not going to be shown, the breeder's contract will stipulate that the puppy is altered and is not to be bred—ever.

The breeder can accomplish this in one of several ways. He can hold the puppy's registration until you send proof that you've altered the puppy (a notice from your veterinarian), or he may give you a limited registration for your puppy. A limited registration is just that: limited. If the dog is ever bred, the AKC will not allow registration of those puppies. Since most people want to buy AKC-registerable puppies, this squashes any ideas of breeding the Chihuahua.

Another approach that breeders can take is to make sure that the puppy is altered before you pick her up. The latest research indicates that no problems are associated with altering male puppies as young as seven weeks, though it is now recommended that female puppies not be spayed until they have reached twelve weeks. All of this is contingent upon the health and vigor of the individual puppy at the time.

 **Alert!**

If a breeder uses any registry other than the AKC, the Canadian Kennel Club (CKC—not to be confused with the Continental Kennel Club) or the FCI (an international registry), it is highly likely that the puppies are not registerable with the AKC. Watch out. You're not dealing with a quality breeder, and it could well be that you're not dealing with a purebred Chihuahua, either.

The health contract is designed to protect you. It guarantees that the puppy does not have any serious diseases at the time of sale. You have between twenty-four and seventy-two hours to have this confirmed by your veterinarian. If your puppy tests positive for a dreaded disease or has a serious pre-existing condition, you generally have the option of returning the puppy and have your money returned to you or exchanging the sick puppy for a healthy one.

Some breeders go even further and guarantee that their puppies are free from hereditary diseases. This may or may not be limited in years. A very few breeders even provide a buyer with the option of returning the puppy and receiving another pup if the Chihuahua is found to suffer from a genetic-based disease at any time in her life.

The Puppy's Parents

You've found a breeder you think you like, and you're going to visit a litter of puppies. What should you be looking for? One of the best predictors of a puppy's temperament is the temperament of the puppy's parents. Temperament is roughly 60 percent inherited, which means pups are born with a predisposition to be easygoing, nervous, timid, or aggressive. The other 40 percent is attributed to environment. In other words, how close a puppy comes to fulfilling its genetic potential hinges on how the puppy is raised by you.

Nature and Nurture

If a puppy that is predisposed to be very shy is raised with an experienced owner who works on the pup's socialization skills, is dedicated to building the dog's self-confidence, and in general, is experienced in bringing shy dogs out of their shells, that puppy may develop into a fairly friendly dog. On the other hand, if raised in the wrong hands, a pup that is born predisposed to be outgoing and gregarious could become intensely fearful or swing the other way and become irritable and snippy.

What You Want to See

Without a doubt, it is best to start off with the best genetics can offer. As noted, the best way to do this is to examine the breeder's adult Chis. Keep in mind that Chihuahuas as a breed are not exceptionally outgoing. This is not a breed that warms up the moment a stranger walks in the door. The Chihuahua, however, is not to retreat to another room with her tail tucked between her legs, nor is she to come flying for your jugular with teeth bared. What you are looking for is a well-balanced Chi. If the dog stays with her owner but doesn't appear fearful, nervous, or aggressive, she is likely to be of even temperament. If she warms up quickly to you and seeks affection, you have an added bonus of congeniality.

 Essential

Do not be alarmed if only the female dog is on the breeder's premises. This is not to be considered suspicious or a red flag of any sort. Quality breeders often seek stud dogs from other lines to improve upon their own breeding. Artificial insemination is also becoming much more common, meaning that the stud dog may actually be thousands of miles away.

The Rest of the Gang

Now you'll want to see the rest of the litter. With Chihuahuas, this may be as few as two puppies or as many as five. Even though many of these pups may already be spoken for, it is still important to see how the puppies interact with each other. Much can be gleaned about the pups' true temperaments by observing them during playtime.

Keep in mind that how a puppy plays on any given day at any given time can differ, which is why it is really optimal if you can see the litter two or three times before selecting a puppy. One day a puppy may appear sluggish and dull because she just ate and is ready for a nap. The next time you see the litter, this same pup could be ricocheting off the walls, tackling her littermates and being mouthy. She just woke up.

When watching the puppies play, you will generally observe one that is bossier than the rest. This puppy is okay; you'd rather have a bold Chihuahua than a shrinking violet. What you don't want, however, is the puppy that is acting like a bully. This is the one that is constantly hassling the other puppies and just doesn't seem to figure out when enough is enough. Be forewarned that she is likely to have this attitude with you, too.

Though it is human nature to want to hold and nurture the very timid puppy, this is not a good idea. As noted previously, those pups predisposed to be timid can be some of the most difficult and complex puppies to raise into calm, less anxious adult dogs. It can be done, but it requires dedication and some experience.

The best puppies are those that seem to have gotten the idea that it's fun to play with other puppies. These puppies understand when enough is enough; however, they're always up for playing. Fortunately, this kind of puppy usually makes up the majority of the litter—or should. If you see a litter and they are all terribly shy, avoid them all. This is another sign of poor breeding and/or poor breeding practices (such as a breeder who has not spent any time socializing the pups with humans).

▲ Chihuahua pups are very playful and love outdoor games.

Finding That Perfect Puppy

After you've observed the puppies together as a group, it is time to examine the pups individually. It's a rough job, but someone's got to do it. What you're looking for are any signs of disease or infection. You will want to make sure that the pup you fall in love with will be a healthy and happy companion for years to come.

What to Look For

When holding the puppy, examine her coat. Is it smooth? Full? Or are there signs of hair loss? Look at the pup's skin. It should be soft and supple without any cuts, gashes, sores, or signs of fleas (such as tiny dark spots of flea dirt), or tick bites. You'll also want to look for any signs of discharge from any of the puppy's orifices. You should not see any material there, clear or otherwise. How does the puppy look overall? The pup's eyes, ears, and legs should all look symmetrical. She should move without any signs of soreness or limping.

 **Question?**

How old do Chihuahua puppies need to be before I can take one home?

That depends. Because toy breeds tend to take longer to wean and are therefore dependent on their mothers for a longer period of time, many breeders will keep their puppies until they are twelve weeks old. Exceptionally small puppies, those that aren't eating as much as they should (which may be susceptible to hypoglycemia), or any puppy that is just not thriving yet, should be kept longer by the breeder.

When the Puppy Picks You

When you've finished handling the puppies, take an objective look at them. Which puppy is the one who keeps coming back to you? Often, if given an opportunity, a puppy will actually pick the owner she wants. If you are so lucky as to have a pup select you, and that puppy is available for purchase, it is very likely that you've found a canine partner for the next decade or two. Matches in which the dog makes the selection are almost always truly made in canine heaven.

 **Alert!**

Be careful when examining Chihuahua puppies. They can break bones when dropped only a couple of feet. Also, many pups have a molera, or an area on their heads that is an open area of the skull. This requires very careful handling; your breeder can point out what this is and show you if any of the pups have it. It is not considered a fault of any kind; it's just something to be careful about.

Take Your Time

If you simply aren't impressed with any of the puppies you see or just aren't taken by any one in particular, don't worry. Wait. With a breed that is as long-lived as the Chihuahua, you don't want to settle for a puppy. Take the time to find a terrific breeder and a quality puppy that you can fall in love with—and then prepare for an incredible relationship.

Adopting an Adult Dog

When looking to adopt an adult Chihuahua, you have several choices. You can search the newspaper and adopt directly from the surrendering owner, check the local animal-control facilities, work with an area shelter, or contact a Chihuahua purebred rescue. Though a good Chi can be found at any of these sources, some require more dog smarts and knowledge than others. Here's a look at what you can expect from each source.

Charming Chis In Search of Good Owners

Want a good reason to consider adopting a rescued Chihuahua? An adult dog can be great in any of these cases:

- You have a Chi and want to add another.
- You lost a treasured senior and want another adult dog.
- Your life is so busy you don't have the time and energy to spend raising a little one.
- You like the idea of giving a great little dog a second chance at life.

Of course, no one really needs a reason to adopt. Adult Chis fit in any home and make fabulous pets.

Toy Breed Doesn't Mean "Toy"

People often think that the only reason a purebred dog would be given up to a shelter or abandoned along a country road is that there is something seriously wrong with the dog. This isn't true 99.9 percent of the time. Usually, the reason is that the dog is being a dog and exhibiting dog-like behaviors—which the owners weren't prepared to deal with.

For the Chihuahua, this is particularly true. Extensive media coverage of the breed in television commercials, print ads, movies, and as a pocket pet to the stars has fueled yet another renewed surge in interest in owning the smallest of the toy breeds. Unfortunately for Chis, puppy buyers often are not fully aware that while the Chihuahua may only weigh a few pounds, it has all the behaviors, drives, and needs of a dog. The Chihuahua is neither a stuffed animal nor a fashion accessory.

 Fact

According to recent estimates, 50 percent or more of shelter dogs are purebred, with breeds differing depending upon the part of the country. Chihuahua populations vary throughout the United States, with the West Coast being a particular hotbed of rescue activity. In the Los Angeles area alone, rescues report hundreds of Chihuahuas needing homes each month.

Just as the trend years ago was for macho guys to seek out tough-looking dogs to establish their manhood, star-struck teens and celebrity wannabes are now seeking out Chihuahuas to carry as status symbols. As soon as these individuals discover that this Chihuahua needs to relieve itself regularly, is not content to sit in a Gucci purse all day (but would rather chase and dismember lizards), requires veterinary care (sometimes a lot of care), and may be either terrified of people (making it hard to show off to friends) or willing to snarl and bite any and all who come near (if not socialized well as a puppy), the Chihuahua is unceremoniously dumped at the nearest shelter.

▲ **Older Chihuahuas is perfect for owners who do not have the time to train a young pup, and they make wonderful companions.**

Other Reasons for Abandoned Chis

Other reasons that purebred Chis wind up in need of rescue vary. Divorce, the arrival of a new baby, inability to pay for the dog's veterinary bills, a job relocation, a move to a property at which dogs are not allowed (sadly, often a retirement community or an assisted-living facility), and the death of the owner are some of the more commonly given reasons for surrendering a dog to a shelter or rescue. Some of the reasons are truly valid, making the surrender even more difficult for dog and owner.

Looking for a Good Home

A common place to find adult Chihuahuas up for adoption is through the local newspaper. Pet owners who really love their dogs but have run into circumstances that are beyond their control, forcing them to give up their Chihuahuas, will often place an ad in the paper so that they can screen potential adopters. This kind of owner isn't looking to make a profit; instead, he wants to have some control in assuring that his dog will have a permanent, loving home.

What to Expect

You can expect to be asked to come to the owner's home in order to meet the dog. While there, the owner will most likely ask some questions about how you will be able to care for and treat the dog. You should also take this time to ask the owner exactly why he is giving up his Chihuahua.

 Essential

Request permission to review the dog's veterinary records with the dog's veterinarian. If the dog has any serious or chronic health issues and requires expensive medications or treatments, you'll want to know these up front.

Even if price is not mentioned in the ad, expect to pay a small price for the dog—perhaps $100 to $200. Though the owner may give you the dog, it is usually recommended that the adopting person pay *something* for the dog. This helps to ensure that the adopter is serious about owning the dog, and it helps to prevent those who try to scoop up unwanted toy breeds for unethical reasons. (In this world there are those who place no value on life and who find enjoyment in torturing poor, defenseless animals.)

Buyer Beware

Be aware, too, that if you take this dog home and things don't work out, the seller of the dog will not be in a position to take the dog back. If he could keep the dog, he wouldn't be trying to place her in a good home. It's a buyer-beware situation. However, if you spend enough time with the animal and the owner, check out the owner's veterinarian, and even consider bringing a Chihuahua fancier along with you to help evaluate the dog's temperament, it is very possible to adopt a charming, lovable dog that will give you years and years of companionship.

Shelters and Pounds

Shelters and pounds, or animal-control facilities, are also a source of potentially adoptable adult Chihuahuas. In fact, these facilities remain the primary sources of Chihuahuas and Chihuahua mixes selected by service-dog training agencies as potential service dogs for the hearing impaired. Many people think that shelters and pounds are interchangeable, that they are set up the same way and offer the potential adopter the same services. Although both facilities do offer dogs for adoption, there are some significant differences between the two that are important to understand when searching for an adult Chi to rescue.

 Fact

Because of antidiscrimination laws, municipal animal-control facilities are required to adopt out any animal to any person without asking questions. For the oft-abused Chihuahua, this adoption philosophy can be tragic. Fortunately, Chihuahua rescues try to network with these facilities and save as many Chis as possible though there will always be too many that fall through the cracks.

Animal-Control Facilities (Pounds)

Animal-control facilities are not privately funded through donations. Instead, they are run on municipal funds. Since most communities don't budget much for this service, animal-control facilities are frequently run on a shoestring budget. They have minimal facilities and can only keep dogs for a very limited time period. Most of the dogs there are strays that have no identification and have been picked up by animal-control officers.

When a stray dog enters a pound, it is tagged with a number and put in a large kennel or run with all other dogs gathered up that day. Because the dogs are not treated for fleas or ticks or medicated for any diseases, unvaccinated dogs run a significant risk of being exposed to deadly canine viruses. The dogs are not spayed or neutered either, as the facility's main concerns are removing stray dogs from roaming the streets. Dogs in estrus can become impregnated if kept with intact males.

 Question?

Why do the dogs have to be euthanized?
It is not that the staff doesn't want to help these dogs or keep them longer. Instead, they are limited by their space constraints. Dogs remain at the shelter only as room allows before they are destroyed to make room for new strays that have just been picked up.

If you adopt from a pound, you will be on your own in determining a dog's temperament, behavior, and physical health. As noted previously, animal-control facilities don't have the money to hire folks to evaluate and place dogs. In fact, because of the city's nondiscrimination laws, the pounds must place any unclaimed dog with any person who is able to pay the adoption fee. Good dogs can be found in pounds; however, it is advisable to bring a Chi expert with you to help you in evaluating any prospective pets.

Nonprofit Shelters

Nonprofit shelters generally offer more evaluation and placement services than animal control. Depending on the number of volunteers, the experience of the staff, and the all-important operating budget, a shelter may provide anything from very limited services (comparable to a local pound but with the ability to screen adopters) to an extensive array of programs.

Some of the very best shelters provide veterinary care (such as altering, vaccinations, heartworm testing and treatment, flea/tick treatment), professional screening of prospective owners and placement of dogs by certified animal behaviorists, extensive temperament testing, and even training by skilled and experienced dog trainers to help difficult dogs become easier to place.

Most shelters will fall somewhere in between those that offer the very best services and those that offer services that are more limited in scope. Regardless of the shelter's abilities, staff members and volunteers can still be extremely helpful to potential adopters.

When a dog is surrendered to a shelter, the staff has the owner fill out a questionnaire detailing the dog's temperament, likes, dislikes, age, and the owner's reason for relinquishing the pet. Keep in mind that an owner who is giving up his pet will frequently make up all kinds of problems so that he doesn't feel as guilty or is perceived by the staff as being a lout for giving up a perfectly good dog. For this reason, take the information you find on the intake sheet with a grain of salt.

 Essential

Chihuahuas are notoriously difficult to housetrain. If you see that the previous owners couldn't housetrain the Chi, don't despair. Unless the dog has a health problem (which your veterinarian can diagnose and potentially treat), with time, patience, and a lot of diligence, most Chihuahuas can become reliable in the housetraining department.

Perhaps more important than the surrendering owner's information is the input and observations from shelter staff and volunteers. Ask everyone you can find what they think of the dog you're interested in and how she's behaved since she's been at the shelter. If she's a great little dog, you'll hear some very enthusiastic responses.

Small breeds and mixes of small breeds are extremely popular, and shelters report that they don't have any troubles adopting out the little guys. In fact, many potential adopters are put on a waiting list. If you would like to adopt a Chi from a shelter, try to be patient and consider being flexible in your dog requirements. If you're set on a female, you might pass up the best possible companion just because he happens to be male. Try to judge each dog on an individual basis.

Working with a Chihuahua Rescue

Without question, the best way to find the Chihuahua you are looking for, the one virtually guaranteed to meet and exceed your expectations, is through a Chihuahua breed rescue. Chihuahua rescues are run by the experts, that is, by Chihuahua fanciers with extensive breed experience. These folks know Chihuahuas. They can differentiate between a truly timid dog and one that hasn't had many life experiences or socialization. Rescue volunteers can determine which dogs are aggressive and which are reacting in self-defense and fear. Most importantly, these people know what to do to help these discarded Chihuahuas become the best dogs they can be and to find them terrific homes.

The Application Process

When adopting through a rescue, you will be asked to fill out a long questionnaire or application. The information from this lengthy form helps rescue organizers match the best dog with the best applicant. The rescue will want to know what your home is like, what kinds of hours you work, where your dog will stay when you are not home, the amount of time you can give to your dog, how you plan on housetraining the dog, your experience with dogs and Chis, why you want to adopt a Chihuahua, and many other facts about your life.

 **Alert!**

Another source for rescued Chihuahuas is through a toy breed rescue. These rescues specialize in all toy breeds and are often found in areas where there is a need for such an umbrella organization. They operate in the same way as a Chihuahua rescue and are an excellent source for rescued Chis.

Once you've submitted your adoption application, a member of the rescue will call you. He'll answer any questions you might have about the breed and the adoption process, as well as fire off a few more questions for you to answer. The reason for the intensive inquisition is that breed rescues want to make sure that you can provide a safe, loving permanent home for an adult Chi in need. Requiring an extensive application to be filled out, following up with a telephone interview, *and* charging an adoption fee generally helps to weed most of these ne'er-do-wells from approaching a rescue.

The Rescue Staff

Once your application has been approved, the rescue will begin introducing you to various rescue dogs as they become available for adoption. The rescue will only show you dogs that they think could be potential matches for you. These dogs come from owners who have contacted the rescue to surrender their dogs, as well as from area shelters and animal-control facilities.

Once a dog is safely in the rescue's adoption program, she is given a complete veterinary exam, brought up to date on her vaccinations, bathed, groomed and then fostered for at least a week or longer by a knowledgeable Chi owner. While at the foster home, the dog's temperament is evaluated. The rescue wants to see how the Chihuahua reacts when around other pets, strangers, and children. They want to know if this Chihuahua has any hot points (places on her body where she doesn't like touched) or if the dog has any behavior quirks or phobias. Basically, the rescue's goal is to know this dog inside and out.

 Fact

To find a Chihuahua rescue in your area, contact the Chihuahua Club of America's breed rescue. (See Appendix A for information.) This national rescue has compiled a network of reputable Chihuahua contacts throughout the country.

Once the rescue understands what makes a certain Chihuahua tick, the foster parent works on helping the new rescue become more adoptable—if she isn't already ready for adoption. Perhaps the most important aspect of adopting a dog from a Chihuahua rescue is that you will be able to adopt a dog that is a known entity. Rescue volunteers sincerely work to help the dog better adjust to home life, and they won't partner the dog until she's ready.

Which One?

If you are adopting a dog through a Chihuahua rescue, you'll receive a lot of help in deciding which dog is the best for you. When working with a private individual, an animal-control facility or a shelter, the decision of which dog is going to be the one you can live with and enjoy for the next decade or two is likely one you'll have to make on your own.

Remember, when looking at adoptable dogs, you're not only looking for an adorable looking dog—you want to find a Chihuahua with a wonderful temperament and good health. The source from which you adopt your dog will determine how much effort you will need to make in determining what the Chi is really like.

Evaluating Health and Temperament

Adult dogs come with baggage. They've had a life largely unknown to anyone other than the initial owner. All of their life experiences up until the present moment have shaped what they have become, and those experiences will also affect what this dog will be when given a good, nurturing home.

Health

Some of what you will see in the shelters and pounds is cosmetic. A dog that has been treated for a bad flea infestation may have healing sores or patches of missing hair. An underfed Chi may appear thin, but if she's eating well and thriving, again, the present look is going to pass.

What you need to focus on are the bigger issues, or those things that will not go away. If the shelter has had a veterinarian examine the Chihuahua, the staff will be able to tell you what problems, if any, were detected. Many heart conditions can be detected with a physical exam and then confirmed using other diagnostics. If a dog is asymptomatic, however, a standard veterinary exam will not reveal orthopedic problems, such as luxating patellas or hip dysplasia.

The good news is that by the time a Chihuahua hits adulthood, many serious diseases or conditions will already be causing symptoms that are more easily observable than in a puppy. If the Chi has skin allergies, for example, you are more likely to see this when the dog is mature.

When adopting a dog from the shelter, it is always a good idea to make your veterinarian one of the first stops on the way home. Regardless of whether the Chi has had a veterinary examination, your veterinarian may be able to spot something the shelter had missed. With the rescued adult, you just want to make sure you know what you're getting into. If there's a problem, it's a good idea to know how involved the treatment will be and how much will it cost.

 **Essential**

If you know anyone who is a longtime Chihuahua fancier or who is very experienced in dog behavior, ask if he will go with you to visit the dog. Often an expert can more easily determine what is imperceptible to novice owners.

Temperament

How can you tell what you are dealing with when looking at a dog in the shelter, sitting behind the cage door? Actually, you can't. In a shelter environment, it is very difficult to determine any dog's temperament. The stress of being locked up with dozens of other dogs in a noisy, frightening environment can terrify even the bravest of Chis.

You'll need to separate the Chihuahua from the noise. Often, shelters have an area in which you can take the dog and spend some time in a relatively peaceful environment. Even then, it may be difficult for the dog to really relax and begin acting more like herself.

If you are unsure of a dog's temperament, try visiting her several times in order that she can get to know you a little better. Of course, if the dog is in the pound, time may be of the essence. Or, if the Chi is in the shelter, she may be adopted out quickly. If you think you are interested in a dog but aren't sure, ask the shelter if you can put a deposit on her while you think about it overnight. It's always better to be a bit safer than to be sorry when you find out weeks afterward that the dog you adopted really is much more than you can handle.

Chihuahua Proofing In and Out

As a Chihuahua owner, your job of making the inside and outside of your home Chi-proof is exceptionally important. Because the Chi is the smallest of the toy breeds, it often takes only a lick, taste, or nibble of certain foods, plants, or chemicals to make your Chi seriously ill. The Chi's diminutive size also puts the breed at increased risk of becoming injured. If this isn't enough, the Chi can be quite saucy with bigger, bolder dogs and has been known to seek out trouble.

Dangers Lurking in the Home

If you've had a crawling baby or a toddler in your home, you understand that a typical home or apartment can be a landmine of danger for a youngster. It is very much the same for a new Chihuahua puppy or rescued adult dog. Everything is new. Corners need to be explored. All unknown items need to be tasted.

If you haven't had to do any childproofing, or if it's been many years since you've had a puppy, it is likely that your home and yard are not quite a safe haven for your new Chihuahua. Don't worry. It just takes a little preparation and some forethought to get prepared. If in doubt, it's a good idea to move the item or prevent access to it until you can confirm the safety of a particular item.

For the Chihuahua, the most common source of danger is the floor. This can include items that have been dropped or left on the floor or those that are naturally present in this area. Most often the danger comes from the Chihuahua trying to sample or taste a dangerous item. Sniffing, chewing, and licking are all ways in which a dog might test an item.

In addition to items that the Chi can ingest, there is also a whole host of physical dangers in the home. Your home may have many areas that the Chihuahua can squeeze into and become trapped—or attractive places for the dog to try to jump off of, risking a broken leg. Though not inclusive, the following topic areas give you some of the more common household hazards to remember.

Foods That Can Kill

Many different kinds of foods have been noted for their ability to make dogs ill, and some can be lethal even in small amounts. The risk of becoming ill from ingesting a substance is much higher in the Chihuahua than in dogs of greater body weights. A small amount of food that might make a mid- to large-sized dog queasy could be more than enough to kill a Chi. The tinier the Chi, of course, the greater the risk of becoming ill, making young puppies particularly susceptible.

 **Fact**

Before an emergency arises, know how to contact your veterinarian after hours or the way to the emergency clinic when your veterinarian is not available. Also, keep the ASPCA's twenty-four-hour poison hotline number available: (888) 426-4435.

Owners often think that just because they find something offensive to eat (such as the garbage, expired dairy products, or rancid cold cuts), their Chihuahuas will also find these items offensive and will completely avoid them. Wrong. There's no accounting for a Chi's sense of taste. Some dogs just don't seem to care and will eat everything and anything. Your best bet is to keep all food items, fresh or otherwise, away from your Chihuahua.

In addition to foods that are more obviously likely to make a Chi ill, there are foods that owners don't realize are poisonous to dogs. These are foods that owners enjoy eating themselves and are more likely to share as a special treat for their Chi. These foods include chocolate, grapes, onions, garlic, and others.

Chocolate

Less than an ounce of chocolate can induce seizures, coma, and even death in the Chihuahua. That's because chocolate contains a high concentration of methylxanthine alkaloids, compounds that include theobromine and caffeine. Both of those are toxic to dogs. The darker the chocolate, the higher the poison concentration. Therefore, baker's chocolate is more poisonous than dark chocolate, and dark chocolate is more toxic than milk chocolate.

A Chi puppy of only eleven ounces could show serious signs of illness by eating only a few candy-coated pieces of chocolate or a bite-sized piece of candy. If you keep candy dishes out in your home, empty them. And don't think that just because the chocolate is kept up on a counter or on a table that it is safe from your Chi. These dogs are extremely athletic as well as clever. If there's something they really, really want, chances are they'll figure out a way to get to it. Store chocolate in closed cabinets.

Grapes

Oft considered the fruit of gods, grapes are definitely not the fruit of dogs. What a shame, too, as dogs seem to love popping seedless grapes and raisins as much as we do. Unfortunately, it has come to light that this fruit is harmful to dogs. Within the last few years a significant number of clinical cases have been recorded in which dogs have become ill or died due to ingesting grapes or raisins.

 **Question?**

My friend thinks it's funny to allow his dog to drink beer—is this safe?
Absolutely not! Allowing a dog to lap up even small amounts of beer, wine, or any other liquor can cause vomiting, diarrhea, loss of coordination, depression of the central nervous system, difficulty breathing, tremors, coma, and death.

To date, no one knows exactly what chemical in grapes and raisins is toxic to dogs, but whatever it is affects the dogs' kidneys. After eating the fruit, symptoms include diarrhea, lethargy, and abdominal pain that lasts for several days or even weeks. If a lethal amount of the fruit has been eaten, death occurs from kidney failure. For the three-pound Chihuahua, these effects could set in with the ingestion of only a few grapes or raisins. As with chocolate, keep grapes and raisins in an inaccessible location.

Uncooked Meats and Fish

There may be nothing more enticing to a dog than a nice hunk of raw chicken thawing on the counter, a pack of ground beef, or some freshly cleaned fish. There are diets in which raw foods are used to create a holistic meal. Many dogs thrive on these raw meat, vegetable, and grain diets. Be aware, however, that bacteria such as E. coli and salmonella are always an issue with raw meats. Raw fish may also contain unwanted bacteria or even parasites.

Other Unsafe Foods

Though not necessarily lethal, other common foods that can wreak havoc with your Chihuahua's gastrointestinal tract include uncooked rice, foods with high salt contents, and meats containing small, hollow bones, such as cooked chicken. Other foods on the no-no list include these:

- Avocado
- Coffee
- High-fat foods
- Macadamia nuts
- Onions and onion powder
- Salt
- Yeast dough
- Garlic
- Any product sweetened with xylitol (a sweetener found in many sugar-free gums and candies)

Even if a food is not generally considered toxic to dogs, too much of *anything* can be a dangerous situation for a Chi. Though Chihuahuas often forget to eat because they are too busy playing, there are some Chis that, if given the opportunity, will gorge themselves on forbidden foods, such as a stash of cookies or a cooling roast. If your Chi gets into something she shouldn't, call your veterinarian and explain the situation. It may or may not require a trip to the veterinarian, but it's far better to play it safe.

Kitchen and Breakfast Areas

What do you keep under your kitchen sink? Chances are you have a variety of highly toxic chemicals stowed in this lower cabinet. Dishwashing liquid or detergent, wood polishers, floor cleansers or waxes, caustic cleaners for the counter and others for the oven and stovetop, and the list goes on.

 Essential

A simple way to ensure that your puppy or dog doesn't get into trouble is to install door and drawer locks. These can be found inexpensively at any baby-supply store and are a good answer to those owning inquisitive, problem-solving Chis.

All of these products are highly toxic; very few, if any, aren't poisonous. The containers they are stored in, usually plastic bottles, are not dog-proof, either. If a dog is determined to have a taste, she will.

Lock It Up

Fortunately, most people stow these items behind a cabinet door or a lower drawer. Keep these areas shut and inaccessible to your Chi. Alternatively, you might consider moving these cleaning items to a high shelf in a room that your Chihuahua doesn't have access to or storing them in a large, plastic container with a tight lid or a container that locks shut (such as a large craft box).

Another item that is kept in the kitchen is the garbage and trash. Don't be lulled into feeling the false sense of security that just because your dog only weighs a few pounds, she won't be able to get into the garbage. Depending on the height, weight, and position of the can in the kitchen, the garbage may or may not be accessible to your Chi. To be on the safe side, put the garbage can behind closed doors. If need be, use a cabinet lock.

▲ Chihuahuas are very small dogs, so make sure there are no small spaces in or around your home that they could get trapped in!

Physical Dangers

Look for physical hazards in the kitchen and breakfast room, too. Often, refrigerators, dishwashers, and stoves are not entirely flush with kitchen cabinets. This could leave little open spaces that could be just big enough for a curious Chi to wedge herself into. This is particularly likely to happen if food bits have fallen between the cracks or if the Chi is in hot pursuit of a lizard. It is quite possible that your Chi could crawl *under* your kitchen appliances.

Make sure there are no gaps in your kitchen or breakfast room that might offer your Chi an opportunity to become stuck. If you do have a Chi-size crevice and can't block it off, do not leave your dog alone in this area unless she is crated or playing safely in a playpen.

Bathrooms and Laundry

As with kitchens, bathrooms and laundries are generally a treasure trove of dangers to a Chihuahua. Very many of these hazards arise from Chihuahuas ingesting items they shouldn't, but others arise from potentially unsafe physical situations. The bathroom—a room commonly used by many owners to keep a Chihuahua safe and contained while they are out—has both varieties of dangers.

Bathroom Dangers

Common sources of poisons in the bathroom are cleansers and cleaning supplies. Virtually anything used to clean a bathroom is going to be highly toxic to a Chihuahua in even minute quantities. Even if your Chi doesn't ingest these chemicals, an accidental spill can cause serious burns and even blindness if splashed in the eyes. Keep all cleansers behind locked doors.

A second source of poisons in the bathroom is what your Chi might find on the floor. Both prescription and over-the-counter medications are easily dropped and forgotten (or dropped and simply not found) on the bathroom floor. These medications are in highly concentrated forms and are virtually always lethal in a dog as small as the Chi.

They may not be poisonous, but for whatever reason some dogs are incredibly attracted to discarded paper drinking cups, used tissues, and feminine hygiene products. Avoid allowing your Chihuahua access to bathrooms in which these items can be found and dragged into other areas of the house to be shredded or hidden for later. Or dispose of these items in trashcans that are behind—you guessed it—closed doors.

 **Alert!**

Other less-obvious sources of danger to the Chi include items discarded in the bathroom trash. Toothpaste formulated for humans is very toxic to dogs, and there's probably enough left in that old tube to make your Chihuahua ill. Additionally, if your Chi were to ingest a long strand of dental floss, it could become entangled in the dog's gastrointestinal tract and also cause serious cuts.

Finally, though drinking out of the toilet itself isn't particularly dangerous (the water isn't profoundly filthy), being around an open toilet *is* extremely dangerous. The Chihuahua is so small that if she is able to get up to the toilet seat (remember: Chis can jump), she could very well fall in and drown. Keep the lid to the toilet closed, or keep the door to the bathroom shut at all times. And, it probably goes without saying, never leave a bathtub filled with water unattended. It, too, is quite dangerous should a Chihuahua jump or fall into the water with no way to climb out.

In the Laundry Room

Potential hazards in the laundry include toxic chemicals (such as bleach, laundry detergent, and spot removers), crawl spaces and crevices in which the Chi can become lodged, and various clothing articles that might present choking hazards, such as socks or knits that have a tendency to unravel. The easiest solution is to keep the door shut. An equally good solution is to keep things off the floor and out of reach of the Chi, as well as blocking off any potential Chi-size crawl areas.

Other Living-Space Hazards

In addition to the previously mentioned household dangers, your home probably contains other threats, such as electrical cords; power cords to computers; squeeze-in spaces; dropped paper clips and push pins; rodent and roach poisons; kitty litter "prizes"; and teetering objects that could fall. You must be ever vigilant to watch out for these and other attractive dangers, like coffee tables. If your Chi gets up on one, don't startle her and make her jump— she could break something.

Electrical Cords

A very common and often tragic home hazard is the electrical cord. For whatever reason, puppies find the texture of an electrical cord irresistible. If the lamp were turned on (with power flowing through the cord) and your Chihuahua chewed through the protective coating and hit live wires, the shock would be enough to kill a puppy or dog. If the electrical cord doesn't have a current flowing through it and the Chi partially chews through the cord, your little dog has now created a fire hazard for the next time the light is turned on.

Ways to prevent cord problems include covering the cords with a rug or heavy plastic protective strips commonly used for computer cords. Applying a bitter-apple–flavored gel or another chewing repellent to cords can also help—unless your Chi enjoys this flavor, and then you're back to trying to cover the cords. Additionally, you can unplug the cords when you are not in the room and wind them around a chair leg or the lamp itself. You can also keep your Chi out of this particular room or let her safely relax in her crate when you can't watch her every move.

Pest Control

Ingestible dangers found in living areas of your home can include rodent, roach, and ant poisons. These poisons in particular are left in areas that a Chihuahua might be able to access—at the base of windows, behind furniture, or against walls. Rodent poisons cause fatal hemorrhaging; pesticides can cause neurological death. They're nasty any way you look at them.

 **Alert!**

Many ordinary houseplants can cause illness, particularly in a small dog. Most of these plants cause irritation in the dog's mouth, but some can be poisonous. For a complete list of poisonous house-plants and their toxicity, visit the ASPCA's National Animal Poison Control Center Web site (online at *www.aspca.org*). In case of emergency, you can also call the center at 1-888-426-4435. A consultation fee may apply.

If you're accustomed to using these methods to keep your home pest-free, you will have to rethink your strategies. You cannot have these poisons out if you have a puppy or dog in the home. It won't be a matter of *if* your Chi will investigate and potentially ingest a fatal dose of these poisons; it will be a matter of *when*. And don't think you can substitute a mousetrap; this could kill a curious Chihuahua, too.

Garage

If you're like many homeowners, your garage is used as much for storage as to house your car (if not more). Much of what is kept in the garage is used for lawn or home maintenance. For the Chihuahua, the garage may be an exciting place to run about and explore; however, it is also full of potential dangers.

One danger is that of falling objects. Paint cans stacked on lower shelves, bikes leaning precariously against the wall, and tools such as shovels, trimmers, and trowels can easily injure a Chihuahua, even if they only fall a few inches. If you allow your Chihuahua to keep you company while you dig in your garage for a lawn implement or try to find a touch-up can of paint, be aware of where she is at all times.

Other hazards that are common to garages are chemicals. Fertilizers, swimming pool or spa treatment supplies, ice-melting products, pesticides, herbicides, and insecticides are just a few items that can make your Chi very ill or even kill her in tiny amounts. Keep these items safely stowed in tightly sealed containers, or prevent your Chi from having access to your garage.

 Question?

Is it true that antifreeze is poisonous?
Absolutely. And it's poisonous in very minute amounts. Compounding the problem is that dogs find the taste appealing; antifreeze is very sweet to them. If you spill antifreeze in the garage clean it up immediately. You might also consider purchasing nontoxic antifreeze to use in your car.

Yard or Patio

Be aware that whether you are welcoming home a Chi puppy or an adult, the Chihuahua is a close-to-the-ground kind of dog. For this reason, the breed is particularly susceptible to contact with chemicals, plants, insects, and animals that can be found in your yard.

Small Animals
As the king of lizard chasers, the lion-hearted Chihuahua cannot resist the urge to chase and kill small, moving creatures. Normally

this prey drive translates to a few insect body parts or a lizard tail gracing your kitchen floor now and then. Depending on where you live, however, contact with certain types of toads, insects, spiders, snakes, and scorpions could prove deadly to your Chihuahua.

Landscaping Items

Items that are commonly used in the garden or patio that are dangerous to dogs include citronella candles, fly baits containing methomyl, and slug and snail baits containing metaldehyde. Do you have a small pond in your yard? The blue-green algae that grows in smaller bodies of water is toxic. What about a compost pile that you're waiting to work into your vegetable garden or cocoa mulch spread in your carefully groomed flowerbeds? These are toxic, too.

Many plants, shrubs, and even trees are highly toxic to dogs. (For instance, all parts of the cherry tree are poisonous.) If you have a Chi who likes to explore and chew, either remove these plants from your garden or devise a way to block your Chihuahua's access to them. If you have any questions regarding a particular plant you are considering adding to your yard or one that is already there, you can check the ASPCA Web site (online at *www. aspca.org*), which maintains an alphabetical list of toxic plants.

Fencing

The importance of having fencing for your backyard or patio is twofold: to keep your Chihuahua in your yard and to keep other dogs, large predatory critters, and even a would-be Chihuahua burglar out. As you might have guessed, the Chihuahua can be a challenging dog breed to keep fenced in.

 Question?

Why would someone want to steal my dog?
The answer is simple: money. Unaltered Chihuahuas—particularly females of breeding age—are common targets because they can be used as brood bitches. Since the Chihuahua is small, she is an easier dog to steal, too.

Choosing the Right Fence

Six-foot privacy fences will work (in wood or plastic). If the slats are staggered to allow air to flow through them, make sure there's not such a wide gap that your Chi can wriggle through. A good guide to figuring out if a fence is escapable is by looking at your dog's head. If your Chihuahua might be able to squeeze his head through the gap, the rest of his body is likely to be able to follow.

When looking at chainlink fences and wrought iron, the same theory applies. If it might be possible for the Chi to get his head through any portion of the fence—whether the fence itself or a hinged gate—it's likely not to contain your Chi.

You can make any type of existing fencing work if you are willing to invest in a secondary fence. For example, you might consider putting up three- to four-foot high chicken-wire fencing against an existing chainlink or wrought iron fence to provide a safe area of containment for your Chi. For a wooden fence with staggered gaps that could become escape hatches, perhaps the addition of a wooden lattice secured to the bottom half of the fence might work.

In addition to making sure that your fence doesn't have any gaps in it that might allow your Chi to escape, take a close look at the fence's condition. Protruding nails need to be removed or hammered back in. Sharp, exposed wires on a chainlink fence should be twisted in the opposite direction or removed.

Other Options

Of course, if your yard is too big to fence, a fence is out of your budget, or you can't fence your yard because of subdivision or condominium rules, you might consider making an enclosed area just for your Chihuahua. If you have a deck outside your back door, you could put a low fence here with a gate for your dog. You can also set up a puppy playpen in a shady spot in your yard for playtime—as long as you're able to watch your Chi.

There's a solution to virtually every fencing quandary. You just need to remember that Chihuahuas can be quite deft at squeezing through small places, digging under things, and jumping over low barriers. With a little foresight and some creative thinking, you can make your backyard a safe environment for your new dog.

CHAPTER  6

Bringing Your Chihuahua Home

You've purchased the perfect puppy, or maybe you've adopted the ideal adult Chi, and you're ready to bring her home. Congratulations! Now it's time to be sure you take off on the right foot and paw together. That means making sure you've made arrangements in advance to see your veterinarian, signing up for a puppy or beginner training class, and purchasing all the supplies you'll need for the ride home as well as the upcoming days, nights, and weeks.

Planning Ahead

In the excitement of bringing home a new dog, many owners forget certain things that can be pretty important. Generally speaking, puppies and rescued adults don't come with collars and leashes or a crate in which to travel home.

Because new buyers frequently do forget to make these purchases, some breeders may stock a few of these items for you to purchase for your Chihuahua. Don't, however, plan on this. The more you can take care of in advance, the less stressful your first twenty-four hours will be with your new Chi and the more time you can spend bonding with your Chihuahua.

It's also helpful to make several key appointments before you bring your new Chihuahua home. Depending on the age of your Chihuahua, her background, and from whom you are purchasing or adopting her, you may need to make several appointments with professionals or perhaps only a few.

 **Alert!**

If you are picking up your Chihuahua at the airport, make sure you know precisely what flight she is traveling on and where you go to claim her. Extremes in weather can preclude a dog from shipping on any given day, as can the presence of hazardous cargo. Your breeder should call you when he has confirmed that the Chi is on the designated flight.

Appointments to Make

Depending on whether you're bringing your Chihuahua home from a quality breeder or a poorly funded municipal shelter, you might have a few or a great many appointments to make for your pup or dog. A quality breeder, a good rescue, and a dedicated shelter will all deliver a Chihuahua that is clean, healthy, and ready to start a new life. In this case, the only appointment you will need to make is with your veterinarian for a basic wellness checkup—and you'll want to have this taken care of as soon as possible after picking up your Chihuahua.

First Stop: The Vet

There are two needs for speed in scheduling this appointment. First, young puppies in particular are notorious for going down quickly if they are ill; they just don't have the resistance to disease and strength that a healthy, larger adult dog would have. In other words, a pup may appear just a little off one minute and within twenty-four hours be desperately ill.

 **Essential**

In addition to ensuring that your puppy is in tip-top health, your veterinarian should also be able to explain the early health signs that might indicate an emergency (such as vomiting, diarrhea, or listlessness). You should also find out where you will need to go if your Chi becomes ill after clinic hours and be familiar enough with the route that you can get there easily after dark.

At this first wellness exam, your veterinarian will check for signs of illness. He will look for signs of existing health conditions, such as heart disease or blindness, as well as infectious diseases. In particular, your veterinarian will be checking for signs of parvovirus and canine hepatitis, which are often lethal to young puppies.

When you take your Chi to the veterinary exam, bring her shot and worming records (supplied by the breeder) so that your Chi won't have to receive any more vaccinations than necessary. If your Chi came from a shelter or pound, these records may not be available. Your veterinarian will need to be aware of this, too, in planning your dog's upcoming health care.

The second reason for scheduling the veterinary appointment within the first day, if possible, is because many breeders' health guarantees only remain in effect if the dog or puppy is examined within a set period of time. Usually, this time period is anywhere from twenty-four to seventy-two hours. This means you may have as little as one day to get your Chi examined for diseases and illnesses.

If your new Chihuahua is ill at the time of examination, your veterinarian will have to provide proof that the dog was sick upon examination in order for you to return or exchange the puppy, depending on the terms of your contract. Be aware that most contracts do not offer to pay for the puppy's veterinary expenses if you try to save the puppy, which is what most puppy owners choose to do who have already become attached to their new canine.

 **Fact**

If your Chihuahua becomes ill outside of the breeder's time window, as defined in the contract, it is normally assumed that you exposed the Chi to a contagious disease. In that case, it is not the breeder's responsibility to return your money or offer to exchange the pup for a healthy one. Breeders' contracts vary, however, concerning their responsibilities if your Chi develops a hereditary disease, such as canine hip dysplasia or epilepsy.

Second Stop: Grooming Shop

If you adopt your Chihuahua from a shelter or an animal-control facility, you will likely want to make an appointment with a professional grooming shop before bringing your Chi home. Many adoption facilities don't have the budget to treat all strays and owner surrenders for ticks, fleas, and mites. These are pests you certainly don't want to bring into your home if you can avoid it.

When setting an appointment with a groomer, make sure to let him know that to the best of your knowledge, the Chihuahua you are bringing in has never been professionally groomed. This gives the groomer a heads-up to go slowly and gently with the dog and use a muzzle, if necessary, to ensure the groomer's safety.

In addition to having any and all pests eradicated from your Chi's skin and coat, make arrangements to have your Chihuahua bathed, dried, and trimmed, if necessary. Long coats may require more extensive work as some of the denser, finer coats can mat and tangle. In extreme cases of prior neglect, part of the coat may need to be shaved, but trust your groomer. He'll avoid anything radical if at all possible.

Don't forget to have your Chi's toenails clipped. It's one less thing you'll have to worry about in the first few weeks that your Chihuahua is home. Additionally, if your Chi is an adult, clipping toenails may not be on her agenda (at the moment) and leaving this potentially touchy job to a professional can save a lot of anxiety for both you and your dog.

 **Alert!**

Some groomers are hesitant about working on unknown dogs that could be potentially ill or easily frightened. Respect your groomer's position and see if he will accept your Chi after she has had her vet check. If this is still unacceptable, call around to other grooming shops and find someone who is willing to work with you and your dog.

Class Reservations

Something that many toy-breed owners neglect is to sign up for a puppy or beginner obedience class. It is a common misconception that little dogs are perfect by nature and that they don't need training or socialization. Here's a news flash: Nothing could be further from the truth.

The Chihuahua is a *dog*. As such, the Chi will display natural dog behaviors, such as jumping up, barking, chewing, snapping, or biting. The Chihuahua also displays many terrier-like qualities, including what some affectionately call "selective hearing." ("If I don't make eye contact with him, I can pretend I didn't hear him call me.") The Chihuahua doesn't need to become an obedience champion (but wouldn't that be cool?), but she does need to learn basic house manners, and you need to learn how to teach her these manners.

Signing up for a training class may not be necessarily easy. Some times of year tend to be busier than others. For instance, the months of March and April are often packed with unruly Christmas puppies. You want to begin your Chi's training as soon as your veterinarian feels it is safe to expose your vaccinated puppy or adult dog to potentially infectious dogs. If you haven't already gotten a spot in a class, you may have to wait weeks or even months for an opening.

 **fact**

Training classes assist with more than manners. They also provide excellent opportunities for dog-to-dog socialization as well as socialization with friendly, experienced dog handlers. For the timid or terribly shy Chi, continued training in this welcoming atmosphere helps to overcome fears.

Investigate the different trainers and training facilities that are available in your community, and get signed up in advance. It may take a while to find someone you want to work with, who is within a drivable distance, and who has an opening in an upcoming class. Don't dally.

Breeder Assistance

Your puppy's breeder can offer you valuable assistance in bringing your Chi home. In particular, he can help you choose the food and supplies you need to purchase prior to your Chi's arrival. Here are a few of the things that you will want to know:

- What size collar does the Chihuahua wear?
- What is her precise weight at time of pickup (so you can continue to make sure she is thriving)?
- What food is she eating and how much?
- What is her feeding schedule?
- Does she have any tendency toward hypoglycemia? If so, what products should you have on hand for her if she has an episode?
- What type of bedding does she prefer?
- Is she used to sleeping on a warming blanket?
- How is she being housetrained? If she's using a litter box, what brand of dog litter is she used to?

- Can you send a hand towel to the breeder for the puppy's mother to sleep on so the pup has something familiar and comforting for her first few nights alone?
- Does the dog prefer a den-like, solid plastic crate or the wire mesh variety?
- In what size carrier can the dog travel comfortably?

As you can see, at a bare minimum you will need to make sure you have the Chi's food purchased in advance (as a sudden change in foods can cause gastrointestinal upset). You may also need to drop off or ship a hand towel to the breeder several days in advance and purchase special bedding and litter. The last thing you want is to be put in the position of having to run out late at night and try to find something you've forgotten.

The Ride Home

Whether you have a relatively short drive home with your new Chihuahua or a veritable cross-country road trip, you'll want to make sure you're prepared for just about anything. In particular, be aware that this could be the first time your Chi has traveled in a car. She may be nervous, anxious, or suffering from motion sickness.

Translated? Your little Chi could transform from Ms. Personality to a shaking, drooling mess that is vomiting and suffering from a most awful case of intestinal distress. And that's just when the car's moving. When you stop at a rest stop to try to clean up, you could potentially have a distraught Chihuahua that is quick to bolt from the car and doesn't know you well enough to come when called. In other words, a short to moderate trip could turn into a disaster.

Unless, of course, you are prepared. For the ride home you should bring with you a collar and leash that fit; a safe means of transporting your new Chihuahua; food and water; cleanup materials, emergency supplies for a puppy that is prone to hypoglycemia; and holistic aids to lessen your Chihuahua's travel anxiety.

 Essential

If you are flying home with your Chihuahua puppy, she will be able to ride in her carrier in the cabin under the seat in front of you if you make reservations for this in advance with the airline. See Chapter 20 for additional helpful preflight information.

Collar

You'll want a flat-buckle collar for your puppy or adult Chihuahua, but getting the exact size will be difficult unless you have the Chi's neck measurement. If you can't get this measurement, try purchasing an extra-small collar or one that adjusts from six inches to eight inches, or even smaller if you are picking up a very petite puppy. If the Chihuahua is quite large (more than six pounds) you may need a collar that measures ten inches in length or more. Again, try to find out what size to purchase in advance of picking up your Chi, or consider purchasing a couple of different sizes and returning those that don't fit.

 Alert!

Harnesses are wonderful for Chihuahuas. These body collars prevent a Chi's delicate neck from getting yanked inadvertently and, since the Chihuahua is a small dog, you don't have to worry about being taken for a drag as you might with a larger breed. To fit a harness properly, however, you will need to try a variety of models on your dog to find the one that fits best.

Avoid purchasing or using a collar that is too big. Chis are quite adept at backing out of their collars. If the collar is not fastened tightly enough (snug but not binding), and your Chihuahua decides to balk or is suddenly frightened, she can pull hard enough on the leash to pop a looser-fitting collar off entirely. Now you have a collarless Chi loose in a strange place with someone she doesn't know well enough to trust to come to when called.

Leash

Initially, all you'll need here is a thin (3/8-inch is fine) four- to six-foot leash with the lightest, smallest clip possible. The last thing you want is a heavy, thick leash with a clip the size of the Chi whacking the poor fellow in the jaw. It's also a good idea to avoid retractable leashes initially. You'll want your Chi to learn good leash manners before allowing her to ziiiiing in and out at will with little control. She can get in trouble pretty quickly this way, and once she's out on the line there's no way to reel her back in other than pulling the leash line with your hands. This is not only awkward, but the line can bruise and burn your hands.

 **Question?**

How do I know if a carrier will fit my Chihuahua?
The carrier should be large enough for the Chihuahua to stand up, turn around, and lie down comfortably. An extra-small or small carrier should be sufficient for most puppies. Very large adults or those weighing more than ten pounds may be more comfortable in a medium crate.

Crate/Carrier

Many people assume that their new Chihuahuas will sleep peacefully in their laps while they drive home. In theory, this could happen. In reality, the exact opposite will occur. A toy-breed dog on the loose in a car is just as dangerous, if not more so, than a larger breed. Chihuahuas, because of their size, can easily wedge themselves into places that can make driving safely impossible, such as under the gas, brake, or clutch pedals. Small dogs have been known to stand on the electric window button, rolling down the window and falling out. If nothing else, the dog's bouncing around from seat to seat in and of itself can be a huge distraction to a driver.

Additionally, a panicked dog can respond aggressively. A terrified Chihuahua may respond by biting you while you are driving. Rescued adult dogs that have never traveled in a vehicle before are really unknowns, and they could respond to fear in a variety of ways. A safely contained Chi may make a lot of noise in her carrier or become ill; however, she will be less of a distraction, and she will not be able to soil or damage the interior of your car on the ride home.

▲ **Give your Chi plenty of time to get comfortable in her new surroundings, and let her explore her new home.**

When choosing a traveling crate, the least expensive option is a hard plastic carrier that is made of two pieces. Though a bit bulky to carry, it is light and easy to dismantle and clean out. Another option is a wire crate. These are nice for Chis that like to be able to see everything around them. If you plan on flying with your Chi, this type of crate is not approved for airline travel. A very popular choice for traveling with a Chi is a soft-sided carrier (many are approved for air travel) that can be comfortably carried over the shoulder when you're out and about and then belted into the back seat of your car while traveling. Soft-sided carriers can be anywhere from rather utilitarian and relatively inexpensive all the way to ultra-chic with super-luxurious fabrics and leathers and very pricey.

Food and Water

If you are traveling any distance, make sure you take along at least one more day's worth of water and food than you think you might need—just in case. The only thing worse than trying to locate a specialty dog food before the pet-supply stores close is to be caught out of town in an unknown area trying to locate a specialty dog food.

 Fact

Some dogs can be very sensitive to changes in water, so it is usually advisable to purchase distilled, bottled water to prevent intestinal distress. Some breeders prefer to fill plastic jugs with their own tap water for you to take along with you on your trip. That's fine, too.

If your trip home is relatively short, you'll still want to bring a supply of water for your puppy or adult. A dog that is particularly stressed or anxious can become dehydrated quickly. Also remember to bring a container in which to pour the Chi's drinking water. A small bowl will be fine for this, or if you'd rather, you might consider purchasing a little collapsible fabric water bowl to keep in the car on a permanent basis.

Cleanup Materials

Whether you are making a long or short trip, it is almost inevitable that your puppy or dog will drool, pant, shed, throw up, eliminate, or urinate (another good reason that you'll want to transport your puppy or dog in a carrier or crate while in the car). Unless the Chi is a seasoned traveler, the first trip in a strange car with strange folks can be borderline traumatic.

In anticipation of a stressful trip, or just normal canine urges, line your Chi's carrier or crate with a thick layer of newspapers or multiple pee pads so that you can just remove sheets as needed. In addition, you'll want to bring along the following supplies:

- Paper towels
- Plastic bags
- Water (to rinse off soiled paws)
- Hand towels
- Spray disinfectant cleaner
- Hand wipes (for you)

Many seasoned dog owners who frequently travel with their dogs keep a cleanup kit in their vehicles at all times. It's pretty much the rule that the one time you forget to bring one of these items it will be the time you need to have that item.

Travel Aids

Not all Chis are terrific travelers. In fact, even puppies and dogs that will develop into terrific travel companions after a few rides in the car are often very stressed with the first car ride. It may not even be the motion of the car itself. Remember, you are suddenly throwing a whole set of new variables at your little Chihuahua: You're new, the car is different, the carrier is strange to her, the smells are completely foreign, and she is leaving the family she has known for her entire life (if she's a pup) or the one person who treated her kindly (if she's a rescue).

To help a dog be a little calmer during the ride, many dog owners have had good success with the holistic flower essence Rescue Remedy. This is a very pure form of five different flower essences or tinctures that are combined for this remedy. Rescue

Remedy can be rubbed on the Chi's gums, or you can put a few drops in her drinking water.

 **Alert!**

Do not ask your veterinarian for any kind of tranquilizers to make your Chi calmer for the trip. Your veterinarian will not write this prescription for the safety of your dog. Except in the most extreme cases, tranquilizers have been shown to be more of a risk to the dog than any stress the trip (even a short one) may cause the dog.

Another product that is showing significant results is dog-appeasing pheromone, or DAP. This synthetic hormone mimics that of a lactating female dog. Puppies and adults alike recognize the faint odor and find it relaxing. DAP can be purchased as an automatic aerosol dispenser, or you can squirt the inside of your Chihuahua's carrier or her bedding with it.

Supplies for the First Night

If you've planned well for the ride home, you will have most of the supplies you will need for the puppy or adult's first night at home. In addition to the basics of food, water, a comfortable place to sleep (the carrier or crate), cleaning equipment, and a way to walk your Chi (collar and leash), you will want to consider a few other creature comforts for your new dog. These items can include any or all of the following:

- A favorite toy
- A "busy" toy or one that occupies the Chihuahua to take her mind off her loneliness, such as a rubber ball that is stuffable with little treats

- The scented towel or other item you were able to secure from the breeder
- A hot-water bottle or a dogproof warming blanket to keep a puppy warm and comfortable

The most important things you can supply, however, are likely to be in supply as soon as you lay eyes on your new dog: a little patience, and a lot of love.

First-Year Supplies and Expenses

How much will care and upkeep for your new Chihuahua cost in the first year? Despite the common thought that small dogs are less expensive than larger breeds (only true of food costs), toy breeds—and Chis in particular—can be quite expensive to maintain and care for.

Vet Care

The biggest expense most Chi owners incur is that for veterinary care. If your Chihuahua is a puppy, you can expect a tab of about $500 for the first year. This will include routine veterinary examinations, a complete series of vaccinations, preventive care (including a heartworm preventive program), and a spay or neuter.

Training

Another substantial first-year expense (that is the same no matter what the size of the dog) is training classes. Depending on your area of the country and with whom you are training, a six-week class could cost anywhere from $40 to more than $100. If you really want a well-trained and superbly socialized Chi that you can trust to take anywhere with you, you'll want to complete at least a year's worth of training. As you can see, this could total up to more than $500 quite quickly—but it is an expense that you will benefit from for the life of your Chihuahua.

 **Fact**

If your Chi is not the picture of health, true of many Chihuahuas, your veterinarian bills could add up into the thousands. For this reason alone, it is always advisable to set aside at least $500 in reserve for unexpected veterinary bills.

Equipment and Accessories

You can spend $20 or so on an inexpensive crate or carrier or literally thousands of dollars on a one-of-a-kind designer carrier. This price range is typical for any other kind of dog accoutrement. Nylon, cotton webbing, and simple leather collars can run from $5 to $20, while those that are made of the finest leather or silks and studded with real gems can cost more than most of us make in a year. And then there are those cute coats, rain slickers, mufflers, and beds. What you spend is really up to you; however, at a minimum, you can expect to shell out at least $100 for collars, leashes, a crate or carrier, and bedding.

 **Essential**

How you choose to housetrain your Chi can also affect the size of your first year's budget. If you are litter training, you'll need to factor in the cost of fresh bags of litter every week, at roughly $6 to $10 each. If you use pee pads, that's another cost that needs to be factored in.

Toys and Supplies

Other expenses to consider are toys, treats, more toys, and healthy chew items. A basket of toys and a variety of chews can be expected to cost $100 to $200 or more. As toys wear down, and as chews are destroyed, you'll need to continue to replace them.

Grooming supplies for the Chi (such as shampoo, brushes, combs, and nail trimmers) may total $30 to $40; however, if you are going to leave this chore to a professional groomer, you'd better factor in a $30 to $40 grooming expense every six to eight months.

As you can see, the first year's expenses for a Chihuahua can range from $500 (the healthy, adult dog that is already altered and up to date on all his vaccinations) to more than $1,000. The sky really is the limit when it comes to shopping for your Chihuahua, and if you can afford the elaborate and ostentatious, terrific. If you are on a more modest budget, you should still make sure that you plan on spending at least $1,000 that first year.

CHAPTER  7

Your Puppy's First Month

Congratulations! Your Chihuahua puppy is finally home! She's gotten a healthy thumbs-up from your veterinarian and is ready to begin a lifetime of adventure with you. Now what? Puppies don't come preprogrammed to accept sudden changes automatically. In fact, for your puppy, the first twenty-four hours in her new home could be the most stressful day she'll ever have in her life. That's where you come in to help her make the adjustments so she can settle in quickly.

The First Day

In the excitement of bringing home a new puppy, many owners can't contain their enthusiasm, and they cart the puppy around from house to house to show her off. Or they invite everyone they know to come over and visit with the new addition to the family.

Visitors

Chihuahua puppies are incredibly cute. It virtually goes without saying that everyone will want to see your new little Chi, marvel at her size, adore her unique personality and intelligence, beg to hold her, and generally make a big fuss. That's just a part of the life Chihuahuas are destined to bear. It is not, however, a good idea to subject your puppy to all this attention on her very first day.

Dropping by friends' houses to introduce your puppy could subject her to contagious viruses and bacteria. Puppies are most susceptible to disease until they have finished their series of puppy vaccinations.

 **Alert!**

> If you must take your puppy to visit someone who has unvaccinated animals—a potential source of disease—do not allow your pup to play on the floor or on the ground. These surfaces harbor diseases and are also the area that a small, low-to-the-ground puppy comes in contact with the most.

Inviting people (no dogs) to drop by the house to see your new puppy provides a safer scenario for your pup; however, there's another problem. Puppies need their rest. With people constantly coming in and out of your home to meet and greet the puppy, your pup won't get the rest she needs. If at all possible, try to spend the first few days with your puppy in a relaxed, calm, and protected environment. Allow her to fall into the day's routines, and then invite folks over when you know your puppy will be rested and ready for play.

Crates

You'll want to provide your Chi puppy with an escape—a safe haven she can retreat to when she's tired or when she's simply had enough excitement for the day. Keep a crate in the room with the door open, comfortable bedding inside, and a favorite toy or chew. This is the crate you'll use when you can't keep your eye on your puppy or have to devote your full attention to something else.

 Question?

Isn't it cruel to keep a dog in a crate?
A crate is the safest place your young Chi can be if you must leave the house or are at home but can't keep your eyes on her. It is also a terrific tool to help with housetraining. Crating only becomes cruel if the space is cramped, soiled, or used in excess. It is generally recommended that puppies not be crated for more than ten hours total during every twenty-four-hour period, and this includes the hours that she is kept crated during the night.

Protecting Your Spaces

You'll want your Chi to be able to explore her new surroundings; however, unless you want to get a bad start on her housetraining, keep her explorations limited to one room. Use baby gates or puppy gates to block off access to other rooms, or set up a playpen in a room with an easy-to-clean floor, such as the surfaces found in most kitchens or breakfast areas. And, allow her to relieve herself frequently—at least every two hours and more often if she is playing hard.

Spread a selection of toys and safe chew items around the floor for your puppy to play with. Sit on the floor with her and spend time petting her, rubbing her, and getting to know her. When she begins to tire—or when you know she should be tired—allow her to rest.

Eating and Sleeping

Be mindful, too, of her feeding times (don't miss any!) and closely monitor how much she is actually eating at each meal. Chihuahua puppies are known for forgetting to eat; they will play until they crash and sleep. Exceptionally small puppies—and those pups that just seem prone to the condition—can become hypoglycemic.

 Essential

Hypoglycemia is a sudden drop in the level of sugar in the blood. (This is the same condition a diabetic may suffer from if he receives too great an injection of insulin.) Symptoms of hypoglycemia include sudden weakness, lethargy, tremors, and seizures. If left untreated, the puppy will become unconscious and could die.

Talk to your veterinarian and your breeder as to the best way to be prepared to respond to a hypoglycemic episode. Honey, corn syrup, or jelly rubbed on your pup's gums will provide a quick, absorbable source of sugar; however, your veterinarian may ask you to keep a high-sugar supplement, such as Nutrical or Nutristat, at the ready.

▲ At first, your Chi could be a little wary of this new place, but after a while he or she will get comfortable and become the king (or queen) of the castle.

Getting Through the Dark Hours

Hopefully, you're rested and have gotten several nights of good sleep prior to bringing home your puppy. If not, then maybe you've thought ahead and taken several days off from work. Just as when a newborn baby arrives in the home, it could be a while before you're able to sleep restfully through the entire night again.

During the wee hours of that first night at home, when your Chi is singing (and barking and crying) the blues, have compassion for the little guy. Remember, all he's known is a loving mom and his littermates. Naptime meant a nice, warm puppy pile to snuggle up in, with lots of little heartbeats to listen to and, most likely, lots of little Chi snorts and snoring.

 Alert!

Do not respond to your puppy's cries by picking her up and saying, "Oh, you poor baby!" Though it is human nature to comfort those in distress, you just rewarded her for crying, which will increase the puppy's crying. As difficult as it may be, ignoring whimpers (unless your puppy is signaling that she needs to relieve herself) and rewarding a quiet puppy will cut down on the number of puppy howling nights you'll have to endure.

Now that you've taken her away from all this, she's lonely. She hasn't had the time to bond closely with you yet, nor has she learned that she can trust that you'll always be there for her and that you'll always come back. She's probably a bit scared and frightened in her new home, and she's certainly more than a little disoriented.

Separation Anxiety

There are many ways, however, in which you can help your puppy feel more comfortable and ease her anxieties. Consider these tried-and-true methods:

The following tricks will help with separation from Mom:

- Place a momma-scented hand towel in the crate with the puppy.
- Spray DAP (a synthetic hormone that imitates the comforting hormone produced by lactating dogs) in the crate or rub it on a soft toy.
- Wrap a ticking clock in a warm towel and place in the crate (to imitate a heartbeat).
- Rub a drop of Rescue Remedy on the pup's gums to ease her separation anxiety.

Here are few ways to help ease sibling separation (a major source of warmth):

- Wrap a hot-water bottle in a towel and place in the crate.
- Insert a dog-safe heating pad in the crate or a battery-operated electric warming pad.
- Keep the puppy warm with a soft pajama coat.
- Provide lots of nestling-down materials in the crate.
- Keep the crate away from any drafts.

You can decrease her disorientation and provide distractions from any source of distress by doing any of the following:

- Keeping the pup's crate next to your bed so your Chi can see you.
- Pulling out the sleeping bag and sleeping on the floor with a hand in the Chi's crate.
- Placing a soft plush toy in the crate with the Chi puppy.
- Giving the puppy a busy toy, such as a scrumptious chew or a hard rubber toy that requires chewing to release tiny bits of treats.

Whatever you do, don't put the Chi puppy in your bed. Even relatively light sleepers are quite capable of rolling over and crushing a young Chihuahua puppy. They are just too small to sleep with you at this point. Wait until the Chi is older and is housetrained. Most puppies don't know to wake you when they have to relieve themselves. They are also so small that the end of the bed doesn't seem like part of their "space," so they're not worried about soiling it. You'll wake each morning to a mess (the best-case scenario) or a deceased puppy (the worst possible—but entirely feasible—scenario).

Handle with Care!

You're now aware that sleeping in bed with a tiny puppy is not a good idea, but this isn't the only time that you will have to exert care and caution with your new Chihuahua puppy. As the smallest of the toy breeds, and at its smallest as a puppy, the Chihuahua youngster can present herself with many opportunities for serious injuries.

Physical Frailties

Falls are one of the top causes of broken leg bones. A Chihuahua puppy can suffer grave injuries when dropped only three or four feet from the floor. That's arm-holding height for many older children and adults. Children of all ages should only hold the puppy while they are sitting on the floor and under the direct and very close supervision of an adult.

A puppy with a molera—a hereditary hole in the dog's skull where the bones do not close—is of itself not a health risk. Chihuahuas live just fine with this unique anomaly. The presence of a molera does require the pup's owner to be careful handling the puppy and to be cognizant of where the molera is. Pushing on this opening can cause serious injury to the pup.

 Essential

It is a common "mythconception" that Chis with moleras are more prone to hydrocephalus, a condition in which fluid collects and exerts pressure on the brain. This is a very serious, potentially life-threatening condition that requires immediate veterinary attention; however, the presence of a molera is neither a prerequisite for nor an indicator of hydrocephalus.

Environmental Hazards

Chihuahua puppies do not retain heat well and can become chilled easily. It is for this reason that you will want to provide your Chi with warm bedding in a draft-free area in your home. Dog coats are necessary in cold weather, and a lighter jacket might even be needed in a very cool, air-conditioned home.

Besides watching the thermostat in your home, you will also need to keep a close eye on other pets in your home. A family dog that is friendly with other dogs will usually recognize that the Chi pup is a puppy; however, that doesn't mean that your older dog won't accidentally injure the pup. If there is a huge disparity in size (for instance, your other dog is a boisterous eighty-pound Lab), you will need to make careful introductions. Keep the dogs crated if you cannot watch their interactions.

Dogs aren't the only possible danger to the Chihuahua. Pets of all species—cats, birds, even a territorial house rabbit—are capable of frightening and/or injuring a Chi puppy. If your other house pet is free roaming and has access to the entire house, always keep an eye on your Chihuahua and supervise any and all interactions. A pouncing cat, a swooping macaw, or a hard-biting rabbit can inflict serious if not fatal injuries to a little puppy.

Do not assume, either, that just because your pets—whether canines or of other species—seem to get along great while you are home that this balance will remain in effect when you leave the house. It is better, initially, to err on the side of caution and crate your Chi so you know she is safe. As with children, if you can't supervise, separate. Fortunately, most pets adjust over time to the new addition and will recognize the Chi as a member of the family rather than an intrusion. Be prepared, however, for a situation in which one or more of your pets will not cohabit peacefully with the Chi. If this is the case, the pets involved will require constant supervision and/or separation.

 **Alert!**

Some high prey-drive breeds (those that enjoy chasing balls or anything else that moves) might not recognize a Chi puppy as a dog, per se. If you catch your adult dog staring hard or stalking your Chi slowly—watch out! Keep the dogs separated, and seek professional animal-behavior training advice immediately in order to defuse this volatile situation.

Setting House Rules—And Keeping Them

It's easier to set the rules of the house when your puppy first comes home than to set them as you go. Do you want to allow your Chi to cuddle with you on the couch or a favorite chair while you watch television or read? Or would you rather the puppy learned that chairs and couches are off limits?

To raise your Chihuahua to be a good companion that quickly learns the rules of home living, the key is to be consistent. If you don't want your Chi up in the recliner with you, it's not fair to allow the puppy access to this chair for months and then suddenly decide at six months of age that this is a no-no. Alternately, it's not fair to expect your Chihuahua to understand why she's allowed in the recliner with you sometimes but not all the time. Make a plan and stick to it—it's easier for your Chi to have consistent rules.

 Essential

If you must err, it is easier to err on the strict side and then later, when the Chihuahua has better housetraining skills or is no longer chewing everything in sight, to relax the rules—permanently. Working in the reverse (lenient to strict) causes a lot of frustration for both dog and owner.

If you live alone, you'll be the only one responsible for making sure the rules are kept. If you live with one or more people, the opportunity for your Chihuahua to break the rules increases exponentially. It is common for at least one member of the family to feel that you are either too strict or too lax with your Chihuahua. This is the person who undoubtedly will complicate your life and your Chi's.

Say, for example, that you don't want your Chihuahua puppy in bed at night. You want her to remain in her crate so that you know where she is and also know when she needs to relieve herself. Perhaps you have a preteen daughter who feels otherwise and who sneaks the pup out to sleep with her at night. Yikes. Now the pup wants to sleep in bed (who wouldn't?), so she yelps more when she's in her crate. It's like the first night all over again. And, to make matters worse, she thinks your daughter's closet is a good place to relieve herself.

Some training experts estimate that it can take up to twenty correct repetitions of the behavior to undo one incorrect behavior. So that one time in bed—or the one time your spouse allows your Chi to cuddle on the couch with him—may take awhile to correct. Before you get into any arguments with family members, have a family meeting to discuss how the puppy is going to be raised, what is allowed and what is not, and what the agreed-upon ultimate rules are going to be. Then, stick to the rules.

Everything Counts

Every incident—big or small—that your puppy goes through makes a permanent impression on her. Every encounter she has, every experience she is exposed to, every interaction she has with other animals, dogs and humans, and every response you make to her behaviors all work to mold her into the adult dog she will be.

 **Fact**

It has long been known that a puppy's potential has a significant genetic influence and that a dog can only be as great as the sum of his parts. However, whether your puppy reaches the best she can be for the genetics she has been given is up to you and how you bring her up in her environment. Your influence, by some estimates, is responsible for as much as 40 percent of your puppy's final adult temperament.

There's a tricky balance to raising a puppy. You want your puppy to experience as many people, places, and different environments as possible, but you also want to make sure that all these experiences are positive. This requires that you, as a puppy owner, think ahead. You have to be a couple of steps ahead of the situation and cognizant of the physical signals of discomfort or approaching anxiety that your puppy is giving.

For example, if she's likely to become frightened by a school bus as it roars by in the morning, don't force her to wait at the corner with you (and a pack of kids) as the bus roars to a halt. Instead, allow her to sit on her leash at a comfortable distance away from the bus. Praise her for watching the bus quietly. If she shows signs of discomfort, move farther away.

The distance at which she can observe "frightening" objects is her "safety zone." Every dog has one—timid dogs will want to investigate unknowns from a greater distance away; bolder dogs will be more comfortable checking something out at a closer distance. From your puppy's safety zone, gradually move a little closer each day, rewarding her for good behavior with verbal and physical praise and a small treat. If you've moved too close for comfort one day, move back to her previous comfort zone and reinforce her good behavior.

 Question?

Shouldn't I make her sit still if she's afraid of something?
Forcing a puppy or dog to be near something that terrifies her will not help her to overcome her fears. Instead, it will intensify them and could lessen her trust in you (since from her perspective you are putting her in obvious danger). Yelling at a timid dog is also a huge no-no, as is verbally or physically comforting her—which teaches her that her fears are founded.

Socialization Begins

Your puppy's mom and littermates played a significant role in teaching her what is acceptable behavior with other canines and what is not. Mom was quick to correct, and littermates yelped and refused to play if a puppy's bites were too hard or her play was getting obnoxious and over the top. Playing with other puppies (and mom) teaches a pup bite inhibition, or how to play-bite without hurting anyone. That is a really important lesson for dogs of all breeds because no matter the size of a dog, a hard bite hurts and can break the skin.

It is also important for your puppy to be introduced to many gentle, kind people while she is still very young. The first critical period for socialization impressions to be made with a pup is over at roughly twelve weeks of age. If your breeder keeps her puppies until they are this age, she will have the initial responsibility for exposing her pups to all kinds of kind visitors.

 Fact

Problems can occur with puppies that are separated too early from their moms and littermates. These pups apparently have not learned their bite-inhibition lessons, and many professional trainers note that this early separation seems to cause more issues later with training. Many Chi pups are not sold until twelve weeks of age. If you purchased a puppy younger than ten weeks, be aware that you may have some catch-up work to do in the pup's socialization and bite-inhibition work.

If he's a quality breeder, he will have done this. Friends will be invited to see the puppies, as well as potential buyers and older children from the neighborhood, and they will get lots of handling and touching from the breeder himself. If you are purchasing a puppy from a breeder who has not done any socialization with her pups, you will have some catching up to do. But don't despair if the situation is not ideal. Remember, everything you do with your puppy makes an impression, and you can go far in bringing your puppy back up to speed socially.

Socialization with Dogs

The experts all agree on the "how" of socializing your puppy with other dogs; they just don't all agree on the "when." Some professional trainers feel the risk of raising a frightened or dog/dog aggressive puppy (by not continuing the pup's socialization with other dogs) is greater than the risk of coming in contact with a dread disease.

If you live in an area that has a high risk for lethal puppy diseases, such as canine parvovirus or canine hepatitis, your veterinarian will not want you to take your puppy out for meet-and-greets where dogs and their owners congregate, such as a dog park. You have no way of knowing which dogs have been vaccinated and which have not, nor can you be entirely sure that the park grounds are free of disease. In fact, you can pretty well assume that in these areas, it is highly likely that your Chi *will* be exposed to a deadly virus or bacterial infection.

What you do want to do is open your home (a safe place) to people who have friendly, unaggressive, vaccinated dogs. Avoid other puppies until they have finished their complete vaccination series.

Socialization with People

Continuing your pup's socialization after she leaves the breeder's home is critical to her future relationships with guests in your home, friendly strangers in the street, or just people in general, of any age, race, size, and shape. If not socialized with people and given lots of opportunities to realize that an extended hand from a nice person means something good is going to happen (such as receiving a small treat), a Chihuahua can become timid of people, defensive, or even a bit aggressive.

 **Alert!**

Many people who have good intentions can be way too overbearing when greeting a toy-breed puppy. You must be your puppy's advocate. Do not hesitate to tell the greeting person exactly how to meet your puppy—by allowing the puppy to make the first move toward the person's outstretched, treat-laden hand.

With a puppy, you'll see that it's very easy to find people to offer your pup treats. Who wouldn't want to "Ooh" and "Aah" over an adorable little Chi? But you must be very careful that you do not overstep your puppy's level of comfort. One puppy may not initially want a person to come closer than five or maybe even ten feet, while another Chi puppy may feel comfortable trotting right up to a stranger and receiving a light pat.

Gauge your pup's starting safety zone with strangers, and work to improve on this or to continue to maintain a happy, friendly dog. Don't think that because you already own an extroverted Chi that she will remain this friendly. Socialization is an ongoing process that should be continued throughout a Chi's lifetime.

Why Little Dogs Need Training, Too

Another ongoing process that should never come to a halt is your Chi's training. A common misconception is that toy breeds don't need any obedience training. This accompanies the misconception that toy breeds aren't really dogs; they are four-legged children who already know how to behave perfectly. Other people feel that toy breeds are so easy to control physically that there's no need for training.

 Essential

Daily training exercises—for even a few minutes a day—are a great way to maintain a healthy dog-leader relationship with your Chi. Without any regular guidance, any dog of any breed will slip into the role of leader in a home. You don't want to live by dog rules, so have fun with training while maintaining the leadership status in your home.

None of these beliefs could be further from the truth. In fact, toy breeds can actually be more challenging, in some aspects, to train than their larger counterparts. Chihuahuas are small (making it harder to reach them while standing), lightning fast (don't think you can catch one of these kids unless they want to be caught), very intelligent (Chis make some of the best service dogs ever), and they have an unending supply of energy (if you don't find something constructive and fun for them to do, they'll find something themselves). On top of all that, they have a terrier-like attitude (a bit independent and a tendency to be feisty).

If you want your Chihuahua to be a great house pet and companion, she needs obedience training. This does not need to be in the form of formal obedience lessons though you might find that it's a lot of fun to train and earn titles with your Chihuahua. At a minimum, however, you need to teach your Chihuahua the basics, such as sit, down, stay, and come, so that she is controllable in and out of the home. You'll be glad you took the time and effort. There's nothing quite like a well-trained dog.

CHAPTER 8

Life with an Adopted Chi

E very rescued adult dog is unique. Each comes with her own life experiences that have molded her into the dog she is today. It is also these previous life experiences that can make your Chihuahua's transition to home life extremely easy or sprinkled with a few challenges. With those dogs that have some obstacles to overcome, time is a great healer—especially when the Chi owner is prepared for virtually anything and is willing to give the dog the time she needs to develop into a wonderful pet.

The First Twenty-Four Hours

If you are adopting a Chihuahua from an outstanding breed rescue or purchasing a former show dog from a breeder, you aren't likely to have many—if any—surprises when you bring your new adult dog home.

If, however, you are adopting a Chi that you really don't know much about, you should anticipate potential challenges. Knowing what to expect and exactly how to respond when issues arise is key in helping your adopted Chi continue to move forward in the right direction. A few training skills and a lot of patience can help even a problem child become an ideal companion.

Just as with a puppy, the first day your rescued Chihuahua comes home is typically the most stressful. Everything and everyone is strange and new. A bolder Chi may walk into your home, look around, figure out which couch is the plushest and settle right in. Often, these are the older Chihuahuas who have experienced nothing but a wonderful life all their years.

 **Fact**

Senior Chis are often overlooked at shelters and rescues because potential adopters fear that they won't have as long to enjoy these dogs. Senior Chis, however, have shown their robust health by making it to their senior years. These are also the dogs that fit most easily into new households, which is a huge benefit.

A dog that was bold and playful at the foster home may take one step into your home and try to scramble back out the door. She may be terrified of everything she sees and start trembling, freeze in place, or pancake (the Chi's way of flattening themselves to avoid predators).

Most likely, however, you will be adopting a dog that falls somewhere between the two extremes. This is the dog that has limited experience with a family but is ready and willing to make your house her home. She's ready for a lifetime bond, but because of her past experiences and limited time with you, she's not quite ready to completely put her life in your hands and trust you implicitly. Trust takes time.

Minimize Stress

Most adopted Chihuahuas are lacking in social skills. Their previous owners most likely didn't spend much time socializing them with all kinds of people and in all kinds of situations. As a result, the Chi lacks self-confidence and doesn't feel comfortable in new surroundings.

Signs of anxiety can include the following:

- Pacing
- Restlessness
- Panting
- Shedding
- Loss of appetite
- Trembling
- Whining, whimpering

To help your Chihuahua feel more at ease in your home, try gating her in a room so she can explore every inch of this area relatively quickly. Provide a crate with comfortable bedding in this room on the floor with the door latched *open*. This gives your Chihuahua a place of refuge. Make sure you have a fresh bowl of clean, cool water available to your new Chi at all times in this room. Stress can quickly dehydrate a dog.

 **Question?**

Can I invite friends over to see my new dog?
A houseful of boisterous people could overwhelm an unsure Chihuahua. Wait until your new dog trusts you, and then begin introducing new people as part of her ongoing socialization. Coach your visitors so they know to let the dog be the one to make the approach and so they resist the temptation to pick her up.

Sit on the floor with your dog, allowing her to come to you for pats and some love. Reward her trust with tiny bits of treats, if she's receptive to food. With a very fearful dog, completely ignore her while you're sitting on the floor. Don't even make eye contact. Allow her to approach you at her own pace. Resist petting her, but allow her to lick your hands and, if she is receptive to food, to take tiny bits of treats out of your hands. Avoid any sudden movements that may send her skittering to the far corners of the room. It usually doesn't take more than twenty minutes to half an hour for even the shyest of dogs to warm up to you if you let her make all the moves.

Gentle Handling

When handling your new Chi, be very gentle. A dog's natural reaction to pain is to bite the source. Until you know if your Chihuahua has any touchy areas, use caution. While stroking your dog, watch for flinching, a quick turning of the head (a warning of an upcoming snap), yelping, and trembling.

 **Alert!**

For many dogs, handling of the paws and nails is upsetting. With an adult dog, this fear could stem from a bad toenail clipping that inflicted a lot of pain, or it could be that the dog has never had this area handled before.

Keep in mind, too, that a sensitive area may not be an area in which the Chi is currently feeling pain. Past injuries or parts of the body that previously experienced pain (for instance, an ear that was horribly infected) can still be reactive areas, or locations to which the Chi will respond as if he is truly in pain.

Watch Your Reactions

It is an unfortunate fact that many rescued adult Chihuahuas have had very limited exposure (if any) to living in a home. You may find that the dog you've adopted takes everything in stride and expresses only curiosity to the various sounds emanating from such things as household appliances, air ducts, rolling garbage cans, and the vacuum cleaner. If, however, your Chi shows fearfulness toward something in your home, you need to know how to react.

To help your Chi overcome her fear of a certain household object, the mantra is, "Ignore bad reactions, but reward good behavior." For example, if the sound of a flushing toilet sends your Chi flying into another room, trembling, just do nothing. Do not attempt to run to the rescue, cuddle, and coo to the shaking dog.

Dogs interpret positive physical contact with their special humans as the greatest reward of all. Since you are rewarding your Chi for running from the flushing toilet, you have reinforced your Chihuahua's reaction to the flushing toilet. It is better to ignore frightened or noisy (barking) responses to ordinary sights and sounds but reward positive responses. Over time, your Chi will show less and less reaction to what she fears.

Danger Zone

Statistically, the greatest percentage of severe dog-bite injuries inflicted to owners occurs when a new dog is brought into a home. This is the time at which the dog is under the greatest stress, and all breeds are more likely to bite at this time. The more quickly the dog adjusts to the home, the less stress she is under, and the faster the risk of a stress-induced bite decreases. It could be a few days or a few weeks.

What this means to you, however, is that you should not put your newly adopted Chihuahua in a position in which she could become frightened, overwhelmed, or feels she is being directly challenged. Give her time to get acclimated and, most importantly, to trust you. Avoid confrontations by limiting the dog's access to one room and preventing her from being able to steal any items that she can't have.

Additionally, don't trust your Chihuahua. Your newly adopted Chihuahua must earn your trust. This takes time and does not occur overnight. Think of it this way: Would you trust a complete stranger to come to your home and watch your children while you were away on vacation? Of course not. But we often expect an adopted dog to behave perfectly, even when under extreme stress. So, keep this in mind. Go slowly with your Chihuahua. Give her a chance to prove her trustworthiness.

▲ With the proper care and love, it won't be long before your Chi looks up to you.

First Night Blues

Your adopted Chihuahua may or may not express any distress during her first night in your home. As an adult, she won't be missing her littermates or anguishing over the separation from her mom. If she's from the shelter, she certainly won't be shedding tears (figuratively speaking) over leaving the other shelter dogs. Even if she's been in a foster home, she may or may not have formed a strong enough bond with her foster mom to feel any separation anxiety.

What your new Chi is likely to feel is a bit of anxiety (again) from being in a strange new place. She may cry a bit or bark at being put in her crate (oh, the injustice of it all!). As she becomes acclimated to her new surroundings—and her crate—this reaction will quickly subside. To help her through the first few nights, here are a few pointers:

- Use a crate at night.
- Make sure the crate is warm and comfortable and away from any drafts.
- Put the crate next to your bed, or sleep next to the crate on the floor so she can see you.
- Ignore crying, yapping, and barking unless you recognize that this is a signal that your dog needs to relieve herself. Do not comfort her when she's crying. (That's a reward, remember?)
- Give her a busy toy that she can work on, like a Kong or other rubber toy stuffed with treats.
- Consider spraying DAP or using an atomizer to help calm your Chi.
- Rub Rescue Remedy on her gums or put a couple of drops in her water bowl.
- Do not put your Chi in bed with you, as you might smoosh her or she could snap.
- Toss her a little treat when you catch her being quiet.
- Be patient; she'll catch on quickly.

An adult Chi *should* be able to sleep through the night in her crate. Keep in mind, however, that this holds true for a healthy, calm adult Chi. If your adopted Chihuahua was anxious during the day, drank copious amounts of water prior to bedtime, or if she isn't sleeping in her crate during the night but is up and very active, you can expect that she will need to relieve herself at least once if not twice during the night.

The Next Few Months

Every adopted dog has a unique and often unknown past. Every experience the dog has had, including those experiences she is having now, molds and shapes her temperament, health, and the amount of personal baggage she brings with her.

Just as every adopted dog is an individual, so is every owner. Some owners are more equipped to handle any potential challenges an adopted dog can dish out. These owners are often veteran dog owners and have lived with Chihuahuas before—maybe even a rescue. They have patience and are confident in knowing what to do to help the dog along. Other owners are new to the Chihuahua world and may even be new to dog ownership.

Add to this equation that every adopted dog has her own timetable for healing, learning, and adapting. Whether you are a novice owner or someone who has decades of Chi experience, patience and persistence are the two virtues most necessary with a rescued adult dog. Don't give up on your little guy. Virtually all problems are solvable given the right training tools to correct them.

 Question?

What is a kid-friendly dog?
When it comes to any breed, a kid-friendly dog is one that enjoys being around sensitive, responsible older children. It does not mean that the dog won't respond with a bark, snap, or bite if it is teased, abused, or hurt—even if the injury is an accident. Nor does it mean that a child can take anything out of the dog's mouth at any time.

Adult Chis and Children

Breed rescues are very hesitant to adopt out an adult Chi to a family with children. The younger the children, the greater the hesitation. From the rescue's viewpoint, Chis and young children are an accident waiting to happen. From experience, they know that it is extremely difficult for even the most vigilant parent to keep both child and Chi from getting hurt.

Risks to Children and Dogs

Babies are at greatest risk of predatory behavior from dogs. Their distinctive cries and the presence of milk or food on their clothing have combined to cause good dogs to do bad things—even as far as to jump into the baby's crib to hurt them. On the floor, a baby is within reach of even the smallest dog. In a swing, the combination of movement, food smells, and baby sounds can trigger a nasty situation.

Toddlers toddle—and fall often, sometimes on the dog whose natural response to pain is to bite. A Chihuahua could also easily be crushed. Children this age investigate their world by tasting and touching, often in the form of biting, poking, prodding, and pinching. If a dog takes a toy away from the toddler, the toddler instinctively grabs it back, possibly provoking an argument over the toy.

 Alert!

Certain aspects of the Chihuahua's anatomy can make this breed particularly susceptible to injuries from well-meaning children. The molera, a hole in some Chihuahuas' skulls, and a Chi's large, protruding eyes can both be critically injured with very little effort.

Young children like to run, scream, and play. A Chihuahua could easily become frightened by these children or decide to give chase. Young children, such as toddlers, can't resist picking up and holding little puppies or small dogs. Holding a squirming Chihuahua is difficult for anyone. Dropping the Chihuahua—even from a distance as short as from a child's arms to the floor—could result in broken bones for the Chi.

Know the Rules

If you have children—or have grandchildren, nieces, or nephews who visit often—you'll need to set the rules down immediately with them if you are to have any hopes of raising children along-side Chihuahuas safely—for all concerned. Here are a few basic pointers:

- The dog's crate is hers and should never be entered.
- Holding the dog is only allowed when sitting on the floor and with an adult helping.
- Never poke, prod, hit, or tease the dog.
- Never try to take a toy or food away from the dog even if it's yours; always get an adult to help.
- Do not scream or run in the house.
- Do not stick your face in the dog's face or try to kiss her.
- Do not wake a sleeping Chi by rubbing or pushing her; call her name to wake her.

As a parent, grandparent, aunt, or uncle your responsibility is to supervise all interactions between the child and the dog. This doesn't mean to watch the kids and the dog in the backyard from the kitchen window. It means being within arms' reach of both children and dog. Even then, things can happen so rapidly that it might be virtually impossible to prevent an accident from happening, but hopefully you can lessen the effects.

If you cannot supervise, then you absolutely must separate child and dog. More things happen when a parent or supervising adult isn't watching than at any other time. And, if you don't see what happened, you might never know the full story. Usually, it's human nature to blame the dog for everything when in fact there's almost always a reason (albeit maybe not a good one) for a dog to snap. Put up a barrier to keep the dog in a room, or allow her to retire safely to her crate.

Typical Challenges of the Rescued Dog

Even if your adult dog has been fostered in a home and carefully evaluated, you won't know everything about her. For example, a

Chihuahua may be fine around other dogs her size and thus be pronounced dog-friendly, when in fact she is terrified of large dogs.

The key here is to be on the lookout for the kinds of challenges that may not have been evident at the rescue or shelter. Characteristically, an adult dog that hasn't had a lot of home or family time may need a little brushing up on the following skills:

- Relationships with strange dogs, as well as living with other household pets (see Chapter 12)
- Socialization skills with people (see Chapter 10)
- Housetraining (see Chapter 9)
- Basic obedience training (see Chapter 14)

 **Essential**

Fearfulness from lack of socialization is a common problem among Chihuahuas. If your Chi is timid or easily frightened, consult Deborah Wood's book, *Help for Your Shy Dog: Turning Your Terrified Dog into a Terrific Pet.*

The good news is that an adult dog learns quickly and will already have many of the skills necessary to become a wonderful companion. You also begin with a dog that wants to please you and has chosen you as her human. Consider your Chihuahua as a work in progress. Some dogs may need a little more work to make progress. Diligence, love, and training can help you achieve the perfect canine companion—that is, if your adopted dog isn't already one!

Who Can Help You

If you have any concerns or questions regarding your adopted Chi's habits or behaviors and need help in addressing them, your first call should be to the breed rescue or shelter from which you adopted your Chihuahua. These folks have heard just about everything when it comes to unusual or problematic behaviors. They also have solutions to the majority of your Chi tribulations.

 **Fact**

If you didn't adopt your Chihuahua from a breed rescue, you can still call a local, regional, or national Chi rescue for advice and help. These people are experts in problem solving, specifically for the Chihuahua breed. There's nothing more they like to do than to help a rescued Chi become a better family member.

If you don't get satisfaction from these sources, or if the situation is more complex, there are several other ways to find the help you need. These professionals include veterinary behaviorists, animal behaviorists, and trainers.

Veterinary Behaviorists

This individual is not only a degreed doctor of veterinary medicine (DVM) but is also a diplomate, or board-certified specialist, of the American College of Veterinary Behaviorists (ACVB). To find a veterinary behaviorist, visit the American Veterinary Medical Association Web site, online at *www.avma.org.*

Veterinary Behavior Consultant

Many veterinarians have an interest in animal behavior but are not board certified through the ACVB. What these veterinarians do have is an in-depth knowledge of behavior, behavior-modification training, and medical therapies. If your veterinarian does not have a special interest in behavior, ask for a referral to someone who is respected in your area. You can also contact the AVMA for a referral to a veterinary behavior consultant. Also visit the Animal Hospital Association of America Web site, at *www. aahanet.org.*

Animal Behaviorists

The certified animal behaviorist holds a Ph.D. in animal behavior and is certified through the Animal Behavior Society (ABS). Certified animal behaviorists can be located by visiting the ABS Web site, online at *www.animalbehavior.org/ABS.*

 Alert!

Many individuals call themselves behavioral experts, animal behaviorists, or any number of other titles. Be wary of anyone who presents himself as specializing in behavior if he has had no educational training in this area or is not certified.

Trainers

To find an accomplished trainer who is good at solving behavioral challenges, contact your veterinarian, breed rescue, shelter, breeder, and other canine-savvy individuals for referrals. You may also try visiting the Association of Pet Dog Trainers (APDT) Web site, online at *www.apdt.com.*

A Rewarding Endeavor

Saving a life by taking in a rescued adult dog and being able to give her a permanent, final home is commendable. Providing the veterinary care and careful nurturing needed to bring back your Chihuahua's health and vigor is inspiring. But perhaps the most exciting and rewarding aspect of adopting and raising an adult Chihuahua is being able to gently mold her over time from reserved or anxious Chi into a "Ms. Personality"—if not around others, at least around you—and knowing that you had everything to do with this amazing transformation.

To say that the ensuing human-dog relationship is nothing short of extraordinary is not an exaggeration. Dogs rarely get to pick their humans; most are selected by a person when the dog is a puppy. Adult dogs, however, generally win over their forever humans by letting them know that they are the one. When a dog picks the person she wants to be with for life, the bond is very strong. You almost can't go wrong.

The experience of owning a rescued dog is singular; it is unlike any experiences you may have had raising a puppy. Once you have earned your Chi's complete trust and she has earned yours, it's pretty much smooth sailing from there on out. But do be forewarned: adopting rescued adult Chis can become addictive. Some Chihuahua owners will be quick to tell you that they'd never want to select a dog any other way.

CHAPTER 9

Tips for Housetraining

Ahousetrained Chihuahua is worth her weight in gold. A dog that lacks housetraining skills—or has recurring accidents—is a common gripe among toy breed owners, Chihuahua owners included. But it doesn't have to be. If you take the correct approach to housetraining your puppy or adult Chi, and you have a little patience, your Chihuahua can be as good as gold when it comes to knowing when and where to relieve herself.

An Easy Principle

Housetraining a puppy or adult does not have to be difficult. While Chihuahuas have an unfortunate reputation for being notoriously difficult to housetrain, this is largely unfair. The reasons that a Chi might take longer to housetrain (or never really be 100 percent reliable) could be due to a couple of factors.

First, the Chi is a toy breed, which means these dogs inherently require a bit more flexibility when it comes to figuring out an effective approach to housetraining. The second factor is that most owners expect too much from their puppies and untrained adults far too soon, which virtually sets up a Chi to fail.

What Is It About Toys?

As a Chi owner, you need to recognize that your Chihuahua cannot be expected to hold it as long as the bigger dogs and will require more frequent opportunities to relieve herself. Four hours is the maximum time you should expect a healthy adult dog to hold if she's on a regular schedule of meals and exercise and has just relieved herself.

Additionally, as the smallest of toy breeds, it follows that when a Chihuahua urinates, the resulting spot is very small—sometimes not much more than a tablespoon of liquid. Accidents often go unnoticed, particularly if they are on carpet or another absorbent flooring, until the spots dry and begin to smell or discolor the carpet. By this time, the Chihuahua is accustomed to using the rug or carpet as her bathroom, and the owner is saddled with retraining his dog.

 **Essential**

No matter how diligent and careful you are in training your Chihuahua, accept the fact that sooner or later an accident will happen. Make sure to have a cleanser on hand that is made specifically to break down urine and remove the smell. Blot the area until no more liquid can be absorbed, and then repeat with the urine-removing cleanser. Cleansers that contain ammonia should be avoided, as the residue smells like urine to a dog.

One Variable At a Time

With housetraining, it is important that you start small and don't move too quickly. You will want to increase only one variable at a time. With housetraining, your two variables are time (the number of minutes/hours the dog is capable of holding) and area (the parts of your home in which the dog can be trusted). If your puppy can hold reliably for two hours in her crate, you might consider increasing her time to two and a half hours *or* keeping her at two hours but increasing her space to include a small playpen encircling her crate.

The Reward System

Give the correct behavior, receive a reward. Give the wrong behavior, nothing happens. It doesn't take long for a dog—a species that has been domesticated for thousands of years and that lives to be with humans—to figure out what behavior gets the most benefits.

When applying the reward system to housetraining, it's really rather simple. When your puppy or adult is in the act of relieving herself, praise her quietly and say, "Go potty" or some other suitable command. If you are too jubilant in your verbal praise, you will startle your Chi and may actually stop the flow of events, so to speak. After she's finished, continue to tell her how good she is and give her a small treat. Do this every time your Chi eliminates in the correct area, such as outdoors or in a dog litter pan. Soon she will not only understand where to relieve herself, she'll also understand the command "Go potty" and will start looking for a spot when you ask her to.

Acceptable Corrections

The only time a mild verbal correction is permissible in housetraining is if you catch your Chihuahua in the act of relieving herself in the incorrect place. If you see this happening, you're allowed to say "Ah-ah!," which should help to startle the Chi and stop what she is doing. Then, with absolutely no anger or malice, pick up the pup and place her in the correct elimination location. When she relieves herself here, praise quietly, give your command, and then treat.

The worst mistake you can make in housetraining your Chi is to call or drag your Chi over to an accident and scold her. Doing this does nothing to speed up her learning; it only teaches her not to come when you call her. In the case of collaring her and dragging her over to the mess, she's not likely to let you grab her by the collar again.

 **Alert!**

Harsh and/or physical corrections do not have a place in housetraining! The Chihuahua is a breed that wants to please her owner. You just need to show her what you want in a consistent manner and follow a reward-based, positive housetraining program. She'll learn much faster without any damage to the human-canine bond.

Your best approach is to go over to the accident and clean it up quietly. If your Chi is curious—and you are having troubles maintaining your cool—place her gently in her crate so you can finish your cleanup work. While you're cleaning, try to figure out what mistake you might have made in her training.

Understand the Signals

If you're not keeping a close eye on your Chihuahua, it is quite possible for her to have an accident right in front of you. Young puppies give very little warning that they are about to relieve themselves, probably because even they don't know they have to go. Just like toddlers, if they're playing hard or otherwise distracted, Chihuahua puppies might ignore their urges until it's virtually too late for them to get to the right place.

If you are watching your Chi closely, she will give you indications that she is about to relieve herself in one or several ways. Here are a few of those telltale signs:

- Sniffing the floor or ground
- Circling
- Running behind furniture
- Beginning to squat (female and young male puppies)
- Sniffing another dog's mark
- Raising a rear leg (older male pups)

Do Not Punish

In some instances, even if a puppy or an adult urinates right in front of you, you should not voice a verbal correction. One of these times is when a Chi leaves a puddle because of submissive urination. A very submissive puppy or young adult may crouch slightly and release a pool of urine on the floor when she greets you. This is a dog's signal that she recognizes you as being her leader and wants to make sure you know this. It is not a sign of disobedience.

 **Essential**

If a puppy or adult Chihuahua suddenly begins urinating with greater frequency or urgency than normal, have her examined by your veterinarian. She could have a urinary tract infection, diabetes, or another condition requiring medical attention.

A person's natural reaction might be to give the dog a correction; however, with a submissive puppy or dog, shouting a correction will only make a submissive dog more frightened. Usually, submissive urination fades away as the Chi matures.

Another common mistake that isn't really an accident is the male puppy dribble. It is not uncommon to see young male puppies dribble urine as they trot across a room or out in the yard when they need to urinate. This situation also disappears as the pup matures, usually around the age of five months or so.

Using a Crate

One of the most effective ways to housetrain a puppy or to refresh an adult is to use a crate. The reason that a crate can be so effective is that puppies and dogs have a natural aversion to lying in their own waste and urine. They don't want to be dirty. In fact, this is one of the first observations you can make with very young puppies: They will relieve themselves in the whelping box away from the area in which they are playing.

When you use a crate in your training, you want to teach the pup to hold until she has alerted you of her needs and you are able to let her out.

 **Question?**

How can I tell if my Chi needs to go out or just doesn't want to be in her crate?
If you just put your Chihuahua in her crate and she relieved herself fully right before she went in, her plaintive whining is most likely due to her confinement. If she's been in her crate for an hour or longer and then starts communicating with you, she most likely needs to relieve herself. Over time, you'll be able to tell what she is communicating by the sound of her bark or whine.

Size and Timing

The crate only works, however, if it is not too large for the Chi and the owner is judicious with its use. For housetraining purposes, the crate should only be big enough for the Chi to stand, turn around, and lie down comfortably. This gives your dog a comfortable place to rest or chew on a good toy but is not so big that if the puppy relieves herself she can lie in a clean, dry area of the crate—far away from her mess.

The Chi should only be crated for eight to ten hours maximum in a twenty-four-hour period. The crate is not a substitute for spending individual time with your puppy or adult and the vigilant supervision that is necessary when the Chihuahua is playing in a larger area. It is only intended for use when you can't keep an eye on your Chi or when you leave the house for short periods of time.

Urge Triggers

Knowing what kinds of things trigger a Chi's need to relieve herself can help, too, in knowing whether you crate your Chihuahua or if you need to give her a quick walk.

In general, your Chi will need to relieve herself at the following times:

- Immediately upon waking up
- Immediately upon being let out of her crate (at any time)
- After playing
- Within thirty minutes after eating a meal
- Within an hour of drinking water
- After or during a lot of excitement
- While under stress, such as a ride in the car
- Every four hours during the day (adult)
- Every two hours or less during the day (puppy)

As you can see, if you have a puppy—particularly a young puppy—the need to go is pretty much a regular occurrence. In other words, you can't give a puppy too many opportunities to relieve herself. As the puppy matures, she will be better able to control her needs. However, always allow a Chi to relieve herself before putting her in her crate for any period of time.

Playpens

When you are confident you recognize your Chi's call to relieve herself, you can expand the crate-training concept to include a playpen or an exercise pen. Put your dog's crate in a small playpen that is located on an easy-to-clean floor surface. You can leave out a stable water bowl (one the Chi cannot easily tip over) and a few toys to occupy your Chi in the playpen.

Initially, you'll only want to use the crate/playpen setup when you can keep an eye on your Chihuahua. You don't want her to use a corner in the playpen as a restroom. Before you leave the house, allow your Chi to relieve herself, and then put her in her crate. When she seems to have caught on to the idea that the playpen is an extension of the no-potty zone while you are supervising her, you can begin leaving the open crate in the playpen when you need to step out.

Moving On

If your puppy or adult Chihuahua has been reliable in the playpen/crate setup for a couple of weeks, you might want to increase her space in your home. A good first choice is to expand the Chi's area to the room in which you currently are keeping her crate and playpen. You can also use another small room with an easy-to-clean floor, such as the kitchen or breakfast room. You'll want your Chi's crate to be open and in this area, just as with the playpen. To block off this room from others, invest in a few dog barriers or baby gates to use in doorways.

 Essential

If you don't want to allow your Chihuahua any more access to your home while you are gone or unable to supervise, it is fine to continue using the crate or the crate and playpen arrangement. If a puppy is teething or an adult suffers from separation anxiety and tends to be a bit destructive, a crate or crate and playpen will keep your Chi safe, as well as limit your rascal's ability to destroy your home.

As you give your Chihuahua more space, keep the amount of time she spends in that space constant. Increase only one variable at a time. Also, if your Chi has an accident in her current space (and it is not because you left her too long or didn't first allow her to relieve herself) then reduce the amount of space until she is once again reliable for several days.

Dog Doors

Once a dog owner discovers the benefits of a dog door, it can be very difficult to return to the restrictive lifestyle of timing walks, meals, crate time, and so on. A dog door that leads to a fenced patio or back yard gives a puppy or adult the ability to relieve herself at will. This is an extremely healthy setup for Chis and is very convenient for the dog owner who may not be able to walk his dog every two to four hours.

Training

A dog door can be incorporated into your Chihuahua's housetraining as soon as she is able to physically push open the door. Doors come in a range of materials and designs, from rubber flaps and Plexiglas swinging doors to locking doors or automatic doors that open when the Chi's special collar is within a set distance of the door.

In order to get your Chi to use the door, begin by removing the door or securing the flap in the open position. Lure your Chi back and forth through the open door with treats, making sure to praise her and tell her how clever she is. Your next step is to do the same maneuver while holding the door or flap open so that she feels the door and has to scamper under it to get through.

Continue holding the door less and less open until you are barely cracking the flap and your Chi is pushing the door open on her own. Then encourage her to go through the door all by herself. If you have a friend or family member whom your Chi enjoys, you can work with two people—one on either side of the flap during the training process.

Now that you've got your Chi going through the door, you can set up one of several arrangements. You can secure the Chi's kennel directly to the dog door when you leave the house so that your Chi can either be outside or resting in her crate. Your second option is to attach the playpen to the dog door with the Chihuahua's crate in the playpen. Or, if your Chihuahua already knows the basics of housetraining and you trust her in one or more rooms of your house, allow her to go in and out at will from the allowable rooms.

 Question?

How do I size a dog door for my Chihuahua?
The most important measurements to consider are the height of the door, its width, and the height at which you are placing it. Most Chis will take a small or extra-small door. However, if you have an arthritic senior—one that perhaps can't crouch down to go under the door flap—you may need a taller or larger door. Most manufacturers of doors and the retailers who sell them will be happy to advise you as to which product will work best; take advantage of this service!

What Goes out Also Comes In

A dog door is not ideal for all dog owners. Obviously, those who live in apartments or condominiums without a yard or patio have no use for a dog door. But even for those who do have a yard, there are benefits and challenges to allowing a Chi twenty-four-hour access to the outdoors that should be considered before investing in installing a good product.

 Alert!

Chihuahuas are very popular and because of this, they are at a higher risk of being stolen. If you allow your Chi free access to your backyard while you are away, make sure your fence is high enough to discourage would-be thieves, and keep your fence gate locked.

One of the drawbacks to a dog door is in what lies beyond the door. If your yard gets muddy, you are sure to have paw tracks through your home on rainy days. If your Chi enjoys hunting lizards or other small prey, you might find a few of these in your home in varying states of life or decay. Setting up a playpen inside the dog door can help contain what your Chi brings in the house, but it won't stop your dog from bringing these items or critters in.

Additionally, there's the risk of your Chi escaping from your fenced yard. (Make sure there aren't any gaps or areas she can dig under.) Another risk is that of predators. If you live in an area with hawks, owls, or other birds of prey, your Chihuahua could become a victim. A way to circumvent this is to run a crisscross of clear filaments over your fenced yard to discourage birds or to provide your Chi with an area outside the dog door that is enclosed and covered, such as large pen.

▲ Be loving but firm with your Chi; not *everywhere* is a bathroom!

Litter Training

An option that many toy-breed owners use for their dogs is a litter box. A litter box provides the Chi the same benefits as a dog door (constant access to an area in which to relieve herself) without having to have an outdoor fenced patio or backyard. With a little patience and a lot of consistency in training, both puppies and adults can be taught to use the litter box.

From the Beginning

Litter-training your Chi involves defining boundaries to the pup or dog's space, just as with crate training. In fact, you'll use a crate from the very beginning. When your crated Chihuahua indicates she wants to relieve herself, take her out of the crate and put her in the litter pan, which initially should be right next to her crate. You'll want about an inch or two of litter in the pan, as well as a little of your Chi's waste or urine in the litter to help her understand what this is all about. Praise and treat her when she relieves herself—and don't forget to give the "Go potty" command while she is relieving herself. When she's out and about playing, try to place her on her litter pan every hour, and reward her when she relieves herself.

 Question?

What if my Chi won't eliminate when I put her in the pan?
Try again in thirty minutes, and in the meantime, watch her carefully! If she looks like she might need to relieve herself, put her on the litter again.

When your Chi is regularly indicating to you when she needs to go and is comfortable using the litter pan, you can increase her space to a crate inside an exercise pen with the litter box. Continue to place her on the litter regularly, and watch closely for signs that she needs to relieve herself. When you're not present, return her to her crate. When she is consistently using the litter pan, you can try leaving the crate door open so she can use the litter box as she needs it.

The Older Housetraining Student

If an adult dog is housetrained, she is usually trained to relieve herself outside. In some cases, she may have been trained to use newspapers or a product that is referred to as a housetraining or pee pad (absorbent layers backed with a waterproof lining). In either instance, the approach to introduce the litter pan is generally the same.

 Essential

> Dog litters are designed specifically for dogs, which produce much more urine for their size than cats. Dog litter, therefore, is a very absorbent, odor-killing, pelletized product. If you own a cat, she probably won't be attracted to the dog's litter because it doesn't have the sandy texture cats prefer.

If your dog is trained to relieve herself outside, begin by placing the litter pan with litter in her favorite spot. Put a sample of her waste or urine in the litter to help her understand what is going on. Place her on the pan and use the "Go potty" command if she already recognizes this command, praising her and giving her a treat when she gets it right. If she hops out, put her back in and repeat your efforts. With patience, she will start to use the litter pan.

When she is using the pan reliably every time you take her outside to her special spot, you can begin moving the pan toward the house. As with all training, move slowly—as little as a foot at a time—until the pan is just outside the door. When you've got the pan to this spot, leave it there for a couple of days to reinforce its use. Then move it inside, continuing to use the "Go potty" command and the reward system.

Once your Chihuahua is using the pan just inside the door without any problems, slowly begin moving the pan to where you want it to be—again, as slowly as a foot at a time. The process will take awhile, but if you take your Chi's training slowly, she will understand what you want her to do. With few (if any) errors, she will be very reliable about using her pan, to the point where you can leave her alone in your home all day and not have to worry about a single mistake.

 **Fact**

When working with a pee-pad trained Chi (or newspaper-trained), begin by putting a pee pad or newspaper in the litter box on top of a very thin layer of dog litter. Put your Chi on the pad or paper when you know she needs to go, such as when you've just let her out of her crate in the morning. (If she knows the "Go potty" command, use it!) Praise, reward, and repeat over and over. Every two days, tear off a piece of the pee pad or newspaper to expose more and more of the litter. Gradually, your Chi will make the switch from the pad or newspaper to the litter.

Determining a Workable Schedule

The more predictable your Chihuahua's needs for relieving herself, the easier her housetraining will be. In order to make your Chi's relief times regular, create a regular routine and stick with it. The three most important factors in developing this routine are meals, water, and exercise.

Feeding

Your Chihuahua's meals should be at specific times. For example, if your puppy is eating four meals a day, you might schedule these feedings at 7 A.M., 11 A.M., 3 P.M., and 7 P.M. Your Chi will need to have a bowel movement very shortly thereafter—usually no more than thirty minutes after eating—so you won't want to put her in her crate and leave for work without this movement. Plan on giving your Chi an hour for eating, exercise, and relieving himself at each feeding. If you cannot keep up this schedule, make sure you have a relative, neighbor, or a pet sitter hired to help when you can't be home.

 **Alert!**

Allowing your Chihuahua to graze throughout the day (in other words, to eat from a never-ending food bowl) can wreak havoc with a housetraining schedule. You'll never be able to predict when your Chihuahua will need to relieve herself.

Water

Fresh, cool water should be available to your Chi at all times. Unlike a constant supply of food, access to water at all times will lessen the possibility that your Chihuahua will overload on water at certain times—which would also make your Chi's urges more unpredictable. The only time you might want to pull up your dog's water is two hours before bedtime. This will give your Chi plenty of time to empty her bladder before she settles down for the night. (This can also be helpful with aging, senior Chis that are having problems with incontinence.)

Movement

Then there's exercise. Exercise is virtually a guarantee that your Chi will need to relieve herself—either during the exercise or within thirty minutes following. Exercise will also increase your Chi's water consumption, so you can also expect that your Chi—though she's urinated during the walk or during a play session—will need to relieve herself again within an hour or so.

Remember that consistency, reward-based positive training, and moving in small steps will help ensure success with house-training your Chi. If your Chihuahua has an accident, step back and re-evaluate the situation. Did you follow your schedule? Did you leave her alone too long? Did you move too quickly with allowing her more freedom in the home? If you can't figure out where you might have erred, then take a step backward in her housetraining. Move back to a smaller space or a shorter time period and allow your Chihuahua to regain her confidence—and yours.

Socialization

One of the most important aspects of owning a dog of any breed and of any size is to socialize him with all shapes, sizes, and kinds of people, as well as with other dogs. Without strong socialization skills, the Chihuahua can become distrustful of people and dogs and can become quite protective of its owner, not even allowing family members to be near that person. With practice and a bit of persistence, however, you can prevent or help your Chihuahua overcome being fearful or aggressive toward people and dogs.

A Must for Every Chihuahua

According to Chihuahua rescues, the number-one behavior problem they see with dogs coming into rescue is fearfulness. The level of a dog's fear can range from pronounced cautiousness to such terror that it causes the release of its bladder and bowels.

Fearful dogs are also the number-one cause of dog bites. As most people incorrectly assume, most dog bites are not the result of a confrontation with an aggressive, dominant dog. Fear biting occurs when a frightened dog is put in a situation in which she feels she is being confronted with a life-threatening danger and has nowhere to escape. In the dog's eyes, the choice is to protect herself or die. This could happen in even an innocuous situation, such as a Chi that is on leash with an owner who is trying to get her to stand still for a little girl to pet her. As the Chi sees it, she has no escape (the leash and her owner are holding her), and she is facing a life-threatening danger (the little girl).

 **Essential**

Signs of fearfulness include a tucked-under tail, ears flattened against the neck, slight crouching, shaking, hiding behind owner, and attempts to run away. In extreme cases, a dog may urinate or defecate or may bite in self-defense.

Fear can originate in the Chi's genetics and be exacerbated by her upbringing (her experiences or lack thereof with people and dogs). In a Chihuahua that has the genetics to be a very outgoing dog, fearfulness can stem from abuse, neglect, and lack of socialization. As you can see, the way the Chihuahua is raised has a great impact on how outgoing she will become as an adult.

So, if you own a puppy, you have a tremendous influence on the outcome of her temperament, whether she is genetically predisposed to be fearful or not. If you own a rescued Chihuahua that is fearful, she is not a lost cause! You can do a lot to help your Chi overcome many if not most of her fears. For both pups and adults, the way to pull a shy dog out of her shell (or to prevent a pup from becoming shy) is through socialization.

Recognizing "Pancaking"

Chihuahuas do have to worry about predators. Hawks, owls, and other large birds of prey can easily swoop down and carry off a puppy or adult Chi. Perhaps as a result of the breed's early ancestry and the necessity for self-preservation, the Chihuahua has a unique reaction to certain sudden overhead movements.

Pancaking, as Chi owners call it, is when a Chihuahua literally flattens herself on the ground. A large shadow passing overhead or the slightest sound in the trees can trigger this defensive reaction. If a Chihuahua pancakes from time to time, it does not mean she is timid, shy, or fearful. This is a natural reaction.

Overreacting

If you find your Chi pancakes frequently for nonthreatening movements (the ceiling fan) or sounds (a jet overhead), you can help her recognize these things are *not* dangerous through one of the following training techniques:

- **Do nothing.** Dogs will take their lead from their humans. If the sound or movement doesn't scare you, and you don't react to your Chi's pancaking, over time the dog will often realize there's nothing to be afraid of.
- **Reward good behavior.** Find your Chi's comfort zone (the distance away from the object at which the Chihuahua remains calm) and reward good, calm behavior. Work in inches toward the object and continue to reward good behavior.
- **Desensitize your dog.** If your Chi pancakes for a particular sound, such as when a jet passes overhead, you may find you have success in eliminating this behavior by playing a tape of jets (softly at first) over and over again until your Chi becomes accustomed to the sound.

Do Not Comfort Your Chi

The one thing you do not want to do is scoop up your Chi in your arms and comfort her—no matter how badly her pancaking pulls on your heartstrings. Comforting a dog when she is frightened will only make her reaction worse the next time. Why? Because your Chi sees your hugging and cooing as a reward for her behavior, thus reinforcing the exact behavior you want to eliminate.

What Is a Timid or Shy Dog?

Though the Chihuahua is loving, devoted, and impish at times with those she knows well, this is not a breed that by nature is an outgoing, gregarious creature with strangers. She is much more likely to want to watch anyone unfamiliar from a distance (her comfort zone) and make her own approach on her own terms when she feels comfortable. With a breed that has a tendency to be a little wary, it is particularly important to work on socializing your Chihuahua.

 **Fact**

A puppy or adult dog that is not exposed to lots of friendly people will only become more and more reclusive. Even a well-adjusted Chi that was well socialized as a puppy can become increasingly suspicious of people if an effort is not made to continually introduce her to friendly strangers throughout her life.

Socialization Is the Key

As a Chihuahua owner, you need to realize that socialization is not a one-shot deal; it is a process that begins when a puppy is whelped and that continues throughout the dog's life.

The well-socialized, friendly Chihuahua will warm up to strangers quickly and should allow herself to be stroked and offered treats by friendly people. She should not cower, tremble, shake or bark, snap, or charge aggressively at people.

So given that the Chihuahua is a breed that is prone to be standoffish initially with strangers, how can you tell if your Chi is truly a timid or shy dog by nature, or whether she has simply not had enough socialization?

Dealing with Fearfulness

If you are working with a young puppy that is already showing signs of being truly terrified of strangers and not the least bit curious about people, even within a reasonable comfort zone (ten feet or so), your Chi probably has the genetics to be fearful. If you have adopted an adult Chihuahua that is timid and shy, there's no real way of knowing whether your Chihuahua's fearfulness is inherited or has been shaped by her environment.

Whether you are working with a naturally shy or well-socialized puppy or dog, your approach to socialization will be basically the same. With the fearful Chi, it will just take more dedication on your part to continue working with your Chihuahua.

Aggression in the Chihuahua

A snappy Chihuahua? Really? Absolutely! This breed is recognized for attaching very strongly to one individual. This is so true the Chihuahua can become aggressively protective of her person and will growl, snap, and charge anyone who dares to come near. This can be a real problem for anybody—even those who live alone.

Preventing this form of guarding requires the same dedication that a person would need to prevent a large, guarding breed from becoming overly protective. The way to teach your Chi that people are friendly and good is to introduce her to as many friendly strangers as possible early on in her life. You want her to recognize an outstretched hand as a sign of a yummy treat rather than an act of aggression.

Threatening Actions

What your Chihuahua interprets as acts of aggression are not necessarily what any person would interpret as threatening. When working on socializing your Chihuahua with friends, make sure they understand what actions your Chi will think constitute bad behavior on their parts and which movements may increase the probability of her acting aggressively toward them. Any of the following may be interpreted by your Chi as aggressive actions:

- Reaching to pat on the head
- Direct eye contact
- Sudden movements
- Squatting to the dog's level
- Sharp, loud, or deep voice
- Leaning over the dog's back
- Going nose to nose or face to face
- Breaching the boundaries of your Chi's space or specific comfort zone

Puppies

Everyone loves a puppy, and Chihuahua puppies are no exception. A puppy's first twelve weeks are her most impressionable as far as imprinting social behaviors, so take advantage of this time period! Until your puppy is fully vaccinated, bring as many friends into your home to meet your puppy as you can. Make sure your friends know to allow the puppy to make the approach and not to attempt to pet her. Give your friends little delectable treats to offer her when she comes close. Once she's really warmed up to a person, then she can be given a pat. If she is still skittering away when she sees a hand, have your friends go back to ignoring her and allowing her to make the approach again.

Take your Chihuahua with you in the car whenever possible so that she can see people and places out of the home. If she acts aggressively to people as they pass by your car windows (as in a parking lot), she must know that this is not allowed. Do not yell at her because this will only excite her more. Put her in a down (See Chapter 14, page 195). Wait a moment to make sure she remains quite and then praise her for the good down and reward her.

The reason a Chihuahua that is showing aggressive tendencies is put into a down rather than a sit is twofold. First, the down is a position of submission, which reinforces that your Chihuahua must listen to you. Second, it is very difficult for a dog to bark when she is in a down, so you quickly achieve a quiet dog that can be rewarded for her appropriate behavior.

 **Essential**

Until your puppy is fully vaccinated, she is vulnerable to several lethal canine viruses. For this reason, your puppy shouldn't touch the floor in places with a lot of dog traffic. Carry her into the veterinarian's office, have her ride in the cart at the pet store, and keep her in a carrybag from which she can peek out and see what's going on without setting foot in high dog-traffic areas.

Additionally, taking a puppy out of her home on a regular basis tends to lessen the pup's territorial aggression or her possessive protection of her home and yard. Taking regular walks, car rides, and visits to other locations, such as parks, can all help in broadening your dog's horizons, so to speak, and lessen her focus on protecting house and home.

Adults

If you've adopted an adult Chihuahua from a rescue or a shelter, you won't have to worry about her showing signs of possessive aggression immediately. She is still working on developing a bond with someone in your household, most likely the person who spends the most quality time with her. This is the critical time period to make sure the Chihuahua does not develop an attitude about other people in the home.

From day one, everyone in your home, as well as those who come to visit on a frequent or infrequent basis (such as the babysitter), should spend time socializing with the new dog and forming a solid friendship. These people should also be able to give your Chihuahua basic commands, such as sit, down, give, and stay. Not only will this give them a little more control over the dog, it will also establish their leadership position with her.

You'll also want to take time walking your adult dog outside the home, taking her for car rides, and visiting other places for play and training sessions. The more time you spend out of the home with your dog, the less territorial your Chihuahua will be of what she considers her space. Also make sure to exercise your Chihuahua. A lot can be said for a tired dog versus one that has pent-up energy and anxieties.

 **Alert!**

If your Chihuahua has already developed possessive aggression with an individual in your family, seek professional assistance in retraining your Chi. Never jeopardize the safety of anyone in your home. Though a bite from a Chi may not seem too serious, it can be not only physically scarring but emotionally scarring as well.

Where to Go for Help

For issues with aggression or fearfulness that is so profound as to cause fear biting, seek professional help. If you are currently working with a professional dog trainer or are a member of a training club, ask if this person or a member of the club works with animal behavior, particularly dogs with aggression or fear biting issues. This is a more specialized area of training, and not every trainer is qualified to give assistance. Go with your gut feelings on this one if you sense that this is beyond the scope of a trainer's expertise or if you don't like the training methods that the individual is suggesting, such as anything involving punishment.

Animal Behavior Specialists

Individuals who specialize in assisting pet owners with their dogs' behavioral issues include certified animal behaviorists, veterinarians with an interest in animal behavior, and veterinarians who are diplomates with the American College of Veterinary Behaviorists (ACVB). Certified animal behaviorists possess a Ph.D. in animal behavior and are certified through the Animal Behavior

Society. To find someone in your area, visit the Animal Behavior Society Web site, online at *www.animalbehavior.org*.

Veterinarians

Veterinarians with an interest in animal behavior are a little more difficult to find; however, your veterinarian should know of any colleagues in the area with this additional training and experience. If not, visit the American Veterinary Medicine Association Web site, online at *www.avma.org*, or the American Animal Hospital Association Web site, online at *www.aahanet.org*.

Only veterinarians that have successfully undergone additional and extensive training, research, and education in the specialty field of animal behavior and have passed a critical peer review by the ACVB can hold the title of diplomate. Because of the amount of time and effort required to achieve this title, there are very few veterinarians in the country that are diplomates in this specialty. To find out if you are fortunate enough to have someone in your area, visit the ACVB Web site (online at *www.veterinarybehaviorists.org*), which includes an up-to-date listing.

Working with Strangers

Getting your Chihuahua to be accepting of family members and friends who visit frequently is relatively easy. These people are around on a fairly regular basis, so your Chihuahua is accustomed to meeting and greeting them. She has time to recognize that she can trust these people, they give her great treats, and they allow her the time she needs to warm up to them.

Then there is the new person, the stranger. Your Chihuahua hasn't ever seen this person before. He could be wearing a floppy hat, sunglasses, a flapping coat, and smell different. The stranger could be tall, short, thin, or heavy. The stranger could be a child, a teen, or a senior citizen. He could be of any race, too. How is your Chihuahua going to react when she sees the stranger? It depends on how much socialization you've done with her.

 **Fact**

With the aggressive dog, your best option is to attend a training school in which all the strangers are knowledgeable dog people. These folks will know how to be as nonthreatening to your Chihuahua as possible and can be an incredible help in assisting you in working with your dog.

If you've worked at taking your Chihuahua to as many different locations as possible to meet and greet as many different shapes, sizes, and ages of people (who all gave your Chi a little treat), your puppy or dog should be relatively accepting of the stranger. It's okay for her to sit at your side and observe the person for a moment and then move toward the friendly stranger—who is holding the treat you handed her.

It's not okay for your Chihuahua to growl threateningly or attempt to crawl up your leg to get into your arms. If your Chi is reacting in this way to strangers, do not force the situation. Remove your Chihuahua to her comfort zone from the person and allow her to observe strangers from a distance. If someone asks if he can pat your dog, politely say, "No, she's in training," or something else to this effect. It is your job to keep people at bay until your Chihuahua becomes more comfortable.

With the fearful dog, you will be able to edge closer to people and reward your dog for observing calmly. Eventually, you'll be able to reduce your dog's safety zone so that strangers can toss her a treat. When she's comfortable with this, you can start to close the gap between the person tossing the treat and your Chi. Your final goal is for your Chihuahua to sit quietly and approach a stranger on her own to accept a treat.

Whatever you do, remember two points. First, you should never put anyone in danger of being bitten. Second, don't give up on your Chihuahua. The Chi that has issues with aggression—whether that stems from possessiveness, territoriality, or fear—is the dog that needs socialization work the most. Your hard work will pay off. It just may take some time, patience, and dedication.

▲ Chis are very social dogs that love to meet and play with other Chis, but it is best to socialize them from puppyhood, especially if you have other dogs.

Introducing Other Dogs

Chihuahuas love other Chihuahuas. Whether they're longhaired or shorthaired, if that dog is a Chihuahua, your Chihuahua is likely to want to engage her in some good old wild Chihuahua play. Introducing two Chis to each other is therefore rarely a problem. The Chihuahuas will want to sniff each other to check each other out, and then typically one or the other Chi will dip into a play bow and the dogs will be off and running.

On occasion, however, Chihuahuas don't get along at first sight. Signs that the meeting is going slightly amiss include rigidness in a dog's body, standing on tip-toes (to look bigger), a stiffly wagging, raised tail, and of course, snarling, snapping, or lunging. Determining why a Chihuahua is aggressive toward another is more difficult. Here are some questions whose answers may provide a clue:

- Where are you making the introduction? If either Chi is on her home turf, she could be territorial. Try introducing the dogs in a neutral area, such as a park.
- Is one of the Chis an intact male? Unneutered males show more aggression toward other males than a neutered male would with other neutered males. Intact males are also more likely to show inappropriate interest in females, to which the female will take exception almost every time.
- Are both Chis dominant, I-want-to-be-the-leader types? If neither Chi will accept a less-dominant role, it could be difficult for these two to play together.
- Are the Chihuahuas on leash? Many dogs that clash while on leash would meet and greet just fine if both were off leash. Consider introducing dogs in a fenced, neutral location without leashes.
- Does one of the dogs have something he's guarding? Even a very submissive dog can become quite ugly if he's got a favorite ball, toy, or chew in the area. Make sure there aren't any of these special objects in the vicinity.
- Is the Chihuahua protecting you? If you are attached to your dog with a leash, this could very well be the case. Again, take leashes off in a neutral place and stand away from your dog.
- Is the other Chi just not getting it? Sometimes a dog just doesn't understand how to play fair. This is the bully that keeps picking on another dog even after that dog has repeatedly told him to back off. The bullying dog should be removed from play and required to sit in time out until he's settled down. If he continues to pick on the other dogs, remove your dog.

Chihuahuas, of course, can and do play well with other breeds. Fearful or timid dogs may not want to interact with any dogs that are very much larger than they are, so these Chis may be more comfortable associating with other friendly toy breeds.

Bold Chihuahuas, on the other hand, may be ready to take on the world, whether this is a safe move for them or not.

 **Essential**

When they are young, Chihuahuas from their littermates learn how to play with other dogs. Once they are in your hands, puppies need to play with friendly, vaccinated older puppies and adult dogs. When your puppy has received her vaccination series, her socialization with dogs will continue in her puppy training class and with your continued introduction to friendly dogs.

If you have a situation in which a larger dog is involved in the play, before you allow your Chi to join in the fun, observe how the larger dog plays with the small dogs. Some large dogs are incredibly gentle and very aware of where their bodies start and stop and sense what would happen if they even nudge a little dog too hard. Most big dogs, however, simply don't realize that they can't use the same force on a little dog that they do playing with another big dog.

Alert!

Some breeds and mixes of breeds have very high prey drives. Depending on the game they were bred to hunt and kill, a Chihuahua bouncing in an open area could be mistaken for prey. Dogs of any breed with a reputation for being cat killers should not be allowed with your Chihuahua—to avoid any fatal chances of mistaken identity.

Allowing your Chi to play with a dog that is substantially larger than she is involves a certain risk. Keep in mind, too, that even the gentlest of dogs could become angered at something your Chihuahua does—though we'd like to think they are, Chis aren't perfect—and decide to make a correction. To another large dog, this controlled chomp would send the message without injury. To a Chihuahua, the correction could literally be fatal.

When deciding on which dogs you will allow your Chi to play with and which dogs you won't, it is always wisest to err on the conservative side. A large dog doesn't have to have any bad intentions to seriously injure or frighten a Chihuahua.

When Your Chi Is Dog-Aggressive

You're walking your Chihuahua on leash and another person approaches you with their dog, also on leash. Your Chihuahua hits the end of the leash, rears up on her hind legs, and begins lunging, snapping, barking, and snarling. What do you do?

First, count your blessings that the other dog, which outweighs your dog by about sixty pounds, is on leash. Two, be thankful that the other dog doesn't respond to your Chi's aggressive overtures. And three, realize that there's nothing unusual about your dog's behavior. Dog-dog aggression is not fun, but it is a form of aggression that can be worked on and diminished or eliminated.

To work on your dog's aggression issues, begin by making sure that your Chihuahua knows the "Down" command. This is a position of submission, indicating to the Chihuahua that he is not the decision-maker in this situation. Physically, the down also makes it difficult for a dog to bark or even growl. If your Chi is in a full down with elbows to the ground, she'll be quiet. If those elbows come off the ground, she won't be quiet. If she looks like she's thinking about coming up off the down, give her the command again and make sure those elbows are on the ground.

When on walks, anticipate meeting other dogs. Know your Chihuahua's comfort zone. In other words, will she remain quiet and just observe another dog if the other canine is fifteen feet away? Twenty feet? Try to keep your Chi at this safe distance when walking past another dog. Talk to your Chihuahua. Tell her just how good she is for being quiet, and reward her with a treat.

Then begin to breech this safety zone. This time you can anticipate that your Chihuahua will attempt to bark at the approaching dog, so put her in a down-stay. Pay attention to your Chi and not the other dog. Praise and reward your Chi for being so quiet. If she tries to bounce out of the down, move her a little farther away and put her in a down (where you know she'll be quiet). Keep trying to move her closer, and make sure she stays in the down.

If your dog is progressing well and you're able to keep her in a down while on the same side of the street as approaching dogs, you can begin to try to walk past other dogs. Move your Chihuahua several feet or even yards back into the new boundaries of her safety or nonreactive zone. At this distance, keep your dog close to you but on a slack leash. Ignore the other dog and talk in friendly tones to your Chihuahua, tossing her treats periodically for paying attention to you. If she tries to bark at the other dog, put her in a down. Pause. Praise her for her down, release her, and continue walking.

Your goal will be to pass by another dog on the same sidewalk without your Chihuahua making a sound. If you've done your training well, she'll have her full attention on you, anticipating your next request. Whatever you do, do not give up on your little guy. The worst thing you can do is not walk your Chihuahua. The second worst thing you can do is walk him but not address his dog-dog issues.

Too Plucky?

If you talk to enough toy-breed owners, you're very likely to hear a tragic tale of how a favorite pet was killed by another dog and just how terrible some of these other dogs are. There are stories of loose dogs attacking and killing Chihuahuas while on a walk with their owners. These stories are horrifying and even more tragic because if the other dog had been properly restrained, there wouldn't have been an incident.

 **Question?**

Someone told me my aggressive dog might actually be afraid of other dogs. How can that be?

Frequently, dogs that are afraid of other dogs will appear to be on the offensive. In actuality, these timid dogs are putting on a good show so that other dogs see them as a dog not to be messed with. The timid dog tends to wait until the dog has passed by before acting aggressively. Give this dog more distance between other dogs on walks, work on meeting friendly dogs off-leash (where she feels she can escape), and don't tense up. The leash is a direct line to your Chi. If she senses you're afraid, she won't realize that you're worried she's going to make a scene. She'll think there really is something to fear and is more likely to appear aggressive.

However, there are also incidents in which the toy dog was the one that was off leash and that initiated the attack against the other dog, which was on leash. The Chihuahua, along with many toy breeds, is feisty enough and has a big enough self-image (that is, doesn't realize she's sorely outmuscled and outsized) to do something like this. Most dogs, however, whether large or small, are going to respond to being bitten and are going to bite back.

Do not ever allow your Chihuahua to run off leash. Do work on your Chi's recall so if she slips away you can avoid a serious confrontation. Also, do work on reducing your Chihuahua's aggressiveness toward other dogs.

Chapter **11**

Puppy Parenting 101

Chihuahua puppies are perhaps some of the cutest puppies to set paw on this earth. But don't let those big brown eyes and tiny woofs fool you; a Chihuahua puppy is able to wreak havoc in the house. Many puppy behaviors that owners find troublesome can be curbed or even avoided if you know what to do and when to do it.

Would You Let a 100-Pound Dog Do That?

Toy-breed owners are notorious for letting their little dogs get away with absolute canine murder. Perhaps it is because Chihuahua puppies are so small that people mistakenly assume their antics won't amount to much trouble.

Wrong. This misconception of how to rear a toy-breed puppy is largely the reason that a portion of the general public views the Chihuahua as a yappy, ill-mannered dog. In reality, the Chihuahua is a great breed, but individuals will behave only as well as they've been raised. If you don't let your dog know how you expect her to behave from the get-go, she'll behave the only way she knows how—as a dog with dog behaviors.

Here's another way of looking at the situation. Why, if you would never allow a child to bite you, shred a pillow, or scramble past you to get out the front door (and run away), would you allow your canine companion to do these same things? You shouldn't.

To succeed in raising a puppy, you have to consider that what might look cute right now will develop into a nasty habit later.

Jumping Up

What harm can an excited, jumping Chihuahua cause that would make you wish you'd worked on training her *not* to jump up on you or other people? Let's consider a couple of scenarios.

Scenario One: You've just dressed for work, you're in a hurry, and your Chi comes barreling into your room and starts jumping up on you, succeeding in: a) tearing your hose or scratching your legs, b) snagging your slacks, c) dirtying your clothing, or d) tripping you.

Scenario Two: Your friend comes over to visit and brings her young niece. Your Chi is very excited and starts jumping up on the little girl, succeeding in: a) scratching the little girl, b) toppling her over, c) tearing or otherwise messing up her clothes, or d) biting her on the hands, which she is flapping around because the dog is jumping up.

There are three solutions to getting pups (and dogs) to stop jumping up. First, ignore the jumping and the Chihuahua until the dog is calm. If jumping up doesn't get your Chi the attention she wants, she won't do it. Second, exercise her more. If your puppy gets enough exercise, she'll have less energy bottled up and will be calmer. Third, provide an alternate behavior. When your Chihuahua is most likely to jump up, give her the "Sit" command or put her in a sit-stay. Reward this behavior. It won't be long before you'll find that your Chihuahua will automatically give you the good behavior in instances in which she normally would have jumped up on you. Reward her!

Begging

Oh, who can resist those beautiful brown eyes? You can—unless you want your three-pound Chihuahua to become a small nine pound table, as broad as she is tall. She may look as if she is starving every time you are eating something; however, if you are feeding her correctly, she is getting all the nutrition and calories she needs. Breaking down and giving in to those soulful eyes will only serve to escalate your Chi's begging. (Next it will be pawing, and then it will be whining, crying, and barking.)

The solution? You can do one of several things, and all will involve ignoring your Chihuahua. First, don't give in, and don't reward your Chi with attention of any kind for begging. Second, you can put your Chi in her crate with an activity toy or favorite chew to keep her busy. Third, if your Chi is good with her commands, you can put her in a down-stay for the duration of your meal.

Needle Teeth

Ouch! It doesn't matter that the Chi pup's mouth is small—she's got teeth. Before her milk teeth fall out and her adult teeth grow in, your Chihuahua's teeth are quite sharp. Adding to your problem is the very nature of a puppy. These guys are very oral creatures and like to explore their environments with their mouths.

Sometimes they can go too far. They bite a little too hard—enough to even draw blood. The best way to stop this hard play is to do what one of your Chi's littermates would have done. Yelp. Loudly. And then turn your back on the puppy and ignore her. There is absolutely nothing worse for a sociable Chi than not to be able to play with someone she loves.

If after yelping and ignoring your puppy she still is attempting to bite you, calmly lift her up and put her in time out, which is her crate. Many times a puppy will bite when she is particularly excited, so placing her in her crate will help to calm her down. If she knows a few commands, you can say, "Aah!" when she bites (distracting her temporarily) and then give her the "Sit" or "Down" command (to initiate new behavior) and reward her for this good behavior.

Another option is to give her something to hold in her mouth. For example, it's not uncommon for a puppy to go wildly happy when you come home. Often times these wild greetings include puppy bites to the ankles, toes, and outstretched hands. You don't want to discourage your puppy's enthusiasm; however, this is not the type of greeting you want to encourage. If the puppy has something in her mouth, she can still wriggle around and show you how much she loves you, but she can't bite. The easiest way to occupy your pup's mouth in a constructive manner is to keep a few small latex dog toys by the front door—or wherever else you might receive an overexuberant greeting. Make sure the toys are something that the Chi enjoys playing with and will want to have in her mouth. Before she can take a nip at you, offer her the toy and say the command, "Take It!" when she has the toy in her mouth. Praise her and give her lots of pats.

 # Alert!

It is important to interrupt the act before giving your puppy a good behavior command. If you don't have this time pause between when the pup has stopped mounting and the moment you give the command, your puppy may actually think she's being rewarded for the mounting behavior.

Humping

Another behavior that is often seen in puppies and even adult dogs that is viewed as inappropriate behavior is mounting. In actuality, mounting another dog in mock mating (or in actual mating) is quite normal for dogs. Puppies of both sexes will practice this maneuver as a part of their play and aren't picky as to which sex the recipient is. Usually, mounting behavior fades as the puppy reaches maturity and is altered. Sometimes, however, a puppy will mount a child, a pillow, or your leg, causing a very embarrassing situation for the owner. In these cases, it may not be possible to ignore the behavior and hope it fades over time. If immediate action is necessary, there are several ways you can proceed.

If the puppy has chosen an object to mount, such as a couch pillow, simply take the pillow and put it in a place where the puppy can't get to it. If a puppy is using a person as her practice object, say "Aaah!" loudly to distract her, which should stop her humping momentarily. Then, give her a command that she knows how to do (such as sit) and reward her for the sit.

What you don't want to do when trying to discourage a behavior, such as mounting, is to yell or holler at your dog. Though it would seem that harsh verbal corrections would lessen the dog's desire to perform the behavior, precisely the opposite is true. With dogs, any attention—whether good or bad—can be rewarding. If a dog finds she is rewarded for a behavior, this will reinforce the behavior, making it that much harder for you to extinguish later.

Barking

Chihuahuas are excellent watchdogs. It is the breed's nature to sound the alert to anyone or anything approaching what the dog considers her territory—whether that's the Chi's home, yard, patio, or favorite person. You will never have a postal worker, delivery person, or stranger ring your doorbell without your Chi enthusiastically alerting you to the individual's approach.

Sounding the alarm is a good thing. But barking at every little thing or at nothing at all can become annoying. Chihuahuas are not beyond becoming yappy if given the opportunity. Some Chis just seem to have something to say about everything. And, conversely to what you would naturally assume, the more you react to your Chi's barking, the more your Chi will bark. What to do?

If your Chi is barking to get your attention or to engage you in playing with her, the best way to extinguish this behavior is to ignore her. If your Chi does not receive a reward for her incessant barking, her barking will lessen or cease almost all together. Engaging in play or turning your attention to your barking Chi (whether in a positive or negative way) will be seen as a reward.

If your Chi is barking as people pass your fence or walk by on the sidewalk, teaching your Chi to keep quiet can be a little more challenging. From the dog's perspective, if the offending person or dog moves away from your yard or home, the Chi thinks her bark chased the individual away. Therefore, if the dog is left unattended and is allowed to bark at will, this pastime becomes a self-rewarding activity. The best solution to a situation such as this is to crate your Chi while you are gone or confine her to an area in which she can't see people or dogs passing by.

▲ It is very important that your Chi knows what is right and what is wrong, so do not back down on discipline.

If your Chi barks at passersby while you are home, you need to recognize the good behavior (alerting you) and reward your puppy when she hushes. This involves teaching the command "Hush." As with teaching many other behaviors, the best way to teach "Hush" is to begin by saying the command any time you catch your dog being silent. Next, give the command "Hush" when your Chi is quiet after barking, and reward. Keep reinforcing the "Hush" everyday, gradually moving to say "Hush" when you know your dog is about to be silent, and finally, while your Chi is actively barking. Within a few weeks, if you are consistent, your Chi will hush on command.

Digging

Chis do enjoy hunting and chasing after little critters, such as the favored lizard. If a critter goes down a hole, the Chi may attempt to go after it by digging. Not having buckets for paws (as some breeds do), the Chihuahua is not very efficient at moving large amounts of earth in short periods of time. Beware, however, the determined Chi that's found a vole underground or suspects a lizard lair. Given time, she can dig. Chis may also dig to unearth cool ground to lie in on a hot day or bury a favorite chew or toy for later. Still other Chis will dig out of sheer boredom.

In working with problem diggers, it is important to determine why the Chi is digging. If there's no reason you can see for the digging, exercise your Chihuahua more. Play more games, and get her active. She is likely digging because she's looking for something to do.

If your Chi is running after critters and is digging in an area of your yard where you don't want holes, make this area inaccessible to your Chi. You can use temporary or permanent fencing to keep your Chi out.

If it's burying and digging things back up that your Chi likes, consider blocking off part of your yard and only giving your Chi access to a small area that has a digging pit in it. Dig out a two- by three-foot area approximately eight to twelve inches deep, and fill it with sand. Put a couple of your Chi's favorite toys partially into the pit and reward your dog with praise and a treat when she digs the toys out. It doesn't take long for a dog to figure out that this digging pit can be a lot of fun.

Chewing and Shredding

Puppies are notorious chewers. When a puppy is losing her milk teeth (at around five to six months of age) and her adult, permanent teeth are breaking through the gum line, the sensation is itchy, painful, and annoying. It is at this time that your puppy really needs something to chew on. Good chew items include puppy toys made of dense or solid rubber, hard chew bones (either synthetic or baked) such as those made by Nylabone, and dog toys made of twisted, knotted, multistrand ropes. These items do not break down into small pieces that could be swallowed or choke the pup accidentally.

 **Fact**

Just as with a teething baby, teething puppies can find icy-cold items to be quite soothing to chew on. For the teething Chi puppy, you can place any of her toys or chews in the freezer and pull them out as needed.

To discourage a puppy from chewing on chair legs and carpet fringes or to discourage idle gnawing on baseboards, cabinet doors, and the occasional low windowsill, consider using a pet product designed specifically for this purpose. Nontoxic products such as Bitter Apple come in gels and sprays that are extremely distasteful to most puppies. Applying a product such as this to an endangered surface will often ward off the chewiest of puppies with just one taste. There are, of course, those pups with no taste. In these instances, keeping the pup away from her favorite inappropriate chewing items is the only way to ensure that these items remain safe.

Escape Artists

Chihuahuas aren't the worst breed when it comes to escaping every means of containment possible. They simply can't scale fences, jump as high, or bite and pull as hard as many of the larger breeds. Chis are, however, very athletic, and they often exceed their owner's estimations.

Jumping

If your puppy is a virtual jumping bean, she will be able to escape puppy playpens, baby gates, and low fences. If you find this is the case, you may need to get a little creative. Use a puppy playpen that has a top or wire roof. For those pups escaping a lower baby gate, consider double-gating a doorway (putting one pressure gate above the other) or using a dog gate that is taller and meant for jumping, scaling puppies. If your outdoor fence is too low to contain your Chi, you'll need to add to your present fence. (Some fences allow the addition of a foot of lattice to the top.) You might also consider replacing the fence with a taller one or always supervising your Chi when she is in the backyard.

Have Head, Will Follow

Chihuahua puppies can be very, very little. The spaces through which they can scramble through to escape their containment or barrier often appear impossibly small. The basic rule of thumb is that if a puppy can wriggle her head through a space, she can wriggle her entire body through. Spacing in your outdoor fence (between slats or the chain links), a window that's cracked open, a crate door that can be pushed open when it is latched on top but not on the bottom, a small tear in a porch screen, or a gap between a door and the floor could all be escape hatches for a little puppy.

Be cognizant of just how small your puppy is, and look for ways in which she could escape, should he set his mind to it. The answer to escape problems is exercise, exercise, exercise! If your Chihuahua is pooped out, chances are she won't be looking for something do—she'll just want to snooze. If your well-exercised puppy possesses a brilliant yet devious mind and is bent on breaking out of all barriers, keep her safely crated when you cannot supervise her every move.

Separation Anxiety

A puppy or an adult has separation anxiety if she becomes distressed—and remains distressed—whenever you leave her. Separation anxiety comes in varying levels, from mild distress to distress so severe that the Chi is in danger of harming herself.

Preventing separation anxiety from occurring in the first place is easiest with a puppy. It is natural for a pup to cry, whine, bark, scratch, and gnash her teeth on her playpen bars or crate. Simply put her in her crate with a favorite activity toy (a toy that she needs to chew on or roll to release little bits of treats) or a chew in her crate to keep her busy while you are gone—and leave. Don't make a big deal out of leaving. Be matter-of-fact about it.

 Essential

> If you are concerned that your puppy is crying the entire time that you are gone, record her activities. Set up a recorder and turn it on before you leave. Most pups will stop crying within minutes of their owner's leaving.

If your puppy or adult is having great difficulties when you leave and is terribly stressed any time you are gone, you can take steps to help your Chi overcome her separation anxiety. Many of the techniques are the same that can be used to prevent separation anxiety from developing. Try any of these:

- When leaving, act as if nothing is happening; don't give her a special farewell hug or tell her it's going to be okay when she starts crying.
- Provide an activity toy or good chew to help occupy your Chi.
- Desensitize your Chi to the sounds that she recognizes as indications that you are leaving. Pick up your keys randomly throughout the day. Put your jacket on and take it off. Open and close the front door. Turn the television on and off.
- Leave your Chi for short periods of time, and gradually extend these times.
- Tape what your Chi does when you are gone to monitor her progress.
- Don't punish her for wetting or soiling her crate; she is most likely voiding due to stress.
- Give her Rescue Remedy, a holistic flower essence that can be rubbed on your Chi's gums or given by dispensing a few drops in her drinking water.
- Spray your Chi's bedding with dog-appeasing pheromone (DAP), a synthetic replication of the hormone that is emitted by lactating female dogs and that all pups and adult dogs recognize and find relaxing and comforting.
- Consult with your veterinarian for additional help. In extreme cases in which your Chi is in danger of harming herself, your veterinarian may recommend medical intervention.

Don't give up on your stressed Chi. Separation anxiety can be an issue with adopted adult Chis, but with time, patience, and a lot of consistency in how you approach your dog's anxiety, you'll be able to make a big difference in your Chi's life. It is often the case with a rescue that the dog simply needs the time to trust that you are always coming home.

Bolting

Chihuahuas are small and lightning fast. If your Chi wants to make a break through the front door when you are talking to someone, has a tendency to scramble out over you when you're letting her out of the crate, or is impossible to catch when you're opening the car door, you know just how difficult it can be to handle a Chihuahua that has learned the art of bolting.

As with most unwanted behaviors, preventive training is the easiest way to avoid the problem entirely. With a pup, you'll want to begin training her to wait whenever you open the crate door. Begin this by gently restraining your puppy while saying, "Wait." Pause and then give the release command, "Okay!" and let your puppy come out and receive lots of patting, stroking and a little treat.

Continue this exercise until your puppy is no longer pushing against you and seems to have caught on to the "Wait" command. Open the crate door and say "Wait" with your hand up (as if you're a traffic guard signaling "Stop"). Pause, and give the release command. Praise and treat such a smart puppy!

Your goal is to work up to being able to give your pup the "Wait" command before you've opened the crate door and have the pup know to stay in his crate with the door wide open until you've given her the release command.

 Alert!

When boarding your trained Chi at a kennel, or if you have someone come to your home to care for your Chi, be sure to tell this person your Chi's release command. Owners who have trained their dogs to wait when a crate or kennel door is opened have recounted stories of the dog refusing to budge when the boarding kennel staff didn't know the proper release command.

Car Door

First of all, your Chihuahua should always be riding in a secured crate in your car or be trained to wear a safety harness that is designed specifically to attach to a seatbelt and restrains your Chi in this way. Bolting from a car should therefore not be too much of a problem.

However, bolting from an opened crate door *can* be a problem, particularly when the Chi squirms around and you can't get a leash fastened to her collar. Use the same training principles as you would for the "Wait" command; your goal will be for your dog to stay in her crate, allow you to fasten a leash to her collar, and then be released.

Begin training as you would with the simple "Wait" command. Make sure your Chi understands this and will sit with the crate door wide open when you are inside your home. Then, with your Chihuahua in her crate, gently restrain her (in case she anticipates the leash as her release command), and repeat the "Wait" command once again as you fasten the leash to her collar. Pause. Then release your Chihuahua.

When your Chihuahua is reliable at this level (gets it right at least nine out of ten times), you can work on the same exercise with the crate in the car. If at any time your Chihuahua anticipates the release (and tries to bolt), take her training back a step until she's solid once again on the basics.

Front Door

It can be downright impossible to grab a scrambling Chihuahua that's determined to slip out the front door and take a run about the neighborhood. With larger dogs, you can usually grab a collar before they burst through the door. But you'd have to be exceptionally fast (not to mention limber) to block a single-minded Mexican torpedo on legs.

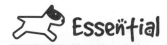 **Essential**

> If your Chi is solid on her "Wait" command when exiting the crate, you can transfer this training to the front door. A few feet from the door, attach a leash to your Chihuahua, give her the "Sit" command, and then tell her "Wait." Pause and give her the release command. Praise and reward.

When she's solid with this (nine out of ten repetitions), repeat the exercise. But this time, take a step toward the door and then back to your Chi before you release her. Praise and reward. Only when she is reliable with this (again, nine out of ten times), move your Chi one step closer to the door. Tell her to "Sit," "Wait," pause and remain in place, praise and reward. Once she's got this down, add taking a step to the door and step back. Then, add grabbing the doorknob and stepping back. This would be followed by stepping forward, opening the door slightly, closing it and stepping back. Your ultimate goal is to be able to open the door, step through the door, turn around and come back to your Chihuahua without his breaking the "Wait" command.

Though it sounds as if this training process of taking incrementally tiny steps would take forever, it doesn't. It allows you to take your Chihuahua as fast as she is able to learn while minimizing her opportunities to fail at any step.

Working with Multiple Dogs

What could be more fun than a pack of Chihuahuas? Depending on the dogs and their environment, the answer to this question could be "Nothing! They are a joy each and every day!" or it could be "A migraine headache because at least that eventually goes away." Owning more than one dog can be a wonderful experience, but it's not a perfect situation for everyone. Before you add a second (or third or fourth) Chi to your canine pack, make sure you know the facts of living with multiple dogs.

The More the Merrier?

Most Chihuahuas love company. In particular, they tend to enjoy living with other Chihuahuas though other sociable breeds and mixes can be tolerated very well. Owning more than one dog can provide additional physical and mental stimulation for your current Chihuahua. Additionally, owning two or more dogs can take a little bit of the pressure off of you for constant attention; Chis can be great companions for each other, not to mention offering a little extra snuggling warmth.

Along with the benefits of owning more than one dog come some challenges. These can include the added costs of added dogs, the situations that two Chis can cause, and working with clashing personalities.

 **Essential**

When you think about it, it's amazing that the Chihuahua is so willing to accept other canines into his home, often living around the clock every day with these dogs for ten, fifteen, and even twenty years with hardly a scuffle. We humans usually have a choice as to whom we live with, and even then we often don't get along.

Show Me the Money

Toy breeds are relatively inexpensive to feed as they simply don't eat the quantity of food that larger breeds consume. Food expenses, however, may be the only expense that is nominal whether you have one Chihuahua or two—or more. For example, most veterinary charges are based on a per-dog fee scale, not per *poundage* of dog. It doesn't matter if your total Chihuahua weight is a mere twelve pounds, if you own three dogs you'll have to pay for three sets of vaccines, three twelve-month doses of heartworm preventives, and three annual exams.

Other expenses to consider if you want to own more than one dog are the cost of supplies (multiple collars, leashes, crates, beds, coats, and so on), boarding and/or doggie day-care expenses (you might get some break because your dogs are smaller but you'll still have to pay per dog), and increased pet sitter or dog walker costs (with rates often set according to the number of visits and the number of dogs).

Double or Triple Trouble

Owners often assume that if they own two Chis that the pair will occupy each other. As the fairy tale goes, two dogs will spend so much time together that they will be less demanding of the owner's attention, and, therefore, owning more than one dog will reduce the amount of time and energy the owner has to put in with the dogs. It's a nice dream, isn't it?

The reality is that yes, the dogs—if they're compatible—will play with each other and keep each other company. The dogs will not accept this as a substitution for time with you. In fact, often a multidog household involves constant trouble as one or the other dog is vying for the owner's attention. Just like a child, the Chi figures out that if being quiet and good doesn't work then maybe doing something bad, such as stealing a sock or tearing up a pillow, will get you to quit petting the other dog and pay some attention to her.

 **Fact**

> Remember how your mother always told you that if you associated with the wrong kids that it wouldn't matter how good you were— bad always rubs off on the good and not the other way around? It's often true of multiple-dog households. The dog with the worst behaviors shows all the good dogs how to misbehave.

Then there's the level of mess and destruction two or more dogs can cause as opposed to one. Housetraining just became more complicated ("Who did that?"), and even if you own altered dogs, you may find that a young Chi (or an older one) is suddenly marking his territory in your home.

In short, adding a second dog does not cut down on the time or effort you'll put into dog ownership. You'll probably laugh more while you're taking care of your Chis, but the amount of attention and care you will need to provide these dogs—not to mention the money you'll spend—increases exponentially.

Who Gets Along Best?

Unless a Chihuahua is dog aggressive, she will usually get along with just about any dog; however, there are some good guidelines to follow that will help ensure a good match. Variables that can affect the success of adding a second or third dog include the breeds of all dogs involved, their ages, and their sexes.

As far as various breeds are concerned, Chihuahuas love Chihuahuas. Even if two Chihuahuas don't know each other, they will often act as if they are long-lost friends the first time they meet. Chihuahuas not only recognize members of their own breed, but they seem to revel in their company. A Chi-Chi pairing is usually best; however, if you already own a sweet toy breed or toy mix, adding a Chihuahua to your dog family will usually go smoothly. Pairing toy breeds together tends to keep the playing field even among dogs.

 Question?

Can a Chihuahua get along with a large-breed dog?
If you own a gentle giant that is not rambunctious and is very aware of his body space (knows where he is lying down, what his front and hind ends are doing at the same time) you can have a toy/giant pairing and everyone will get along happily. Basically, the safety of your Chihuahua is the primary issue here.

If you're looking for an age of dog that is virtually assured to get along, littermates or puppies of roughly the same age almost always grow up to be best buddies. They are, however, holy terrors for the first year of their lives. If you have a lot of energy, training experience, and patience, you might consider this option. Another age combination that works well is a puppy with a mature dog. In this case, the puppy usually grows up accepting the older dog's alpha status and does nothing to challenge this situation. A puppy with a senior Chi is also considered a good combination; studies have shown that the senior dog benefits greatly from the added mental and physical stimulation of a puppy in the house. An adult Chi paired with another adult Chi can work well, too, if you know that the incoming adult Chi likes your present Chi and vice versa.

As for the sex of your second dog, opposites not only attract, but they tend to get along better with fewer squabbles. Neutered males and spayed females of any age can often get along fabulously. Same-sex pairings can end up in serious rows if both dogs want to be alpha, but if the temperaments are good together or one is a pup and the other an older dog, same-sex pairings may work out fine in your home.

▲ Chis are dogs that love friends: the more the merrier!

Introducing a New Dog

If you've purchased a puppy or adopted an adult rescue, you want the initial introductions to your older Chi to go as smoothly as possible. One of the best ways to introduce two dogs to each other is in neutral territory. For example, try to have the pair meet in a park or on the sidewalk in front of someone else's home. The reason for picking a neutral location is to allow the dogs to meet and greet each other without the older Chi trying to protect her home and people from this new intruder.

The advantage to arranging a meeting at a fenced-in park is that the dogs can meet off leash. This makes the meeting of the dogs less confrontational. Apparently, being joined by a leash to an owner often gives a dog the feeling that she must protect her owner or, if she is timid, the frightening sensation of not being able to escape.

 **Fact**

Another way to introduce two dogs is to bring the new addition into your home when your older dog is not home. This is the same method used when parents are bringing home a newborn baby. Keep the new dog in your home for several hours or even a day before bringing the older dog home again. With the new dog's scent already in the home, the older dog is not as confrontational as he might be if a new dog crossed the threshold to your home.

Supervise the two dogs whenever they are together, and never leave them home alone without crating either one or both dogs. Until the dogs have accepted each other completely, which may take several days or even several months, anticipate that they will have a few squabbles. The worst of the squabbles will naturally occur when you aren't home, so you'll have no idea what led up to the situation except that you have two injured dogs.

How will you know when your Chis are cohabitating well? They will play together nicely, and when they're not playing, they'll either cuddle up next to each other or completely ignore each other. What you don't want to see is constant picking by one of the dogs or an overly excited sustained interest in the new Chi. If you see any signs of predatory behavior in your older dog (stalking, creeping, intense staring, body stiffness, or rigidness), safely separate the two dogs and seek professional help from an experienced trainer or animal behaviorist immediately.

Pack Ethics Essentials

Remember the saying, "Two's company, three's a crowd"? When it comes to dogs, as soon as you add that third dog, the balance and relationships between your dogs will shift. You now have a pack, and along with it, you will see your dogs displaying pack behavior, which they never have displayed before.

Though the change in power and dog-dog relationships in your home may be very subtle, it's important to understand how your dogs' behaviors might change and what kinds of situations you might see emerge over time.

Pack Power

The most dramatic—and to some unsuspecting owners, the most traumatic—is a change in attitude toward other dogs. Three or more dogs running loose together tend to be much more aggressive than a single dog or even a pair of dogs, and these groups have been known to attack dogs many times larger than themselves. The surprise to the owner comes in that the individual dogs in this pack previously may not have shown any aggressive tendencies at all when by themselves. Somehow the safety in numbers of being in a pack is empowering to the dogs. Never allow your Chis to run loose for any reason together unless it is in your own backyard and you can control the situation.

Gang Mentality

You will also see your dogs pick on a sick or injured dog in the pack. This is very disturbing to most owners, who would like to think that their dogs would be more empathetic to the disadvantaged dog. Not so. If you have five Chis and one gets involved in a squabble with another, all of a sudden the remaining three Chis will side with the stronger of the two Chis. For this reason, it is wise to separate your Chis into smaller groups or put them in individual crates when you must be gone. And, be particularly aware of any potential changes in pack order that could trigger a free-for-all.

Changes in Pack Order

When you have more than one dog, you will see your Chis develop a ranking from the Most-Powerful-and-to-be-Obeyed One (the alpha) to the I'll-Do-Anything-You-Say-If-You-Won't-Hurt-Me dog (the omega). In a large pack of dogs, you will find an alpha male and an alpha female. Though the female may appear to be the ultimate alpha, she's usually not. The supreme alpha male just puts up with her bossiness until he's had enough.

Pack Dynamics

If you have only two or three dogs in a home, the leader is generally the oldest dog or the one who's been with you the longest. The leader in a small-dog family could be either male or female and may actually be the smallest and physically weakest of your dogs. Age has its value in the dog kingdom.

 **Alert!**

Signs of submissiveness include submissive urination or defecation, rolling over on the back (exposing the belly), licking another dog's mouth, "smiling" (in which the dog exposes her teeth without aggression), allowing toys and chews to be taken away by the other dog, and lying down and waiting for the higher-ranking dog to finish eating before beginning her meal.

But the alpha position in a larger group of dogs can be tenuous. If among the pack there is a rising wannabe leader-of-the-pack, he will be looking for his chance to topple the alpha. If he sees any physical or mental weakening of the alpha dog (and this includes a health problem in the older dog that you're not yet aware of), you may see increasing irritability between the alpha and the beta dogs as the beta starts jockeying for position. This irritability may lead to arguments and possibly all-out fights with serious injuries.

What to Do

If you see the beginning of a power shift within your group of Chis, and you suspect the shift may not be a peaceful one, don't leave the two competing Chis alone together. Supervise them at all times, and prevent arguments by removing potential triggers, specifically, attention, food, chews, and toys. For example, don't praise, lavish love on, or punish one Chi when the other Chi is present. The Chi not receiving attention is likely to take exception to this and will jump in and attack the other Chi on the spot.

Make sure the sparring Chis are fed separately and don't have any opportunities to create issues over the last piece of kibble in a bowl. Give highly valued items, such as chews and favorite toys, to the Chis in their crates to enjoy.

Resource Guarding

Most people assume that a dog that guards her resources (such as food, bones, chews, toys, or stolen goods) is a very bad, dominant, aggressive dog. Precisely the opposite is usually true. Usually, and this is most obvious in a pack of dogs, the alpha Chi (who is the dominant force in the pack) doesn't need to guard her resources from the other dogs. They know not to take anything away.

The submissive dog or puppy is the most likely candidate to display resource-guarding tendencies, which are natural dog behaviors and not deviant in any way. Why? Because she is the dog that is constantly getting her things taken away by the other dogs. She never gets to keep anything. So, when she does manage to capture a prize, she doesn't want anyone to take it away—including you.

Dealing with Resource-Guarding

If the object being guarded is hers, leave her alone. Don't take the chew, food, or toy away. In our society, we too often expect too much from our dogs. Think of it this way: Would you like it if someone in your family came up and yanked a book out of your hands? A steak off your plate? Or took your favorite jacket? No, of course you wouldn't. It's very much the same for our dogs.

There are times, however, when it is absolutely necessary to take an item away from your Chi. To do so without getting bitten involves a trade. Find a delectable food item that your Chi can't resist and offer to swap your item for hers, holding the delicacy as close to her nose as possible. Usually, the Chi will drop the item she has, and take your offering. Praise her! What a good dog.

Practicing the Swap

To prevent future confrontations over items your Chi can't have, practice offering tidbits of treat for toys that she doesn't feel so possessive about, rewarding her with praise and giving her back her toy when the exercise is over. Your Chi needs to learn that if you take something away, she can trust you to give it back. Then, on those hopefully rare occasions when the item she is guarding is toxic, dangerous, or destructible, your Chi will trust you and will willingly swap the item for a treat.

If your Chi is stealing a particular item, such as a sock, facial tissue, toilet paper, or a pillow, the easiest way to solve her resource-guarding is to make the dog's fetish item inaccessible to her at all times. Pick up the socks, close the door to the bathroom, and place the pillow in a closet. It's really a small sacrifice that will help to avoid any confrontations with your Chi.

Alert!

Children are never to take anything out of the Chi's mouth, and this is a concept that is very hard for young children. It is a child's nature to snatch back a toy that the Chi has stolen. You must make sure your children understand this rule, in addition to supervising their interactions with the dog or separating them.

Feeding Solutions

The two most common issues that arise when feeding two or more Chis at the same time are arguments and giving each dog her proper portion. The easiest way to solve both problems is to feed each Chihuahua in her own crate. You might be able to separate the Chis by placing their bowls in different rooms; however, you may find that one dog (usually alpha) will go around the house, eating the other dogs' food in addition to her own. Feeding out of a community bowl may be okay for dogs that get along well; however, you'll never know who is eating how much. Watching portion sizes and appetites of your individual dogs by feeding them separately enables you not only to prevent obesity but also to detect early warning signs of illness. One of the first symptoms of many diseases is loss of appetite.

Determining Illness

Owning multiple Chihuahuas requires more time and vigilance in handling and closely observing each dog every day. If a Chi is off her feed, there's likely to be something wrong. If you feed each dog separately, you can spot a loss of appetite immediately.

Other warning signs of illness are harder to observe in a group canine environment, such as individual water intake, vomiting, diarrhea, or lack of bowel movements. With water intake, copious amounts of drinking could signal diabetes or another disease. If your Chis drink out of a communal bowl of fresh water, you may not pick up on this very quickly unless you make it a habit to keep an eye on their drinking habits.

A problem with a dog's gastrointestinal tract is easy to spot, but unless you actually see the Chi vomit or defecate, you'll have no idea "whodunit." Again, the only way to determine which dog did what is by close observation.

Raising Two Puppies Together

If you think keeping two or more dogs in the home sounds like a chore, triple that headache if you're considering raising two puppies together. On the positive side, the pups will have a built-in playmate and will grow up learning a lot about bite inhibition from each other and what's fair in dog play and what's not. They'll keep each other company, will suffer less separation anxiety from being separated from their mother, littermates, and breeder, and they'll snuggle together in a puppy pile when they sleep—even when they are all grown up.

On the negative side, your first-year expenses will be large. According to some estimates, these first-year expenses run up to $1,000 or more per puppy. Then there's the challenge of house-training two puppies at the same time. This process often takes longer since it can be hard to determine which puppy is not keeping up with the training. Sometimes the puppies may appear to bond more closely with each other than they do with you. Other times, both puppies are very needy and are constantly clamoring and wrestling for your attention. And then there's the whole issue of obedience and good-dog training. You'll have to carve out time to train both puppies at the same time. (If you are adding only one puppy to an existing older Chi, hopefully the older dog will already be trained, and you'll only have one year of beginning training to go through.)

CHAPTER 13

A New Way of Training

No more choke chains. No more harsh verbal or physical corrections. No more squashed enthusiasm or so-called "stubborn" Chihuahuas. Hooray! The dark ages of training are gone, and a new era of positive, reward-based training is in. Today's fun training methods are just what the doctor (the veterinary animal behaviorist, that is) ordered and make the goal of owning a well-trained Chihuahua within reach of everyone.

No Excuses!

"I'd train my dog but I just don't have time." "I can't find a training class nearby." "He's a toy. He doesn't need training." Excuses, excuses, excuses! And what's this about toys not needing training? Just because the Chihuahua is not heavy, strong, or tall doesn't mean a few manners wouldn't help around the home. And, in the case of some training, a command such as "Wait" or "Come" may be the very thing that saves your Chihuahua's life in an emergency. It's easy to put off something you've never done before, especially if you think it might be difficult or time consuming. We've all been procrastinators at one time or another. With obedience training, however, there's no time like the present. So, no more excuses! Train for you and for your Chihuahua!

Time Commitment

Training requires only a few minutes of your time scattered throughout the day. In fact, you can incorporate some aspect of training in every interaction you have with your Chihuahua. For example, you can work on your Chi's sit every time you feed her or offer her a treat. "Wait" can be worked on each time you release your Chihuahua from her crate. And, while playing with your Chihuahua, you can work on skills such as "Take it," "Give," and "Fetch." All that is needed is a basic understanding of how to train your Chihuahua.

 Essential

Old dogs do learn new tricks. In fact, because their focus tends to be more directed, an older dog is often attentive to what you ask of him and may learn a skill in less time than a rambunctious youngster.

Classes

Finding a training class that offers positive, reward-based training is becoming easier as the benefits of training in this manner receive more and more publicity. You may find, however, that you happen to live in an area that hasn't embraced this new, effective form of training (that's actually been around since the 1980s), or you may live in a remote area of the country. No problem. You'll find an incredible number of training guides and, in particular, training videos that can help you learn the basics on your own.

Benefits of the Well-Trained Chi

Where to begin? A puppy Chi (or one that is still learning the ropes of housetraining) that knows to wait won't rush out of her crate with poopy paws first thing in the morning. The Chihuahua that understands she must sit or lie down before you will place her bowl in front of her makes feeding spills (from an excited dog) a thing of the past. And a Chi that will lie quietly in a down while you eat dinner will never trouble you with begging.

A well-trained Chihuahua is not only a pleasure to own, she's also a pleasure to take with you wherever dogs are allowed. That includes road trips! Knowing that your Chihuahua will obey basic commands makes traveling in the car or plane safer. A well-trained Chihuahua is also much more likely to be welcomed into other people's homes, too.

 Question?

Can training help my shy adult dog?
Absolutely. Training is a confidence-building activity for your dog. Your Chihuahua learns to trust that you will never do anything that would put her in harm's way. As a result, she feels safer, learns new skills that she knows pleases you, and, most importantly, gains confidence in herself.

And then there's the benefit of gaining a much deeper bond with your dog. Owners who work with their puppies and dogs on training skills are spending quality time with their dogs. It is natural that the bond in this situation would be much greater than if an owner doesn't have time to spend with his dog. Additionally, the process of training your Chihuahua gently reinforces your leadership in the dog-human relationship. You also gain an appreciation for just how smart and clever your Chihuahua really is.

Choosing a Training Collar

The best collar for your Chi will be one that fits well—in other words, that she can't slip out of—but that is still comfortable and will not hurt her or restrict her delicate windpipe. The following sections describe some of the more common types of training collars used with Chihuahuas.

Slip Collars

If you can believe this, some trainers still insist that a Chihuahua puppy should wear a metal choke chain or a nylon slip collar for training. A trainer who is very, very skilled and has the lightest of touches may be able to use this training tool successfully; however, for most of us, one pop with one of these collars could literally flip your Chi around or injure her cervical vertebrae. Ouch!

 **Alert!**

A dog that appears to be stubborn or resistant to training is usually always a dog that has received negative reinforcement training, such as that used with a choke chain. Once a Chihuahua's enthusiasm for training is squashed in this manner, it is exceedingly difficult—if not impossible—to regain this joy and eagerness to please.

The reason these slip collars (metal chain or nylon) are too harsh for the Chihuahua is that they work by tightening around the Chi's neck (which explains the term "choke" chain). The way the collar works is that a dog hears the uptake of the chains and knows a correction (pop) is coming unless he quickly figures out what he's doing wrong and fixes it.

Negative reinforcement training, the manner of teaching in which a dog tries to avoid punishment, can be very effective. But at what cost? Small dogs are easily injured and frightened, and they sour quickly on training.

Better Choices

A great choice for a training collar is the simple flat buckle collar or the adjustable collar with a snap closure. These collars don't inflict pain on the Chi, and the wider the collar, the less pressure is placed on the Chi's neck structure should she hit the end of the leash on occasion. The adjustable collar is another good option, especially if you have a puppy that might need two different sizes of collars before she's finished growing. Since the Chihuahua will never exert very much pressure on the collar, you don't need to be as concerned with the strength of the clip as a large-breed dog owner would.

Another collar you might consider is a greyhound collar. This collar involves two pieces: a wider band that nearly encircles the dog's neck and a slip of nylon or light chain that loops through the ends of the wider band. When the dog strains against the collar, it tightens; however, since the throat band is quite wide, it does not choke or injure the Chihuahua. Additionally, this kind of collar prevents a Chi from backing out of her collar (that is, pulling backwards until the collar pops off over her head).

 **Essential**

Collars come in several different materials: flat and rolled leather, nylon web, and cotton-covered nylon. Rolled leather tends to rub a dog's coat the least and lasts the longest (unless gnawed on by the pup). Nylon web is tough and comes in a huge variety of colors, but it can rub off a soft coat. Adding a cotton cover provides even more style options but it is less durable. The cover will require washing and will eventually fray.

A harness can be used with great success on a Chihuahua, too. The harness has a chest band that fits around the front of the chest and a second band that fits under the chest behind the dog's elbows. The dog cannot back out of a harness. A Chi is not so big that pulling is an issue, and the harness ensures you won't accidentally injure the dog's neck. The harness does, however, need to be fitted to the dog to ensure that it is comfortable and doesn't rub or restrain the Chi's movements in any way.

Basics of Operant Conditioning

The theory behind operant conditioning is that an animal can be conditioned to give a specific behavior. You perform this conditioning by either giving the dog a reward for exhibiting the desired behavior or punishing the dog for exhibiting an incorrect behavior.

In the first approach, the dog performs the behavior because she wants to please you. Inappropriate behaviors are extinguished because the dog doesn't receive any pleasure or reward (your praise) when she performs them. In the second approach, the dog gives a specific behavior to avoid pain. The correct behavior is molded by punishing all the incorrect attempts.

Both approaches garner equal results. The rate at which a dog learns with either negative or positive reinforcement is equally fast. Studies also show that the dog's retention rate is similar with both methods. With negative reinforcement, however, the Chihuahua is not providing the behavior you want because she wants to please you; rather, she performs because she is trying to avoid pain. Dogs trained in this manner often show it in their demeanors. Their performances are lackluster, and the obvious sense of joy seen in a dog trained with positive reinforcement is missing. Negative reinforcement training does little to bolster the human-dog bond and doesn't take advantage of the Chihuahua's strong urge to please her human.

Primary and Secondary Reinforcements

When working with positive, reward-based training, you will be working with primary and secondary reinforcements. The primary reinforcement is the dog's ultimate reason or reward for performing the task you've asked of her—your physical praise. For dogs, physical praise such as rubbing, petting, hugging is the most highly regarded reward. However, treats, toys or a quick game of tug may be used as the reward for a task with great success, too. Just don't forget the ultimate reward of following up with some gentle physical attention.

▲ **Start training your Chi early in puppyhood if you would like a show dog in the future.**

In positive, reward-based training, a secondary or conditioned reinforcement is the signal that the dog is doing something right and that a primary reinforcement is coming. For example, one of the most common secondary conditioners used in dog training is verbal praise, such as "Yes!" or "Good!" Other secondary conditioners that are extremely effective are treats, clickers, and toys.

Free Shaping

When rewarding the good and ignoring the bad, the Chihuahua has to exhibit the desired behavior in order for you to be able to reward her. One way of doing this is by waiting for the dog to give the behavior on her own and then rewarding her. This method is called free shaping.

 **fact**

Primary and secondary reinforcements for a negative training approach would be the sound of the chain collar tightening or the slight buzz of an electric collar (secondary reinforcement) and the sharp choke of the tight collar or the full shock of the electric collar.

For example, if your Chi tends to sit a lot, you can use this to help your dog make the connection between the command "Sit!" and actually sitting. You would begin by saying "Sit!" when your Chi is sitting, reward with your chosen secondary reinforcement, and then physically praise (rub, pat, love) her.

After a day or two of saying "Sit" whenever your Chi is sitting, you would next say "Sit!" when you catch your Chi in the act of sitting. *Click* and *pat.* You would then progress to saying "Sit!" when your Chi is just starting to sit, followed by "Sit!" when you know your Chi is going to sit, and finally, "Sit!" when your Chi is paying attention to you and you want her to sit.

Using Food Lures

Sometimes waiting for a Chihuahua to produce the desired behavior on her own may take too long. Or perhaps your Chi doesn't produce the behavior you want. In these cases, using a tiny bit of food as a lure to shape your Chihuahua into position is very effective and is absolutely nonconfrontational (if the dog has a tendency to resist your leadership) and nonthreatening (particularly good for the timid, fearful, or particularly sensitive dog).

A really good example of using a food lure to shape a behavior is the sit. Holding the Chi gently by the collar with one hand and a treat in the other, you would slowly move the treat from the tip of your dog's nose slowly over her head, skimming closely over her muzzle and the crown of her head. By the time the treat is overhead or between the ears, the dog will have folded back on her hind legs, giving you a perfect sit.

 **Essential**

> For simplicity's sake, a secondary or conditioned reinforcement will be referred to as click, whether you're using a snap of the fingers, clicker, cluck of the tongue, or an "Okay!" The primary reinforcement—treat, ball, or play followed by physical praise—will be referred to as pat.

Timing is important when using a food lure to shape the correct behavior. Just as with free shaping, you want to give the command only when the dog is in the correct position. So with the sit, you would not say "Sit!" until your Chi was squarely on her haunches. You would then *click* and *pat*.

Repetition is very important for the dog not only to recognize what it is you want her to do but also to build her confidence that she is doing the right thing each and every time. Where many novice (and experienced!) trainers fail is that they don't reinforce each step of the process enough. Every trainer has his percentage, but it is generally agreed that the dog should provide the desired behavior correctly and with confidence at least eight out of ten repetitions before moving to the next step.

Small Steps to Success

In addition to not allowing enough correct repetitions of an exercise, another common error is increasing more than one variable at a time, setting the dog up for a mistake. Of course, this means that as a trainer, you'll need to recognize what variables are involved in the exercise you are working on.

 **Fact**

> Setting a dog up for success means setting up an exercise so that the dog literally can't fail the task. Free shaping incorporates this philosophy well, as does shaping using lures—as long as the handler increases the difficulty of the exercise slowly.

For example, with the sit-stay, your variables are time and distance. You would never want to increase your demands for both the amount of time your Chi must remain in a sit as well as how far away you move from her. Instead, you could increase the time you expect your Chi to remain sitting by thirty seconds for a total of ninety seconds. When she can accomplish this reliably (and with confidence) nine out of ten times, you can then increase your other variable, distance. Depending on where your Chi was with this exercise, this might mean adding one additional step away from her for a total of four steps.

A variable that is often forgotten is location. If your Chihuahua sits reliably on command anywhere in the house, this does not mean she will sit on command when you are on the sidelines of a kids' soccer game. When adding a new variable to the mix, start at the beginning. If you're working on a sit, begin with the lure to shape the sit. You will progress more quickly this time; however, you are setting your dog up to succeed by giving her an easier, confidence building task.

How to Find a Good Trainer

Are all of these technical training terms make your head spin a bit? Don't worry. It's not important that you remember the exact terms, but it is important that you understand how your dog learns and the best approach to take in training. A key for novice trainers is to find a professional dog trainer or training club that has experts who can coach you on how to train your dog.

Training Method

One of the most important qualities you want to find in a training facility is the method by which they teach. For the Chihuahua—even one you might consider a problem Chi—positive, reward-based training is a must. This breed is too easily frightened and the bond too easily fractured between handler and dog if the handler uses harsh training methods, and this includes harsh verbal corrections.

To find out if a trainer or training school uses positive, reward-based training, ask if you can observe a class. Look for the types of collars that the trainer or school encourages or requires. If you see choke chains and a trainer who insists on physical corrections, run. If you see nylon slip collars but the students aren't popping their dogs, ask the trainer if flat-buckle collars are allowed for toy breeds. Sometimes a trainer will require slip collars so that a dog can't back out of his collar and wreak havoc.

 Question?

How are the dogs separated in the class?
Toy breeds can be targets of larger, more aggressive dogs. Problem dogs are in training classes—where they should be—but the owners of these dogs frequently can't control their canines. Trainers will sometimes offer separate classes for toy and small breeds, or at a minimum they will ensure that dog-aggressive dogs are trained separately.

Watch to see if the owners are using treats, toys, and clickers to shape behaviors. Some schools only allow verbal praise and incorporate limited physical corrections. You want to be able to use the reward that excites your Chihuahua the most.

Where to Look

To help narrow your search, begin by asking your veterinarian for recommendations. Your breeder, if he is in your area, will be able to give you a good referral. Another source is your local shelter or Chihuahua breed rescue. These folks are in the business of helping dogs find permanent, loving homes—which involves a lot of problem solving. They'll know who to call in your area.

Another source that lists certified trainers—trainers who have met specific training criteria—is the Association of Pet Dog Trainers (APDT). This national professional organization can be contacted for referrals to trainers in your area. Before you sign up with a trainer, make sure that the trainer enjoys working with Chihuahuas, employs the training style you are seeking, and that you get along personally with the trainer.

CHAPTER 14

A Few Basic Commands

With just eight easy-to-teach commands, you can literally transform even the most unruly, destructive Chihuahua into a really special family pet. A Chihuahua that recognizes these basic commands is not only more obedient but also more attentive, waiting for your next command. Carrying out tasks gives the Chihuahua a mental challenge, and the trained Chihuahua not only enjoys training sessions but also develops a very deep bond with her owner. A well-trained Chihuahua is literally worth her weight in gold as a canine companion.

The Well-Mannered Chihuahua Is Welcome

One of the most common reasons for dogs of any breed to wind up in shelters and pounds is that their owners didn't do any basic training with their dogs when they were puppies. What were considered "cute puppy antics" quickly become bothersome behaviors as the puppy matures. By the time the untrained Chihuahua reaches eight or nine months of age—and has nearly reached physical maturity—she's "misbehaving" on a regular basis.

The untrained Chi runs away when called, evades anyone trying to grab her by the collar, nips the children when they try to pet her gently, growls and snarls when anyone tries to displace her from her favorite chair, won't let anyone put a brush through her coat or clip her nails (lest they feel like letting blood), and is entirely unhousetrained.

Now the family is up in arms with the young dog, and outside to the back yard she is banished. At this point, the young dog is one step away from the shelter. She doesn't like being separated from her family. She barks incessantly, digs, and scratches at the back door. ("Why am I out here?") Outside living is not for a Chihuahua. She's dirty and has fleas. And that's the beginning of the end. The saddest part is that this Chi was just being a dog and was displaying very natural dog behaviors.

 **Fact**

Dog behaviorists recommend a solid year of attending training classes with your new puppy or rescued adult dog. If more owners made this effort (and the effects last a lifetime—which could be twenty years) there would be far less unwanted dogs.

Without guidance, nurturing, and molding from us as to what we expect from them, it's impossible to suppose that our canines— yes, even the loving Chihuahua—will behave perfectly. We must teach our Chis the rules of the house, and the best way to do this is to make sure that they know how to sit, down, stay, come, jump off the furniture, take and give objects on command, and walk nicely on the leash. With these few training tools, socialization becomes much easier, and your leadership role is firmly established in a gentle and reassuring way.

Choosing Your Reward

In order for the positive, reward-based system of training to be most effective, you will need to figure out what secondary or conditioned reinforcement drives your Chi nuts. Some Chis will do anything for food, so tiny bits of training treats might do the trick. For others, toys or use of a clicker might be the answer.

Treats

If you are purchasing prepackaged training treats, make sure you read the nutrition label. Many of these treats are high in salts, sugars, and preservatives. You want to make sure that the treats you are using are not only delectable to your Chihuahua but also nutritious.

 **Question?**

What's a really healthy treat that most dogs can't resist?
A favorite training treat is baked chicken chopped in small pieces. Chicken is a wonderful source of protein, but if you use this make sure that you adjust your Chi's food portions to take into account the calories from the added treats. Ask your veterinarian for nutritional advice; you don't want to skimp on any vitamins that your Chi would be receiving in her missed supper portion.

As a toy-breed owner, however, you'll need to be aware that it doesn't take many treats to overfeed a Chihuahua. For this reason, you may want to explore a few food options. One option is to portion your Chi's daily food allowance in a fanny pack and carry it with you all day. Her rewards will be bits of food. For this to work, however, you'll need to ask her to learn and/or perform different exercises throughout the day. If you aren't able to work in little segments throughout the day, you might consider using a low-calorie option for your training treat, such as cut-up carrots.

Toys

A favorite reward for many Chihuahuas is a highly desired toy, one that is very special to the individual dog. (This is the most common reward used for Chihuahuas that work as service dogs for the hearing impaired.) The toy could be one of many different objects, such as a ball, which must be big enough to hold but not so small as to be swallowed, a small tug toy, a squeaky toy, a balled-up sock, or a rope toy.

 **Essential**

If you can't find a rope toy that is small enough for your Chi, check out the bird supply section in a pet store. Often this department has toys that are similar to those for dogs but that are smaller and more easily handled by the Chi.

It is important that the Chihuahua only has access to this toy when she is being trained. As with children, if she has access to the toy all day, it becomes not so special anymore. Additionally, some of these toys are those that must be enjoyed under close supervision. For example, a Chi can tear apart a squeaky toy to get the squeaker and choke. A balled-up sock can be a choking hazard, too.

Clicks

For those Chi owners who have good dexterity, a clicker may be an excellent training tool. Many professional and amateur trainers prefer a clicker to verbal praise or a treat because the *click* is very precise. Your dog knows exactly when she did the right thing—even if you are at quite a distance. The *click* also serves as a signal to the dog that the exercise is over and is an automatic release, too.

To use a clicker in training, you must first condition your Chi to make the connection between the *click* and a food reward. To do this, you will *click* only when you have your Chi's rapt attention, and then you'll immediately treat. After practicing this for several days, your Chihuahua should be anticipating a treat whenever she hears the *click*.

 **Question?**

What if I can't juggle the clicker, the leash, and a treat at the same time?

You're not alone! Police K-9 trainers use a cluck instead of a clicker because it is impossible to juggle a handgun and a clicker at the same time. If you're all thumbs with the clicker, you can substitute a verbal click with a cluck of the tongue, a finger snap, or a short, sharp whistle toot.

The Importance of a Quiet Place

Intense focus is not always the Chihuahua's forte. In fact, as a puppy, the Chihuahua gets distracted easily. For this reason it is important to set your Chihuahua up for her greatest possibility of success. This means that you need to choose a quiet, distraction-free environment in which to train.

Have Patience

Once your Chihuahua is executing the desired behavior reliably and with confidence, then you can consider working on the skill in a slightly more distracting location. A key word here is "slightly." You don't want to jump from training your Chihuahua in the privacy of your living room and then expect a perfect performance in a crowded city park.

A better step would be to progress to the quiet of your backyard, then your front yard, followed by some work while walking around the neighborhood and finally moving to a park (while it's empty), the park while it's crowded (but working at a healthy distance away), and then moving closer to the crowd over time.

Remember that when you change the location, you've changed a variable. Rather than expecting your Chihuahua to perform an exercise at the difficulty level at which she had been performing in your home, you'll need to begin the exercise from its most basic level and work back up to the proficiency level your Chi had shown in the home. This allows your Chihuahua to work at a good confidence level even if she finds the new location a little distracting.

▲ If trained properly, your Chi will be obedient and very attentive to your commands.

Position Tips

When training a Chihuahua, it is also important to set yourself up for success. It's no secret that bending over to shape a Chi into a sit or another task can be a backbreaking experience. Kneeling or sitting on the floor to work with your Chi is perfectly acceptable and allows much more comfortable access to your dog. If you prefer to stand, consider training the initial elements of these basic commands using a grooming table or another counter high surface that is slip-proof.

When starting your training on a raised surface, you'll work your Chi until she is reliable and confident (eleven out of twelve repetitions correctly) before moving her to the floor. Treat changing positions (table to floor; seated floor to standing floor, and so on) as a variable. In other words, when you move to a seated floor position, begin at the beginning of the exercise again—as if your Chi didn't learn anything the first time around. She'll quickly fly through the beginning stages, which will build her confidence despite the uncertainty of this new location.

 **Alert!**

For ease of description, click has been used to signify a verbal or mechanical signal that the Chi has done the right thing. Reward signifies the primary reinforcement using treats, toy, ball, or verbal praise followed by physical praise. The phrase "Repeat eleven out of twelve reps" indicates that you should repeat the exercise until the dog achieves a proficiency of eleven out of twelve correct and confident repetitions.

Sit

If there is only one command you teach your Chihuahua, the sit is perhaps the most useful of all. It is easier to settle an excited Chi that sits on command. A good sit can make it easier to snap a leash on a bouncing Chi's collar or keep your Chi from jumping up with muddy paws on your clean slacks. And, being able to give your Chi the "Sit" command while feeding her dinner prevents many spills.

Free Shaping the Sit

If you choose to use the free shaping method of teaching the sit, you will need to carefully watch for each and every opportunity you might have to catch your Chi in a sit. You'll also want to carry a clicker (if you're using this training tool) and a concealed favorite toy or bag of treats with you whenever you are with your Chihuahua. You need to be prepared to reinforce this behavior at any moment.

As soon as your Chi sits fully and squarely on her haunches, say "Sit," then *click* and *reward*. Because you are only clicking and rewarding when you catch your Chi in a full sit, you can't do any immediate repetitions. You'll need to wait for the next opportunity. After you've been able to *click* and *reward* your Chi's sits for a day or two, then you can say "Sit" when your Chi is almost all the way in a sit. As soon as her haunches are on the floor in a full sit, *click* and *reward*.

 **Essential**

With any exercise, it's important to begin by saying the command only after the dog has performed the exact behavior you want. If you say "Sit" before your Chi is all the way to the floor in a full sit, you will teach your Chi that it is a semicrouching position, not the all-the-way-down-on-the-floor sit, that you are looking for.

Your next step will be to give the "Sit" command when your Chi is starting to sit and then *click* and *reward* when she hits the full sit. Next, you would give the command when your Chi is close to you and has her full attention on you. When she sits squarely, then *click* and *reward*. At this point, you can now begin repetitions as opposed to waiting for the moment.

Using Lures

If you are taking a training class, your instructor is likely to use the food lure method of shaping the sit. You'll take your Chi gently by the collar to hold her in front of you. In your other hand, you'll have a treat. Take this treat and slowly move it from the tip of her nose, between her eyes and over the dome of her head. As she rocks back for the treat (she can't step backward because you're gently restraining her) she will fold into a sit. As soon as she is in the correct position, give the command "Sit" and immediately *click* and *reward*. Repeat this exercise until your Chi is easily rocking back. Repeat eleven out of twelve reps.

Next, still using the food lure, say "Sit!" as your Chi is rocking back to sit. When she is in a full sit—and only then—*click* and *reward*. Repeat this until she's correct and confident eleven out of twelve reps. Now say "Sit" when you first start moving the food lure, waiting until she gives the full sit and then *click* and *reward*. Finally, you will only hold the treat, say "Sit," and *click* and *reward* when she sits.

Down

The down is very close to the sit when it comes to in-the-home usefulness. It's a comfortable position for your Chi if you are asking her to remain in the same position for any length of time, such as while you eat dinner. She can even be on her side and sound asleep and still be obeying the "Down" command.

What you may not know though is that the down is a submissive position for a dog. This command can therefore be a wonderful training tool to help establish leadership with a challenging dog or to control dog-dog aggression. Because the down is a submissive position, however, a dominant dog that challenges your leadership position will be very resistant to learning this command. This is the dog that needs this command the most, of course, so keep working on it! If you really are having difficulties, consult a trainer for assistance.

Begin by holding your Chi gently by the collar while she is standing and facing you. With a treat in your other hand, slowly move the treat from the dog's nose downwards and toward your Chihuahua's chest. She will rock back and fold into a down. When she is all the way into her down, then say, "Down." *Click* and *reward*. Repeat eleven out of twelve reps.

 **fact**

You can, of course, free shape any of the commands in this chapter. The principles are the same for all—initially, you'll need to catch your pup or adult Chi producing the behavior you want independently. Only when you've established a solid link between the command and the behavior you want can you begin to ask her to repeat the exercise on command.

When your Chi is performing this solidly, still using the treat, you'll now give the command "Down" when she is almost all the way into her down. *Click* and *reward*. Repeat eleven out of twelve reps. Next, give the command when your Chi begins to go into the down. Only when she drops fully to the floor and is in her down do you *click* and *reward*. Repeat eleven out of twelve reps. Finally, say "Down" while holding the treat at her nose. As with all levels of difficulty, only *click* and *reward* when your Chihuahua is in the down position. Repeat eleven out of twelve reps.

Stay

The "Stay" command is a variation of the "Wait" command (described on page 160). The difference is subtle, but your Chihuahua will catch on quickly. The "Wait" command indicated a momentary pause before a release, while the "Stay" command is for a longer time period that can be followed by another command or series of commands.

To teach the stay, your Chi must be comfortable and proficient with either the sit or the down. Both the sit-stay and the down-stay are taught in the same manner but to keep things simple, the stay exercises described here will only be referred to as the sit-stay. Another prerequisite for teaching the "Stay" command is that you must know your right from your left. When you step away from your Chi with your right foot first, this will indicate that you expect her to stay in place and in position. Conversely, stepping away from your Chihuahua with your left foot first will signal that you expect her to move and keep up with you.

 **Essential**

When giving commands to your Chihuahua, be careful to always keep your voice upbeat and positive. In fact, you should only train your Chihuahua when you are in a great mood and have lots and lots of patience. This will help ensure a productive training session while maintaining your Chi's enthusiasm and confidence.

With your Chihuahua in a sit by your left side on leash, lean over and put your right hand in front of her face, palm toward her. Say, "Stay." Stand back up, but do not step away from her. Remain still. After only a few seconds, *click* and *reward*. Repeat eleven out of twelve reps.

Your initial variables in the sit-stay are going to be the time you ask your Chihuahua to stay in position and the distance away from you that she is expected to stay in position. To increase the difficulty of this exercise, you'll first increase the amount of time. To make sure your Chihuahua continues to succeed, increase the amount of time between the command "Stay" and the *click* and *reward* in no more than fifteen-second increments until you've reached a successful sixty-second sit-stay.

 **Alert!**

Don't forget to release your dog verbally with an "Okay" after every correct repetition of an exercise, followed by lots of physical and verbal praise.

Now you'll begin increasing the distance variable. Give your Chihuahua the "Sit-stay" command. Rise back up to a standing position, and with your right foot first take a step to the right side and immediately back again. *Click* and *reward*. Repeat eleven out of twelve reps. Give the "Stay" command, take two steps to your right, and go immediately back again. *Click* and *reward*. Repeat eleven out of twelve reps.

To reintroduce the variable of time, give your Chihuahua the "Stay" command, take one step to the right, pause a few seconds and step back. *Click* and *reward*. Repeat eleven out of twelve reps. Next, give the "Stay" command, take one step to the right, pause fifteen seconds and step back. *Click* and *reward*. Repeat eleven out of twelve reps. Continue increasing time and distance incrementally until you can perform various activities—such as walk around your dog, jump up and down, or walk away from her and stand for several minutes—while she remains in her stay.

Come

Teaching your Chihuahua to come when called will not only save a lot of frustration, it could also save your Chihuahua's life someday. Countless pet owners retell stories of narrow misses when a dog or puppy got loose and only avoided a car accident or encounter with an aggressive dog because she actually came when called.

As important as this command is, novice handlers frequently botch training the recall because they forget the basic rules. Here are the most important things to remember:

- "Come" is to be treated as an emergency command only.
- Always practice this command when your Chihuahua is on leash so that your Chihuahua always comes in response.
- When your Chihuahua is off leash (whether in the backyard or in the house) and thus out of your direct control, use her name as a signal for her to see what's up.

- For every time you utter the command "Come" and your Chihuahua doesn't respond, it will take a minimum of twenty repetitions at an equivalent level of difficulty (which will take a long time to work up to) to overcome the fact that now your Chi thinks she doesn't have to come.
- Never call your Chihuahua with an angry voice. Who wants to come to be punished?
- Consider using a whistle or other loud sound in place of the verbal command. That way, your Chi will never hear the anxiety in your voice when you're frantic for her to come to you. (Always carry the whistle, however.)
- Make "big" over every brisk, fast recall. It's gotta be a great reward.
- Say "Come!" only once; if you repeat a command two or three times your Chi quickly learns that only after you've said "Come!" two or three times does she have to respond.
- Make sure all other family members understand the rules of "Come!" Any inconsistencies in training a command will confuse your Chihuahua and will lengthen the time required to train the skill.

To train the "Come" command, snap a leash on your Chihuahua and start walking. Suddenly, start jogging backwards, saying your Chi's name, and acting as silly as possible to encourage your Chi to run after you. The moment your Chi whips around and starts running to you, say "Come!" Immediately *click* and *reward*. Repeat eleven out of twelve reps. Next, do the same exercise except give the "Come" command as you begin to step backwards. When your Chi spins around and is running toward you, *click* and *reward*. Repeat eleven out of twelve reps.

Now you'll want to begin recalling your Chihuahua when she's in a sit-stay or down-stay. Place your Chi in a stay of your choice, step out on your right foot, and walk to the end of the leash. (Your prerequisite here is that you've mastered this level of stay with your Chi.) Turn to face your Chi and say, "Come" as you begin running backwards. *Click* and *reward*. Repeat eleven out of twelve reps. Use a longer line to work the stay at longer distances. Only progress to an off-leash recall if you are considering competing in performance events.

Essential

To get your Chi really wound up for the recall, once she's running toward you, you turn around and really start running. Chihuahuas love to chase their owners, and this unexpected twist is great fun for them. As always, stop, click and reward. Once you've got your Chihuahua running in from a long line, toss a favorite toy through your legs for your Chi to grab. This unexpected surprise will get your Chi really running to you!

Off

This is a great exercise to work on to prevent a pup or an adult from developing the opinion that a specific spot, cushion, or chair is hers. A Chihuahua that thinks she's right and you're wrong can get quite ugly if you attempt to remove her from her spot. To prevent this issue from even arising, begin by working from a low surface—you don't want any injuries! Use a food lure to bribe your Chihuahua to leave her comfy roost and follow the treat to the floor. When your Chi hits the floor, say "Off!" Click and reward. Repeat eleven out of twelve reps. Practice the same exercise with the lure when your Chi is on the low surface. *Click* and *reward*. Repeat eleven out of twelve reps.

Take It and Give

These commands are taught in tandem and are wonderful in preventing issues over what your Chihuahua can and can't have in her mouth. Begin by finding objects around the house that you know your Chihuahua will take readily from you, such as a favorite squeaky toy or ball. Offer your Chi the object and as soon as she takes it, say "Take it!" *Click* and *reward*. Repeat this exercise without asking her to give back the toy.

Once she has caught on to the "Take it!" command, find an object that she will hold in her mouth but that she won't be possessive about giving it up. Offer her this object, say "Take It!" and then—before the *click* and *reward*—offer her an incredibly scrumptious piece of food. When she opens her mouth and begins to drop the object, say "Give!" *Click* and *reward*. Repeat eleven out of twelve reps.

Walk Nicely

If you want your Chihuahua to walk briskly by your side without crisscrossing in front of you and tangling you up in the leash, resist using a retractable leash for walking for at least a month. Your goal is to make sure that your Chihuahua can walk without pulling or darting around without any external control.

One of the easiest ways to gain your Chi's attention is to continue changing directions. Instead of walking straight down the sidewalk, go in the opposite direction your Chihuahua is going the minute she starts pulling. For example, if your Chi is pulling you forward, go backward. When she realizes you're going in the opposite direction and she darts back after you, *click* and *reward*. Is she straining to the left? Go right. *Click* and *reward* when she's with you again. Pulling to the right? Go left. *Click* and *reward*. She'll catch on right away that she needs to stay with you.

And, as always, keep training fun! It really is fun to work with puppies and adults and watch as they progress in their skills. And you, too, can take pride in having trained your Chihuahua to be a wonderful, well-mannered companion.

CHAPTER 15

Nutrition

What you feed your Chihuahua has a significant impact on her health—either positively or negatively. The Chihuahua is not recognized as an easy keeper that can eat virtually anything and thrive. In fact, with puppies, it is not only what you feed but when that's important. To be at her best, your Chihuahua requires a highly digestible, nutrient-packed, quality diet throughout her life.

Choosing a Healthy Diet

Gone are the days when dogs were expected to survive on whatever scraps a family could scrounge up for their pets. Gone also are the days of one-size-fits-all dog food. As consumers, pet owners now have an incredible array of food choices not only for adult dogs but for all life stages: puppy, adolescent, adult, senior, and geriatric. Food choices now include the convenience of commercial pet foods, all-natural diets, and home-prepared meals developed by veterinary nutritionists.

When choosing a diet for your Chihuahua, there are several basic characteristics that play key roles in whether your Chi will thrive or just survive on the food you've chosen:

- **Aroma**—Some researchers believe that toy breeds do not have a finely tuned sense of smell, which in turn can affect their perception of whether something is tasty or not. The better a food smells to your Chi, the more likely she is to taste it.

- **Palatability**—Not only does the food have to hold the promise of tasting good (aroma), it has to be scrumptious, too.
- **Bite size**—The Chihuahua needs foods that can be easily eaten. Larger chunks of kibble or raw foods can be difficult or impossible for a puppy or small Chi to eat.
- **Digestibility**—It can taste and smell great, but if a food cannot be digested and its nutrients aren't absorbed, a Chihuahua could become malnourished.
- **High quality in, less quantity out**—The less filler that is used in a food and the higher the digestibility of the ingredients, the less stool a Chihuahua will produce. This is a good thing if you are using a litter box or pan.
- **Odor**—A food that is highly digestible will produce less gas and, depending on the ingredients used, less fecal odor, too.

Commercial Foods

Most of the information we have today regarding the nutritional needs of dogs comes from ongoing research being performed by commercial pet-food manufacturers. Manufacturers are continually trying to get a leg up on their competition, and one of the best ways to do this is to incorporate the latest and greatest research discoveries they've made into their dog-food products. Of course, it's the pet owners and their dogs that benefit the most from this research.

Despite the rapid gains that are being made in developing high-grade pet foods, you'll still find inexpensive, low-end products with poor protein sources, fill (indigestible roughage), and mineral and vitamin sources that can't be absorbed into a dog's system.

It's not easy to tell, however, if a dog food is made of high-quality ingredients or is the equivalent of junk food. Each state regulates how ingredients must be listed in pet foods and what claims pet manufacturers can make on their packaging.

 **Fact**

Ongoing research has helped develop specific formulas for a wide range of dogs, including puppies and adults of various sizes (toy/small-breed, medium-sized, and large-breed), active/high-performance adults, overweight adults, and senior dogs. You can also find specialty formulas for improving skin and coats, strengthening immune systems, and preventing or improving joint degeneration.

In order to create more uniformity nationwide in feed regulations and as pet-food manufacturers grew from local to regional and national companies, the Association of American Feed Control Officials (AAFCO), an association of state and federal feed officials, developed recommended nutritional minimums (and a few maximums) for two life stages: puppies and lactating dogs, and adult dogs. The AAFCO also provides methods by which pet-food manufacturers can test their products to prove they meet the AAFCO's nutritional profiles. The AAFCO continues to review new studies and research, updating the nutritional profiles as needed.

Feeding Trials

Commercial pet foods must meet a minimum nutritional content, which is recommended by the Association of American Feed Control Officials (AAFCO). A food that is tested in a laboratory and shown to contain the recommended vitamins, minerals, fats, proteins, and so on, can print the statement: "This food meets the AAFCO's nutrient profiles." This statement only attests to the food's content. Even foods so labeled might be virtually indigestible.

A better food will be labeled "Complete and balanced," and reference will be made to "animal feeding tests" or "animal feeding trials" using AAFCO procedures. Foods that contain this wording not only have the necessary nutrients, they have been shown to be palatable and digestible because dogs thrived on this food in feeding trials.

Essential

The most frequently used meats are chicken and beef. Lamb appears as a key ingredient in foods for sensitive stomachs or allergies; salmon is a favorite for those foods promising soft skin and luxurious coats.

▲ **Make sure your Chi eats nutritious foods everyday—and be careful that they don't pick up any bad habits when they're pups!**

Deciphering the Label

The ingredients that are contained in a dog food are listed on the label according to the quantity with which they appear. So, if a particular pet food's primary ingredient is beef, "Beef" will be the first ingredient listed. For most puppies and dogs, it is best if the first ingredient listed in the food is a protein source, such as any one of several meats or fish.

Within the various protein sources that are used in dog foods, you want your Chihuahua to eat the highest-grade meats or fish possible. If commercial foods using human-grade ingredients are not available to you or are cost prohibitive, your next best option is to find a food using a premium grade of meat. Whether the meats contained in the dog food are all meat (premium) or are of a lesser grade of meat containing organs, such as livers and gizzards, the meat will be listed simply as "beef" or "lamb."

 **Quesﬁoñ?**

What is human-grade meat?
Human-grade chicken, beef, lamb, and other meats must meet the standards set by the United States Department of Agriculture (USDA) for feeding, raising, and slaughtering. Human-grade chicken, for example, must come from chickens that were fed an alternative feed for a minimum of six to eight weeks prior to slaughter to ensure that the meat will have acceptable levels of growth hormones and steroids.

The lowest grade meats are listed as by-products. These meats include both digestible and indigestible parts. Indigestible parts could include hooves, claws, feet, or feathers. Unfortunately, how much of the protein source is digestible and how much is indigestible can't be determined from reading the label.

Changing Formulas

What a lot of dog people don't realize is that commercial dog-food manufacturers will vary the ingredients and their proportions in a food. The labels will always reflect what is in the bag, but if a savvy dog owner saves a few labels, you may find that the food you are feeding is inconsistent. The formula changes because the manufacturer takes advantage of the lowest market prices and substitutes ingredients. If corn is at a better price than rice one month, the manufacturer will use the less-expensive corn in its packaged food.

A dog food that varies its ingredients regularly can be upsetting to a sensitive dog's system, causing gastrointestinal distress. For many dogs, the variation in formulas is so subtle as to have no effects at all. However, if your Chi doesn't always seem to enjoy her food, or if you notice a change in her ability to digest her food, you may want to track the product's labels for a few months and see if there is any variation in the ingredients.

 **Alert!**

Dry foods can help improve your Chihuahua's dental health greatly. Crunching hard kibble slows the development of plaque and dental tartar that leads to periodontal disease, which is particularly prevalent in this breed.

Dry, Semimoist, and Moist

Commercial dog foods fall into one of three categories of textures: dry, semimoist, or moist. Dry foods are inexpensive to feed. They store well and have a reasonably long shelf life, but they do contain the largest amounts of preservatives. Semimoist foods (chewy morsels) have fewer preservatives and a shorter shelf life. They typically contain high amounts of sugars, as well as artificial coloring. Moist foods, such as canned dog food, have the least amount of preservatives and sugars but are the most expensive to feed. Additionally, once the wet food is placed in a dog's bowl, it becomes rancid quickly and must be picked up within thirty minutes.

Semimoist and moist foods, because of their high palatability, can induce a dog to eat beyond her normal capacity. It's similar to humans eating to satiation and then making room for dessert, except it's your Chihuahua at her dinner bowl. Dry foods—if not moistened with gravy or anything else enticing—are generally eaten as needed. Unless the Chihuahua perceives that there is competition for her food, she will rarely overeat dry kibble.

Preservatives

Many leading pet-food manufacturers have moved away from packing dog foods with synthetic preservatives. Instead, the preservative of choice is becoming such natural ingredients as ascorbic acid (vitamin C), rosemary extract, or citric acid. If possible, avoid foods that list the controversial synthetic preservative ethoxyquin. Though there have been no definitive studies that prove a link with cancer, it is still better to avoid chemicals when at all possible.

 Essential

Some people believe they must add even more vitamins and nutritional supplements to their dog's diet, thinking that a lot of the vitamins and minerals are cooked out of the food in the manufacturing process. Manufacturers report that the nutritional content of a food is determined from the final product—the same as what your Chi would eat.

Chelated Vitamins

Vitamins are added to commercial dog foods to meet the AAFCO's nutritional minimum recommendations. Many dog foods, however, exceed these minimums and add additional vitamins and nutrients to their foods. How much a food is supplemented is determined by the manufacturer's research as to what the optimal nutritional requirements are for the food's targeted market. Since much of this research is proprietary information, buyers sometimes must trust the integrity of the manufacturer.

Can you supplement your Chi's diet with various vitamins, nutritional extracts, and powders? Yes, but be aware that too much of a good thing can be bad. Only supplement your Chi's diet under the supervision or advisement of your veterinarian. Excesses of some vitamins, for example, are flushed from the dog's body, whereas others are stored in various organs and can reach toxic levels.

Natural and Home-Prepared Diets

Natural and home-prepared diets are free of preservatives, coloring, and chemicals. If you want the benefits of feeding an all-natural product but don't want to give up the convenience of commercially prepared foods, you may be interested in feeding your Chi one of several natural dog foods that are available. All-natural dog foods come in dry, canned, and frozen varieties and are regulated by the same state feed officials that regulate other commercial pet foods.

Home-prepared diets are without a doubt the best way to make sure your Chihuahua is receiving human-grade meats, organically grown whole grains, pesticide-free vegetables, and vitamins, minerals, and other important nutrients in their most digestible forms. These diets cannot be thrown together, however, and they must follow very precise measurements developed by veterinary nutritionists.

Home-prepared diets are time-consuming to prepare; however, because of the small amount of food the Chihuahua consumes, these diets can be made in larger batches and frozen in individual portions. The biggest mistake owners make with a home-prepared diet is that they become lax in measuring and weighing ingredients or start making substitutions. To feed a home-prepared diet successfully, you must be vigilant in not varying the recipe in any way.

 **Alert!**

Safe food-handling hygiene is critical when preparing raw home-made diets. Raw meat carries the risk of exposing you (and your dog) to E. coli and salmonella bacteria. Hard freezing meats prior to handling may decrease this risk; however, the only sure way is to cook the meats thoroughly and clean all surfaces that come in contact with the raw meats.

Feeding the Puppy

The care and feeding of a Chihuahua puppy is likened by some breeders to the nurturing of an egg. Their health can be profoundly affected by a missed or even a late feeding. For this reason, the Chihuahua puppy's meals must be monitored closely.

 **Essential**

Most breeders will keep a very tiny or frail puppy under their watch until the puppy is thriving; however, you may be in a situation in which this didn't happen. If your puppy cannot eat much at a feeding or is particularly frail, consult with your veterinarian immediately.

Scheduling

If a Chi misses as little as one meal, her blood sugar level may drop low enough to cause hypoglycemia, a condition that can be fatal if untreated. Many breeders recommend keeping a high-caloric, easily digested product, such as NutraCal, on hand to rub on a pup's gums to re-elevate her blood sugar level in emergencies.

Arrange your puppy's meals as equally throughout the day as you can. A young puppy will eat four times a day, so feeding times could be at 6 A.M., 10 A.M., 2 P.M., and 6 P.M. When a puppy is eating well and obviously thriving, she can be fed three meals a day.

What to Feed

Puppies require nutrient- and calorie-rich foods to keep up with their rapidly growing bodies. Feed your puppy a high-grade, quality puppy food up until ten months of age, when puppies have almost completed their full growth. If your breeder has great success with a certain food, continue using this food and closely follow his recommendations as to amounts to feed and when to feed.

If you don't know how much your puppy should be eating, try this method. Measure a half cup of dry puppy food in a bowl, and allow your pup to eat as much food as she'd like. After twenty minutes, pick up and measure the remaining food to calculate how much your puppy ate. Continue feeding in this manner for a full day. You should have a good idea how much to feed at each meal, as puppies rarely overeat dry puppy food and will eat only what they need.

 **Fact**

Your Chihuahua puppy will double her body weight within the first ten weeks that you have her home. A puppy weighing one pound, four ounces at eight weeks should weigh two pounds, eight ounces by the time she's eighteen weeks old.

Make sure the kibble is a comfortable bite-size for your Chihuahua puppy. Many puppy foods are geared toward small to medium breeds and don't take into account how tiny the Chi puppy's jaws really are. Manufacturers are producing quality foods specifically for toy- and small-breed puppies. You might also consider a puppy food that is tailored specifically to the Chihuahua puppy, such as that produced by Royal Canin. If your Chi's jaws aren't capable of managing even toy puppy food, you may want to moisten her food for her until she grows a bit more.

Maintenance Diets

As the Chihuahua puppy reaches maturity, it is time to begin transitioning to an adult maintenance diet. As an adult, the Chihuahua has finished growing and is not burning fuel like she did as a pup. The Chihuahua's nutritional needs also change; adult formulas reflect this shift in protein, fat, vitamin, and mineral requirements.

 Essential

When changing foods, gradually incorporate the new food with the old food over a period of seven to ten days. Sudden changes in diet can cause severe gastrointestinal distress.

Appropriate foods for the adult Chihuahua include those designed for toy or small breeds, which provide the correct balance of nutrients for an adult dog but in kibble size that is easily managed by the Chihuahua's jaws. Adult toy- and small-breed foods often address the extensive dental problems toy breeds tend to suffer by producing a crunchy kibble that helps reduce tartar.

Adult Chis can be fed two small meals, twice a day. If you've adopted a rescued Chihuahua and don't know how much to feed her, you can administer the free-feed test. If your Chihuahua is not overweight, allow her to eat undisturbed from a half-cup serving of dry dog food. After twenty minutes, pick up the leftovers and record how much your dog ate. Continue this for three or four meals until you have a basic idea as to what your dog is eating.

If your Chi is overweight, you'll need to consult with your veterinarian as to how much your Chihuahua should be eating and ways to help reduce her weight.

Obesity: Number-One Health Risk

Just as the Chi has a problem with not eating enough food as a puppy, the mature adult Chihuahua has the opposite problem. She eats too much food for her slower activity level. Overeating is largely an owner-induced problem. The Chihuahua is very adept at convincing owners that she is starving and needs more food. Those big, brown eyes are hard to resist.

But resist you must. The overweight Chihuahua puts extra stress on her joints, wearing down cartilage and increasing her likelihood of developing arthritis at an early age. Additionally, obesity puts additional stress on the Chi's heart, putting her at greater risk of suffering a more severe form of several heart diseases that affect Chihuahuas.

If your Chi is already overweight, here are some tips to help your dog shed her excess weight and live a healthier life:

- Reduce your Chi's food portions by 10 to 20 percent.
- Consider feeding a weight reduction food; you can keep the portion size the same but reduce calories 20 percent or more.
- Eliminate feeding any leftover people food.
- Incorporate training snacks into your dog's total food allowance.
- Take action; start walking your Chihuahua and play indoor games at least three times a day.

The ultimate cause of obesity is the same for all dogs: too much food in and not enough energy expended. Research has shown that dogs can lose weight by either cutting back on their food portions or by increasing exercise; however, a combined effort of decreasing the amount of food and increasing the dog's exercise was shown to be most successful.

CHAPTER  16

Grooming Your Chihuahua

There's nothing that looks quite as good as a well-groomed Chihuahua. Keeping your Chihuahua in tip-top shape is not difficult, and the benefits are many. Regular grooming provides quality, bonding time between you and your dog, and it improves your Chi's health. Being hands-on with your Chihuahua enables you to spot potential health problems much sooner, too.

Coat Care

The Chihuahua comes in two coats: short and long. The short-haired Chi is the classic wash 'n wear dog, requiring very little grooming, while the longhaired Chi can require more care, depending on just how long and thick her coat is.

Shorthaired

Though the shorthaired Chi would love to be brushed every day, her needs are far less demanding. A gentle brushing once or twice a week should suffice quite well. When choosing a brush to groom your Chihuahua, look for a small brush in order to be able to negotiate all the small curves, nooks, and crannies of her body.

A soft bristle brush or slicker brush for sensitive skin are good choices for soft, relaxing grooming sessions, and repeated use can help produce a glossy coat. Whatever brush you choose to use, begin your grooming session by gently brushing against the lay of the coat to pull up dander, dirt, and oils. Then brush with the lay of the coat to finish removing loose hairs and dander and to more equally distribute the skin's natural oils. Finish off with a rubdown (front to back) with a clean cloth.

 **Fact**

Regular brushing is good for a dog's skin. The bristles gently massage the Chi's skin, increasing the blood flow at the surface. Skin with good circulation tends to be much healthier and suppler. Brushing stimulates skin, reduces dander (scale, dirt, and oils), and distributes natural oils, which protect the hair shaft.

The most challenging part of caring for a shorthaired Chi's coat may well be the Chi's attitude toward brushing. You can't expect a rescued adult dog to sit still for a major grooming session, just as you wouldn't expect a squirmy puppy to remain quiet. For those Chis that haven't had much grooming experience, start slowly. Begin with a few brush strokes at a time and stop the grooming session before the adult or puppy starts becoming impatient. Reward good behavior with treats, praise, and lots of love. Gradually increase the amount of time you spend brushing your Chihuahua until she will remain still for several minutes. If your Chihuahua shows any indication of snapping or biting you, use a plastic cage-type muzzle. This muzzle allows plenty of airflow while protecting you from a nasty bite. Whatever you do, don't allow the Chihuahua to make the call when the grooming session is finished. You make that call, always rewarding good behavior and working through (and ignoring) poor behavior.

▲ Chis that have long coats must be brushed, especially after a venture outside—wood ticks and other bugs are an unwanted menace.

Long Coats

The Chihuahua's long coat varies greatly within the breed. A longhaired coat can mean wispy, soft hairs that feather from the Chi's legs, tail, ears, and belly, or a thick, full, long coat. The thinner, wispier coat will require only one or two grooming sessions a week. The thick, full, and long coat requires daily attention.

Alert!

Some shorthaired Chihuahuas have very thin, smooth coats. Others, however, can develop a very thick coat during the colder months. If your Chi carries this thicker short coat, you can use a small pin brush with rounded ends to help remove some of the thickness when moving into the warmer months.

The biggest problem some owners have in grooming their longhaired Chis is not using the correct brush. If you use a bristle brush, you can brush and brush and never actually brush the coat hairs lying closest to the skin. These hairs then tangle to form mats. These mats harbor dirt and moisture and can cause secondary infections. Once a Chi has a mat, grooming becomes an uncomfortable experience for both dog and owner.

 Question?

Do longhaired Chis get split ends?
Not exactly, but their coat hairs are more prone to breaking if you brush them when they are completely dry. Some groomers recommend spritzing the dog's coat with water prior to brushing. Never force the brush through the dog's coat; if you hit a tangle, gently pick it apart without tugging—and breaking more hair. Really bad matting will need to be cut out by a professional groomer.

A better brush to use is a pin brush. The pin brush has short pins spread through the head of the brush. The pins have rounded ends so as not to irritate the dog's skin. With a pin brush, you're able to reach the coat hairs closest to the skin, removing dead hair and preventing mats. Once you've brushed through your Chi's coat both against the lay of the coat and with the lay, then take a fine-toothed comb and make sure your Chihuahua's coat is free of tangles.

If your Chihuahua puppy grew up to have a lot more coat than you anticipated when you fell in love with her, you may consider having her professionally trimmed by a groomer. Trimming her coat not only shortens it a bit but thins it out, too, making it much easier to groom. Trimming a Chi's coat does not, however, mean you get out of daily grooming chores. It just makes the process a bit easier.

Shedding

All dogs shed. All Chihuahuas shed. Your Chihuahua will shed. Granted, the Chihuahua is not a huge dog and doesn't have the surface area on her body to shed such quantities of hair as to make wafting "Chi puppies" float through your hallway and settle in your butter. But, don't expect your Chihuahua to be shed-free.

 **Fact**

If you own a tan Chihuahua, she will shed on your black plants. If you own a black Chi, you'll find her hair on your white carpets and love seats. That's just the universal law of canine shedding: the hair will go where you'll notice it the most.

Daily brushing goes a long way in removing dead hairs for both short and longhaired Chis. If you are diligent with your brushing, you will find far less fallen hairs. Bathing is another good way to rid your Chi of dead, shedded hairs.

Bathing

If you are brushing your Chihuahua regularly and taking care to remove any dander or dirt, your Chi should look and smell quite clean. There are always occasions, however, in which your Chihuahua gets dirty, muddy, or finds something dog-wonderful to roll in and becomes awfully stinky. It's bath time!

How to Bathe

You can give your Chihuahua a bath in one of three ways: the right way, the wrong way, or by taking her to a professional groomer. Obviously, if you use a professional groomer it will cost you a few dineros; however, the job will be done quickly, professionally, and without incident.

Then there's the wrong way: Wait until your Chihuahua desperately needs a bath and try to wash her. Here's the problem. Chis do not take to water very well. Many Chihuahuas have been known to demand being carried to their potty spots when it's raining to avoid getting their paws wet. If you fill up your sink with warm water and try to plunk your Chi in it for a bath, you'll witness her amazing ability to spread all four legs out in such a fashion as to make it impossible for her to be lowered into the sink. You'll also discover that despite what you thought, your Chi is made of muscles of steel and a will of iron. And if you're really lucky, you *won't* see how sharp those teeth really are.

 **Essential**

Before you begin bathing your Chihuahua, make sure you've already washed and dried all of the dog's bedding. There's nothing more frustrating than to have a clean, sweet-smelling Chi lie down in a stinky bed.

The right way to approach bath time is to start working on this skill weeks (even months in some cases) before you ever need to bathe your Chihuahua. Here are some tips:

- Put nonslip strips or a washcloth in your sink bottom to keep your Chi from slipping.
- Lift your Chi into the sink, give her a treat, and take her back out. Practice this.
- Fill the bottom of your sink with half an inch of warm water. Lift your Chi into the sink and immediately back out. Treat and practice.
- Increase the time that your Chi is in the sink.
- Increase the amount of water by half an inch.

- If you have a spray attachment, hold your Chi in the sink while you turn the spray on and off without wetting your Chihuahua.
- Wet only your Chi's legs with the spray attachment and immediately take her out of the sink.
- Wet more of your Chihuahua until you can wet her entire body except for her eyes and ears—you'll do these by hand.
- Introduce a tiny amount of shampoo (a little bit goes a looooong way), rub your Chi in a massage-like fashion, and then rinse thoroughly. Rinse again.
- Once bath time is down pat, continue to practice wetting your Chi in the sink in between baths to further acclimate her to this whole process.

You may never get your Chihuahua to like taking a bath, but you can get her to tolerate it. Never yell at your Chi while trying to acclimate her to this whole process; it will only make her more frightened. Take things slowly, and use lots of praise and rewards for good behavior. If all else fails, make an appointment with a professional groomer.

Drying

Chihuahuas have a difficult time maintaining their body temperatures, and they chill quite easily. For this reason, it is important that you bath your dog in a warm, draft-free location and dry her in an equally comfortable place. Use clean soft towels to blot and gently rub her dry. If your Chihuahua is longhaired, you might consider using a blow dryer to ensure that the hair closest to the dog's skin is completely dry. Moist, warm skin and hair that is insulated with dry outer hairs can be a breeding ground for bacteria, skin irritation, and potential infections.

If you are blow-drying your Chihuahua's coat, be careful that the forced air does not become too hot. Try to maintain a nice warm temperature that will keep your Chi from becoming chilled and yet won't harm the hair shafts in your Chi's coat by heating them too much and causing them to become brittle.

 **Alert!**

If you are going to crate your Chihuahua after you've toweled her dry, make sure she's got lots of clean dry bedding to snuggle down into and that she's in a warm, draft-free area of the home.

Shampoos

When choosing the perfect shampoo for your Chihuahua, you have only two points to remember. You want the shampoo to be made specifically for dogs and in a tear-free formula. Dogs have a different pH to their skin than we do, making human shampoos too harsh for a dog's skin. The necessity of a tear-free formula is that try as you might, there will come a day when you will get some soapy water in your Chi's eyes. If you are using a tear-free product, the effects will be far less uncomfortable for your dog.

From there, the sky's the limit as far as shampoos are concerned. You'll find shampoos specifically to make white coats white, black coats black, itchy skin not so itchy, dry hair moist, and long hair luxurious. Specialty formulas may be more expensive, but if you'd like to give one a try, go ahead. (You don't need a large bottle.) Again, as long as the shampoo is for dogs and is tear-free and you like it, then it's a good product.

Trimming Nails

Keeping your Chihuahua's toenails trimmed is important to your puppy or dog's health. When a dog's toenails grow too long, it causes the Chi's foot to splay and makes it difficult and even painful for the dog to walk. Even moderately overgrown toenails can affect the dog's ability to walk properly and can exacerbate existing joint problems.

▲ **Smaller Chis are not equipped to deal with extreme cold, so it never hurts to have a sweater on hand to keep them warm.**

The ability to trim a puppy or dog's nails, if you've never done this before, is an acquired skill for the owner. Fortunately, Chihuahuas do not have large thick toenails that take monster clippers to trim, but they do require a sharp eye and a gentle hand.

 **Essential**

Toenail clippers come in two styles: a scissors type and a guillotine. Either trimmer can be suitable; it's more a personal preference. Just be sure to replace your trimmers as they become dull.

Depending on the coloration of your Chihuahua, she may have white or clear toenails in which you can see the pink quick, where blood flows into the nail. She may also have black toenails in which you can't see anything. Or you may find that your Chi has a combination of dark and clear toenails.

If you're trimming a clear toenail, the process is much easier. Look for the end of the pink quick, and trim the toenail a little longer than the quick. If you're trimming a dark toenail that is next to a light toenail, you can usually gauge how much to trim from the lighter nail. If your Chi has all dark nails, look at the shape of the nail. You'll be able to see the part of the nail that is starting to form a point. Underneath the nail, you'll be able to see where this point begins; it's usually smooth. Clip here.

Quick! I Quicked Her!

No matter how careful you are with your dog's toenails, you will someday misjudge the trim and quick the nail, causing your dog to bleed. For a little dog, the Chi's toenails can really bleed, too. Unless you do something, it could take up to thirty minutes or more for the toenail to stop dripping, and as soon as your Chi bumps something, the nail will start to bleed all over again. You can imagine what a mess this could cause.

Luckily for dog owners, there are ways to stop the bleeding. Canine styptic pens can be applied to the end of the bleeding nail, or the nail can be dipped into a sulfur powder mix made specifically to prevent infection and stop bleeding. Both these products can be purchased without a prescription and are recommended to have on hand whenever you are trimming nails.

Not My Paws!

In addition to learning how to trim your Chihuahua's toenails, your Chihuahua will also need to learn how to remain still and tolerate all sixteen of her toenails (eighteen if she has dew claws) to be trimmed. If you have a puppy, begin this training early. If you have an adult Chi that is not used to toenail trimming, you can use the same gradual approach that you would with a pup.

Every day, take a tiny nubbin off a single toenail. Treat and praise your Chi for sitting still. Work up to being able to trim an entire paw at a sitting, then two paws, then all paws. Praise only good behavior, ignore bad behavior, and cut her toenails anyway. If at any time you think your Chi might bite you (that qualifies as bad behavior), use a muzzle and continue working with your Chi. She'll eventually get the idea.

If all this sounds too much for you—or if you have difficulty seeing the tiny (and it is tiny) little pink quick—take your Chihuahua to a professional groomer. The toenail trimming will be quick and relatively painless for both you and your Chihuahua.

The Ears and Eyes Have It

Chihuahuas have large, protruding eyes, which make them more susceptible to injury. For this reason, Chi owners need to make sure that they regularly inspect their puppies' and dogs' eyes for injury or the presence of a foreign body.

Chihuahua's eyes tear regularly, so the presence of tears below your Chi's eyes is not unusual. If, however, you notice that your Chihuahua seems to be rubbing her eyes with her paws or trying to scratch them, this would call for a trip to the veterinarian. Even if the object that was in the eye is no longer present, it could have scratched or punctured the eye.

 **Alert!**

If you see that your Chihuahua's eyes are bloodshot, that tearing is excessive, or that they are producing a milky or thicker discharge, it could be that your Chi's eyes are infected. Take her to the veterinarian immediately for treatment.

Tear Stain

Because the Chihuahua's eyes do tear, those Chis with white, cream, or light fawn-colored coats will develop a tear stain. This is a rust-colored discoloration of the coat beneath the eye. Though this tear stain does not hurt the Chihuahua in any way, it is noticeable and in some cases can be a bit unsightly.

To help keep tears from staining, regularly wipe beneath your dog's eyes with a cotton ball soaked in saline solution (the same as you would purchase for contact lenses). For stubborn stains, you can work on the stain with a saline-soaked cotton swab or place a warm rag with the solution over her eyes while she lies in your lap. The more care and attention you give to your Chihuahua's eyes, the less likely she will be to develop tear stains.

Listen Up

Chihuahuas are not a breed that has abnormal or excessive problems with ear infections. Because the breed's ears are erect and open, airflow is better to the ear canal. If an ear infection is brewing—due to an imbalance in the ear's natural yeast or bacteria content—the infection will not take off as quickly as it would in a drop-eared dog. That's the good news. The challenging news is that dogs with open ears are more susceptible to foreign bodies entering the ear, which can be the cause of an ear infection.

Regardless of the cause, as a dog owner you should be aware of the symptoms of an ear infection. These include scratching the ears, rubbing the ears on the floor, shaking the head, excessive waxy substance, holding the head at an odd angle, and in severe cases, loss of balance. In all cases, there will be noticeable redness from inflammation deep in the ear, possibly swelling, and a distinct, foul odor.

An ear infection calls for an immediate trip to the veterinarian. If your Chihuahua suffers from chronic ear infections, your veterinarian may suggest an ear wash that, if used weekly, can help ward off future infections by keeping the ear canal dry.

Basic Ear Cleaning

To keep the outer portion of your Chihuahua's ears clean, use a cotton ball dampened with saline solution. Wipe this on the inside of the dog's ears to remove dirt and oils. Never, however, use a cotton swab or any other object in an attempt to clean the inner workings of your Chihuahua's ears. If you suspect this area needs cleaning, it could be the onset of an ear infection, so back to the veterinarian's office you go.

 Essential

Chihuahuas with allergies often suffer ear infections. If the allergies are seasonal, the ear infections will be seasonal, too.

Teeth Are Number-One Priority

Chihuahuas have a reputation for bad teeth. Periodontal disease is so common among Chihuahuas that many owners just accept this as a Chi thing. It doesn't have to be. Bad breath, loss of teeth, and inability to eat dry food do not have to be part of your Chihuahua's fate. But you have to take the situation into your own hands.

First, feed your dog a dry food so that she must sink her teeth into the kibble, which helps to scrub tartar from her teeth. Next, provide your Chihuahua with lots of delectable chew toys and treats. Rope toys serve as floss, if your Chi will chew on them. Hard-baked artificial bones can encourage even the pickiest chewer to work on removing tartar. And stuffable toys that make your dog chew to release the biscuits are also a good idea.

You must also learn to brush your Chi's teeth. If your pup or adult Chi hasn't had her teeth brushed before, begin brushing with a rubber-knobbed finger brush. When she accepts this activity, you can begin using a toothbrush.

When brushing your Chi's teeth, be sure to use only toothpaste that has been made specifically for dogs. Human toothpastes contain fluoride and other chemicals that can't be swallowed, which is exactly what your Chihuahua is going to do with her toothpaste. Additionally, dog toothpaste comes in chicken and beef flavors.

And finally, if your Chihuahua is undergoing a procedure that requires anesthesia, such as a spay or neuter, take advantage of this opportunity to have your puppy or dog's teeth deep cleaned and given a fluoride treatment.

CHAPTER

Basic Health Care

Nothing beats a bright-eyed, vibrant, healthy Chi. One look at a dog like this and you know she is being well cared for. In addition to excellent nutrition and good grooming, providing your Chi with quality veterinary care throughout her life is perhaps the most critical aspect of maintaining a Chihuahua's good health and vigor.

Prevention Is Key

Of the varying age groups, young puppies are at the greatest risk for dying from a disease, followed by older puppies, seniors, and geriatrics. Also at an increased risk are dogs of any age that are already in a weakened state from illness or suffering from an immune system that is not functioning correctly (immunocompromised). Even robust, healthy adults are not without some risk for becoming seriously ill.

In addition to your Chi's age and general health, other factors that affect how at risk your Chihuahua is include the area of the country you live in; what type of housing you own (such as a farm with livestock or a city apartment); how much and where you travel with your dog; how often you board your dog; and the number of dogs your Chihuahua regularly comes in contact with (as at a dog park that dozens of dogs use daily or dog shows with hundreds of dogs).

Alert!

Many deadly diseases are regional in nature. If you travel a lot with your dog, it's important to research what diseases are common in the area to which you are traveling. Protecting your Chihuahua may be as simple as making sure she only drinks bottled water, or it may require that your Chi receive a specialized vaccine prior to traveling.

You can't, of course, keep your Chihuahua in a protective bubble all her life. Even if you are meticulous about reducing the chances that your Chihuahua will come in contact with disease, it's not a matter of if your Chi will be exposed but when. Simply said, it's unavoidable. What you can do, however, is provide her with as much protection from contagious diseases, bacterial infections, and parasites as possible through preventive veterinary care.

Keep It Moving!

Exercise is one of the best ways to keep your Chi healthy. Tired of the same walks around the block and looking for more to do with your Chihuahua? From noncompetitive to performance events, there are many activities that you can enjoy with your Chihuahua.

Agility

Agility is perhaps the most popular canine sport in the country. There's a reason it's so popular; agility is fun. The objective is to send your dog around a ring filled with obstacles, such as a teeter-totter, a tunnel, or an A-frame, with the least amount of mistakes in the fastest time. A lot of people play with agility just because their dogs enjoy the training so much.

Obedience and Its Cousins

If you've enrolled your Chi in a basic puppy class or beginner adult class, you're already learning obedience! Competitive obedience is an extension of these early classes with a few new tricks to learn. With obedience, your goal can be to achieve passing scores to attain a title or it can be to achieve the highest score in the ring on that day. You may not be interested in competitions, but if you and your Chi enjoy training, there's no reason why you can't train your dog to the top levels.

Other versions of obedience are rally obedience (or Rally-O), in which the ring is set up with signs that tell the handler and dog what skill to do at that place. The skills that competitors are asked to complete are actually training segments or parts of the more complex skills required in formal obedience.

Then there are sports in which obedience meets music. In canine freestyle and canine musical freestyle, participants work to set maneuvers to music. Canine freestyle is a bit more structured, whereas canine musical freestyle involves costuming and choreography for both dog and owner.

Volunteer Opportunities

If sports aren't really your thing, and you have a well-socialized, friendly Chihuahua, you might consider doing therapy work with her. Therapy dogs are no longer limited to social visits in nursing homes. Depending on the need in the community and on your interests, you might train to assist in one of many scenarios, such as school reading programs, rehabilitation centers, assisted living communities, and children's hospitals.

With the Chihuahua, size is not a limiting factor when it comes to being involved in a wide range of activities. The key is to find an activity that both you and your Chihuahua enjoy.

Finding a Veterinarian

If you've owned dogs in the past and have a veterinarian whom you know and trust, you're lucky! If your Chi is your first dog, or if you've moved to a new area, you'll need to get set up with a good veterinarian as soon as possible. The three factors you will need to consider are the veterinarian's qualifications, the location of his practice, and the type of facility and services the veterinarian offers.

Qualifications

In order to be able to practice, a veterinarian must hold the degree of doctor of veterinary medicine (D.V.M.) or veterinary medicine doctor (V.M.D.). Most veterinarians will be happy to tell you where they received their degrees and any special interests (such as behavior) or subspecialties they hold.

 **Fact**

Veterinarians who have received their veterinary degree in Ireland or Great Britain are licensed through the Royal College of Veterinary Surgeons. The degree MRCVS stands for "member of the Royal College of Veterinary Surgeons," which means the vet is registered by the RCVS to practice veterinary medicine.

A special interest in a specific aspect of veterinary medicine is different than a subspecialty. To have a special interest in an area of veterinary medicine means that the veterinarian attends seminars and training in this area and keeps current in the very latest information available. A veterinarian with a special interest can be very skilled and a great asset to his clients and patients needing this extra expertise.

A veterinarian who has undergone intense, additional post-graduate education in a specialty, passed rigorous examinations and who has been board-certified by an AVMA-recognized veterinary specialty organization (a board or college) receives the title of diplomate. A diplomate of the American College of Veterinary Behaviorists would have D.V.M. after his name and then the designation "Diplomate ACVB."

 **Question?**

Do I need a veterinarian with a specialty?

Only if your regular veterinarian determines that your Chihuahua has a disease or condition that would benefit from the attention of a specialist. For example, a Chi with an eye ulcer could be referred to a D.V.M. with a diplomate from the American College of Veterinary Ophthalmologists.

Location, Location, Location

How convenient is your veterinarian to your home? For some people, convenience is of the utmost importance. Who wants to spend forty minutes driving across town if you can take your Chihuahua to a veterinarian two miles away? For many other people, it is the combination of an excellent veterinarian coupled with convenience. These folks will skip the veterinarian on the corner and drive a little farther to reach the best practitioners for their dogs. And for others, a long drive means nothing if they can get the absolute best veterinary care for their dogs possible. Where you fit into this mix is a personal choice.

Facilities and Service

What kind of veterinary practice are you most comfortable with? Do you enjoy a veterinary clinic in which there is only one veterinarian? Or do you prefer a larger animal hospital with several veterinarians on staff? Smaller practices tend to be more limited in that they often don't have their own operating rooms, laboratories for blood work, or diagnostic tools, such as X-ray or MRI machines. Animal hospitals have expanded facilities (some even have boarding kennels); however, some pet owners prefer the personal, one-on-one nature of the single practitioner. Again, it's a personal choice, but one to consider when you are searching for a veterinarian.

▲ Keep your Chi active by taking walks and giving plenty of toys.

 Essential

To begin your search for a veterinarian who meets your criteria, ask for referrals from your breeder (if he's in the area), local rescues and shelters, and other Chihuahua owners who rave about their veterinarians. You can also contact the American Animal Hospital Association (AAHA) for contacts in your area.

When you make an appointment to visit a new veterinarian, don't be afraid to ask questions. Perhaps the most important quality of a good veterinarian is the ability to communicate easily with his clients. When talking with your veterinarian, you should get a sense that he not only welcomes but encourages all sorts of questions from very basic health care to more complex issues, such as those surrounding vaccinations or the genetic basis of a particular disease. The bottom line is that if you don't feel comfortable asking this individual what you think might be some of the dumbest questions in the world, you will never be able to fully reap the benefits of the veterinarian's extensive knowledge.

The Holistic Alternative

Holistic veterinary medicine, alternative veterinary medicine, and complimentary veterinary medicine are all the same. Depending on whom you ask, it's either the only way to practice medicine, one of many tools that can be used in a veterinarian's practice, or complete mumbo-jumbo-voodoo-magic that should be avoided at all costs.

Well, we know the latter opinion is false—at least for the better-researched and tested modalities that fall under the definition of holistic medicine. For example, the AVMA has noted that acupuncture and chiropractic do have healing abilities and can be valuable to veterinarians in their practices. Other practices, such as homeopathy (the practice of giving very dilute quantities of substances that cause the same symptoms as those the patient is having to purge the system), flower essences (using extremely pure dilute essences of various flowers to treat emotions), and nutraceuticals (the use of certain nutrients in pure or concentrated forms to treat disease) show great clinical promise, but they lack the double-blind trials and substantial research that Western medicine relies on to prove efficacy.

 Fact

Conventional veterinary medicine uses pharmaceuticals in its treatment program only after these drugs have been proven to be effective through double-blind studies, or research in which a study group is divided between those given a placebo and those given the medication being tested. Most holistic nutraceuticals, herbs, and other substances have not undergone these trials; however, many substances show excellent results clinically in individual patient cases.

Holistic Versus Conventional Medicine

The difference between holistic veterinary medicine and conventional veterinary medicine is in the approach to healing the animal. Conventional veterinary medicine, which is taught in veterinary colleges across the country, is based on treating disease through analyzing a dog's symptoms and using diagnostic tools such as blood, urine, and fecal tests, X-ray, MRI, and CT scans to pinpoint the cause of the symptoms.

Holistic veterinary medicine is based on treating the whole or entire animal—physical and emotional—and not basing treatment on a dog's symptoms alone. Holistic veterinarians are schooled in conventional veterinary colleges and hold DVMs or VMDs. After attending veterinary school, these veterinarians then research and educate themselves on one or many different holistic or alternative modalities, such as the use of herbs, Chinese medicine, acupuncture, or chiropractic. In some cases, expertise in certain modalities is certified by organizations through continuing education courses, seminars, research studies, experience, and formal training. For most modalities, however, there is no certification, and the pet owner must trust the veterinarian's interest, experience, and knowledge when treating his dog.

 Question?

How can I find a holistic veterinarian in my area?
The American Holistic Veterinary Medical Association (AHVMA) has an excellent search engine on its Web site, online at *www.AHVMA.org*.

Talk to a Vet

Holistic modalities are noted for taking longer to have an effect but having few detrimental side effects than are often seen in conventional medications. If you are interested in this gentler approach to veterinary medicine, talk to the veterinarians on your list and see how they feel about holistic medicine. You will find that many conventional veterinarians implement one or two modalities into their own practices or regularly refer their patients to holistic specialists for specific treatments. Other veterinarians offer practices that are entirely holistic, or are holistic but also take advantage of modern diagnostics tools.

Vaccinations

The world of vaccinations is quickly changing. For years, puppies received a series of combined vaccinations beginning at four to six weeks and continuing every two to four weeks until the pup reached sixteen to twenty weeks of age. Boosters were recommended every year thereafter for the life of the dog.

Booster Shots

The reason for the annual boosters was that the vaccinations had only undergone duration-of-immunity tests for a twelve-month period. In other words, a dog might still have 100 percent protection from a deadly virus twenty-four or even thirty-six months after the booster was given. But because testing had only been completed for a dog's immunity at twelve months, the vaccinations could not be approved by the United States Department of Agriculture (USDA) for longer periods.

Veterinarians were faced with a dilemma. Vaccination protocols were emerging from veterinary schools encouraging a three-year protocol (boosters every three years) but since there weren't duration-of-immunity tests for this time period (except for the rabies vaccination), veterinarians were faced with a liability issue. If they recommended vaccinations after the initial puppy series be given only every three years, in the unlikely case that a dog became ill with a disease, the veterinarian would be faced with a nasty law suit.

Some veterinarians offered to test their clients' dogs' blood to find out what their immunity levels were; however, this test was more expensive than the actual vaccines, so few dog owners took their veterinarians up on this offer.

When it comes to vaccines, the size of a dog doesn't matter. Whether your Chi pup is only twenty-four ounces, she will receive the same dosage of vaccine as a thirty-pound puppy. The reason for this is that the injection contains the minimum amount of vaccine necessary to stimulate a dog's immune system to create antibodies, and this is the same regardless of size.

Now, as of April 2005, veterinarians have been able to offer a combined canine vaccine for distemper, adenovirus, and parvovirus that carries a three-year duration-of-immunity approved by the USDA. With this vaccine, the puppy vaccine schedule also is modified: the puppy is now to receive only two injections—one at eight or nine weeks and the second at twelve weeks.

Adverse reactions to vaccines are not uncommon in Chihuahuas. An adverse reaction usually occurs within the first twenty-four hours after injection. These can range from heat and inflammation at the site of the injection to complete anaphylactic shock or falling ill from the disease for which the vaccine is meant to produce protection. Talk to your veterinarian to make sure you know exactly what to look for, and remember that an adverse reaction is an emergency!

Core Vaccines

Vaccinations are divided into what are called core vaccines—or those deemed absolutely necessary for the protection of your Chi's health—and non-core vaccinations, which are recommended only if the risk of falling ill from a disease is substantially higher than the risk of suffering an adverse reaction to the vaccine itself.

The core vaccinations, as recommended by the AVMA, are canine distemper, canine parvovirus, and adenovirus-hepatitis (usually packaged as a combined vaccine in one injection); as well as a vaccination for rabies.

Non-Core Vaccinations

Non-core is the name given to vaccinations that may or may not be necessary for a puppy or dog, depending on the individual dog's risk of coming in contact with a disease. Among the non-core vaccinations are those for bordatella, canine adenovirus-2 (CAV-2), and parainfluenza (the three most common causes of respiratory infection, also known as kennel cough), giardia, Lyme disease, and measles.

 **Fact**

Coronavirus, formerly a core vaccine, is no longer considered a deadly threat to puppies. Research has found that the virus is self-limiting and does not cause very serious illness. Therefore, the risk of an adverse reaction to the vaccine far outweighs the risks of becoming ill with the disease.

Kennel Cough

Vaccinations for kennel cough are recommended for puppies and dogs that regularly come in contact with large numbers of dogs. If you plan on showing your Chihuahua or competing in performance events, your veterinarian will likely recommend vaccinations for these three diseases. Additionally, if you plan on traveling without your Chihuahua, she will need to be up to date on her bordatella vaccine in order to be accepted into any boarding kennel.

Giardia

Giardia is also known as beaver fever. Unless your Chi will be regularly exposed to water sources that have the potential to contain this protozoan, your veterinarian is not likely to recommend this vaccine. Dogs become infected when they drink from streams, brooks, puddles, or other natural water sources that contain giardia in cyst form. The cysts are passed into water by an infected animal, often beavers.

Lyme Disease

Lyme disease is a concern mostly for those dog owners whose dogs hunt, work, or play in tick-infested areas that are known to carry Lyme disease. However, the disease is not limited to these areas; pet owners walking their dogs in suburban neighborhoods have been infected by ticks carrying this disease. Most likely, providing your Chihuahua with a daily once-over after walks to check for ticks and/or applying a tick repellent to your Chi will provide enough protection for your dog with less risk of side-effects than the Lyme disease vaccine itself.

Measles

And then there's measles. Surprisingly, the human measles virus shares some antigens with canine distemper virus. In areas where canine distemper is literally running rampant, your veterinarian may recommend vaccinating with the measles vaccine (along with the canine distemper vaccine) to provide your Chi with some crossprotection.

External Parasites

The two most common parasites to affect your Chihuahua are fleas and ticks. Both are obnoxious, bloodsucking, disease-carrying pests. Ticks are carriers of many different diseases, including ehrlichiosis, babesiosis, Lyme disease, and Rocky Mountain spotted fever. Fleas can cause uncomfortable skin irritations, as well as severe allergic reactions in some dogs. Fleas can also pass tapeworm larvae to dogs if ingested. And yes, your Chi is quick enough to snap up a flea or two.

 **Question?**

Does my Chi have fleas?
Fleas are hard to spot. An easy way to test for fleas is to place your Chi on a damp piece of tissue paper and carefully comb through your Chi's coat with a flea comb. If your Chi has fleas, you will see tiny brownish black granules (flea dirt) that will leave a rust-colored ring on the paper.

Removing Ticks

If you find a tick on your Chihuahua, use tweezers to remove it. You may even wear gloves to prevent transmission of any potential bloodborne disease to you. Grab the tick with the tweezers, being careful not to puncture the tick, and pull straight out without any twisting. Save the tick in a container with rubbing alcohol (this kills the tick) in case your veterinarian needs to test or identify the insect. Clean the bite area with soap and water and then rubbing alcohol.

Eradicating Fleas

If your Chi has signs of one flea, he's probably got a whole host of them living in his coat, his bed, your carpets, your bed, your furniture—basically anywhere he's been in the last month. Not only do you need to treat your Chihuahua for fleas with a medicated shampoo, dip, or powder, but you will also need to vacuum your floors well every day for a month to catch all life stages of the flea (from eggs to new hatchlings). Wash all bedding in the hottest water possible, vacuum your mattresses, and repeat this cycle every week for at least four weeks.

Prevention

Of course, the easiest way to keep your Chihuahua from suffering any potential tick- or flea-related illnesses—and to keep your home clean—is to prevent fleas and ticks from ever infiltrating your Chi. Currently, there are several products on the market that are suitable for use on Chihuahuas. Products containing Fipronil, a neurotoxin specific to invertebrates (such as fleas and ticks), causes fleas to die within a few hours of contact and ticks within forty-eight hours. Fipronil is applied to the dog's skin, typically between the shoulder blades, and spreads over the entire body using the natural oils in a dog's skin.

 **Alert!**

If your Chihuahua has an adverse reaction to Fipronil, contact your veterinarian immediately. Shampoos containing benzoyl peroxide may be effective in removing this topical insecticide; check with your veterinarian for the latest information prior to use. If your Chi becomes lethargic or irritable when wearing a tick collar (with Amitraz) remove the collar immediately and contact your veterinarian for further help.

Products containing Amitraz, such as some tick collars, target only ticks (not fleas) and work by paralyzing the mouthparts of the tick, preventing the tick from attaching to the dog. Amitraz also kills ticks that have already attached, but this product can take twenty-four to forty-eight hours to have an effect.

If you live in a multidog household, be aware that Amitraz is highly toxic. Because this product is used on tick collars, it is possible for a Chihuahua to decide to chew on another Chi's collar—or to pull a collar off during play. If this happens, contact your veterinarian immediately. She will have an antidote for ingestion of

Amitraz, but be sure to bring the collar with you to ensure that this product contains this particular chemical.

▲ Chis love to run and play, especially with their owners! This is great exercise for your Chi and also gives you the chance to spend some time together.

Worming Around

Puppies and dogs can become infested with numerous types of worms; however, the most deadly of all worms is heartworm. Heartworm is aptly named because in its mature form, adult-sized worms inhabit and reproduce in the dog's heart and lungs. Other worms—like roundworms, hookworms, tapeworms, and whip-worms—occupy and wreak havoc in the dog's digestive system.

Heartworm

Even though heartworm treatments are generally effective, these treatments aren't without their own health risks to the dog. Even with treatment, a dog infected with heartworms can still die. There's no need for this to happen. Effective, safe preventive medications are available and are reasonably priced so that every Chihuahua can be protected.

In cold, northern states, heartworm preventives may not be necessary during the winter. In more temperament climates or in areas in which you can have a few freak warm days in the winter, year-round protection is recommended. Areas that are particularly bad for heartworm year-round are those that are 150 miles inward from either coast or in the heart of mosquito country, the Mississippi Valley.

 **Essential**

Chi owners need to be aware that dogs receiving heartworm medications sporadically (on four months, off one, on three months, late five weeks, and so on) seem to be at greater risk of becoming infected in their unprotected months. For this reason, be vigilant in giving your Chi her prescribed dose. Your veterinarian will require a yearly blood test to make sure your Chihuahua is free of heartworms prior to renewing her preventive prescription.

Heartworm preventives are available in pills and chewable tablets that can be given daily or monthly, as well as topical solutions that are applied monthly. In addition to protecting against heartworm, some preventives include protection from several intestinal worms, as well as fleas, ticks, and mites. Many of these products are gentle enough for young puppies and are recommended as early as three months of age.

Intestinal Worms

This category includes roundworms, hookworms, tapeworms, and whipworms. All can sap your Chihuahua's health quickly, with some infestations being more damaging than others. Your veterinarian will require that you provide an annual fecal sample in order to test for the presence of worms. If you own a puppy, expect your veterinarian to require that your Chihuahua puppy undergo one or more wormings to rid her of roundworms, a parasite commonly passed from mother to puppy. Roundworms can cause a puppy to have a pot-bellied appearance and, if the infestation is severe, can block the puppy's intestinal tract and cause death.

The other worms, hookworms, tapeworms, and whipworms, rarely cause an infestation in a healthy adult dog that is so great as to jeopardize the dog's health. However, because these worms can be passed on to humans, it is important that you watch for any changes in your dog's health (including vomiting, lethargy, and anemia), and bowel movements (especially diarrhea) that would indicate an infestation of worms.

Preventive measures are key in keeping your dog healthy, and it is no different when it comes to worms. Clean your dog's feces up when walking your dog, and prevent her from sniffing or ingesting other dogs' feces and dead critters that may be infested with parasites. Additionally, discuss with your veterinarian your options with several different heartworm medications that protect dogs from several types of intestinal worms, too. These medications are effective and, since you'll already be giving your Chi heartworm preventive, you can administer them at no additional cost.

CHAPTER 18

Advanced Health Care

The Chihuahua, as with all purebred breeds, has a higher risk than the general dog population of developing several serious conditions and diseases. Responsible, quality breeders work hard to lessen the risk of a puppy inheriting a genetically based disease; however, many conditions don't have a known hereditary factor at this time. Whether you've purchased your Chi from an outstanding breeder or not, it behooves all Chi owners to recognize the most serious diseases of the breed.

Protecting Your Chihuahua

You can't change your Chihuahua's genetic potential for developing a particular inherited disease or condition; however, you can greatly improve her odds of surviving or overcoming an illness if you can spot the disease in its early stages.

Since most Chihuahua owners do not schedule more than one veterinary wellness checkup a year for a healthy adult dog, eleven months out of twelve the owner is the dog's first line of defense against disease. If you are keenly aware of your dog's usual behaviors, temperament, activity level, appetite, and overall character, you are far more likely to spot subtle changes that could indicate the early stages of disease than a more distant owner.

Veterinary experts agree that the earlier any disease is detected, the greater opportunity the practitioner has for successfully treating the disease. Even with diseases that may not have a cure, prompt diagnosis and treatment can go far in slowing or halting the disease's progression and/or improving the Chihuahua's quality of life.

Luxating Patellas

If you've ever suffered a knee injury, you can commiserate with a Chihuahua with luxating patellas. When the dog's patella, or kneecap, does not fit neatly in a track with the femur or thighbone, the off-kilter or misaligned patella can luxate, or literally slip off to the side of the joint, causing the knee to dislocate. A dog's patella may be misaligned due to trauma to the area, or it can stem from a malformed kneecap.

Regardless of why the kneecap is not tracking correctly, a luxating patella is extremely painful. The patella does tend to right itself—or "pop" back in—but the aftermath leaves the entire joint sore, tender, and inflamed. If you happen to catch your Chihuahua when she dislocates her knee, you may notice her slip and then hop a few steps before gingerly putting weight back on the rear leg.

In more severe cases, the patella doesn't realign itself, and the Chi's rear leg locks and becomes stiff. When the patella remains misaligned, it is necessary for your veterinarian to move the patella back into place.

Regardless of the reason, when the knee dislocates, the supporting tendons and ligaments are stretched and pulled and are now even less equipped to hold the kneecap in place. With everything loose in the joint, the Chi is likely to dislocate her knee repeatedly on an intermittent basis—or with a severely misaligned patella, the situation could be chronic. With a joint problem such as this, arthritis is more likely to appear at an earlier age, too.

In addition to hopping (temporary dislocation) or a stiff rear leg (requiring veterinary assistance to realign), symptoms that your Chihuahua has suffered a dislocation include stiffness in either or both rear legs, difficulties rising from the floor, limping, tenderness in the knee, and a reluctance to exercise. The severity of the situation usually dictates what treatments might be prescribed, but in general, moderate to severe cases benefit greatly from surgery.

Upper Respiratory Issues

Chihuahuas suffer from a variety of upper respiratory conditions, not all of which are medical problems. The following sections describe some of the most common you are likely to observe in your Chi.

Collapsed Trachea

This condition is one that is almost exclusively seen in toy and miniature breeds, especially the Chihuahua. It is considered to have a genetic factor; however, it can be difficult to eradicate because symptoms often don't appear until the Chihuahua is middle-aged and has already been bred (potentially) many times.

Tracheal collapse is the inability of the inner rings of the trachea (the air tube from mouth to lungs) to keep their circular shape, causing the trachea to narrow significantly or collapse while the dog is breathing. When this happens the Chihuahua will make a harsh, honking cough.

 **Alert!**

Obesity, heart disease, and chronic respiratory infections are thought to play a role in exacerbating the extent of a dog's tracheal collapse. All of these factors can apply added pressure to the trachea, forcing faulty cartilage in the trachea to collapse even further.

The coughing tends to occur in fits, with the coughing spells becoming more and more frequent and debilitating over time. Periods of exercise, excitement, pulling on a leash during a walk (putting pressure to the trachea), drinking, and eating will often initiate these coughing fits.

At this time, there is no known cure for trachea collapse; however, it can be managed relatively well with bronchodilators, nebulizers, and vaporizers. In some cases, corticosteroids (as a fast-acting anti-inflammatory) and sedatives may be necessary. In all cases, Chihuahuas with this condition should be walked on a halter or harness to avoid any direct pressure on the trachea.

Reverse Sneezing

Chihuahuas are notorious for a condition called reverse sneezing, which could be mistaken for a collapsing trachea. Reverse sneezing is brought on by periods of excitement and exercise, and the sound a Chi makes when reverse sneezing is quite alarming. Rest assured, however, that this condition is neither related to trachea collapse nor dangerous.

When a Chihuahua starts reverse sneezing, she usually stops moving and becomes a little hunched as she starts sucking air in hard through her nostrils, making a dreadful wheezing sound. The episodes don't last more than a minute at most. If you want to help your Chi halt the reverse sneezing, you can try blocking her nostrils with your fingers or encouraging her to swallow a few treats.

Snoring

Many new Chihuahua owners are amazed the first time they hear the melodious sounds of a Chi enjoying a deep, luxurious sleep. In other words, Chihuahuas snore. Snoring has nothing to do with a collapsing trachea—it happens because they have shorter muzzles. It's just a cute little thing that Chihuahuas do when they're very relaxed and comfortable. Smile and enjoy.

Eyes: Injuries and Diseases

The same physical aspects of the Chihuahua's large, luminous eyes that make them so appealing and beautiful also make their eyes more susceptible to injury. There are also a number of eye diseases to which Chihuahuas are particularly prone. Here's how to spot some common eye problems and what to do about them.

 **Essential**

If a Chi is experiencing severe pain in her eye, she will close the lids together very tightly. Any efforts to see why she is closing her eyes will be met with significant resistance. Don't force the issue! Get her to your veterinarian immediately.

Injuries

A sign that your Chi has something in her eye or that something has scratched or punctured the eye is the presence of the third eyelid, or nictitans (a protective membrane that is usually present over one-third to one-half of the eye when the dog is sleeping). The presence of this third eyelid when a dog is awake indicates that she is experiencing pain in her eye.

If you suspect something has gotten into her eye or that she was exposed to some kind of irritant, you can attempt to give the eyes a saline wash, using copious amounts of saline solution. Whether or not this seems to help, it is important that you take your Chi to your veterinarian immediately for a closer examination and further treatment.

Diseases

The Chihuahua is susceptible to several eye diseases, with the most prevalent being corneal dystrophy, glaucoma, and progressive retinal atrophy (PRA). Corneal dystrophy appears in three different forms. The Chihuahua is prone toward one form, endothelial dystrophy, which causes a build-up of fluid in the dog's cornea, making the cornea appear cloudy or bluish and significantly decreasing the Chi's vision. Additionally, this type of corneal dystrophy can cause painful water blisters to develop that then burst and cause erosions on the dog's eye. There is no cure for this disease; however, your veterinarian can prescribe medications to limit or control the development of water blisters.

Glaucoma refers to an increased fluid pressure within the eye that damages the retina and optic nerve. It is the leading cause of blindness in Chihuahuas and dogs in general. If the rise in fluid pressure is acute, the dog may become irreversibly blind within just a few hours. A slower rise of fluid pressure can result in blindness over a period of weeks or months.

Symptoms that your Chihuahua has increased fluid pressure in her eyes include redness, pawing or rubbing of the eyes, sensitivity to light, cloudiness in the eye, and enlargement or protruding of the eye itself. Glaucoma is an emergency. If not treated immediately, blindness is a near certainty.

PRA, another eye disease found in the Chihuahua, is often referred to as night blindness. The disease usually appears in adult Chis between the ages of two to five years or older. The progression of the disease is slow and begins with the Chihuahua having difficulties navigating at night or in the dark. Gradually, the Chihuahua's vision worsens until over time she can no longer see even in strong light. There is no treatment for this disease at the time; however, the genetic testing that is available for many forms of PRA is the only promise that the genetics for this disease are not passed to another generation.

Heart Conditions: Grave and Chronic

It seems an ironic shame that a breed capable of such love and devotion can suffer from diseases of its generous heart. Heart disease is not rare among Chihuahuas. Moreover, several forms of heart disease are found to occur three to six times more frequently in Chihuahuas than in most other breeds. Since bad luck appears to come in threes, perhaps it's not so coincidental that the Chi suffers from three heart diseases: patent ductus arteriosus (PDA), pulmonic stenosis, and chronic valvular disease, or endocardiosis.

PDA

This disease occurs when blood is abnormally moved through a shunt from the left to the right side of the Chi's heart, causing increased blood to flow to the lungs. This in turn causes a buildup in fluid and a strain on the left side of the heart. Symptoms that a Chihuahua is suffering from a serious case of PDA include coughing, weight loss, exercise intolerance, and (eventually) congestive heart failure.

If a Chihuahua is diagnosed with a more serious form of PDA, and the disease is caught within the first two years of the puppy's life, surgery can resolve the shunting of blood from one side of the heart to the other. If PDA is not discovered until later in life, surgery is not as successful at this time.

 **Question?**

Is it possible to have PDA and not be seriously ill?
Yes. Some Chihuahuas have an incomplete shunt or one that allows only a trickle of blood through from left to right. In these cases, a Chi may live without symptoms or any significant health repercussions.

Pulmonic Stenosis

This heart disease is caused by a malformation that creates an obstruction in the right side of the heart that prevents full flow of blood from the heart into the lungs. The extent of this obstruction dictates how seriously ill your Chihuahua could become. If the blood flow is restricted to the point that the heart must work very hard to function, this work overload will result in congestive heart failure. On the other hand, a slight obstruction may go completely undetected. In severe cases, surgery is often recommended to remedy the situation.

Endocardiosis

Chronic mitral valvular disease (CMVD), also known as endo-cardiosis, is an acquired heart disease that results from the degeneration or loss of elasticity of the heart's valves. Male Chis tend to be affected more often than females and older Chis more often than young adults. When the edges of the heart valves degenerate, they lose their perfect seal and allow the backflow of blood into the heart, which can be heard as a murmur. Whenever there are leaks, the dog's circulation is compromised, and eventually the Chi will begin to show signs of heart failure. Symptoms include the following:

- Lethargy
- Loss of appetite
- Depression
- Coughing, difficulty breathing
- Weakness
- Dizziness, disorientation, fainting
- Distended abdomen

At the current time, there is no cure for heart valve complications; however, there are many drugs available to help ease the Chihuahua's discomfort and help extend the length and quality of life, in some cases substantially.

Puppy Perils

Your Chihuahua is also at greater risk of suffering from additional diseases or conditions that can severely impair her health. Several conditions are unique in that they appear during the puppy's first year.

The most common health issues that Chi puppies are susceptible to include water on the brain (hydrocephalus); juvenile hypoglycemia (a drastic drop in blood sugar levels); cryptorchidism (one or both testicles do not descend); and shark teeth (puppy's milk teeth do not fall out and adult teeth erupt and grow in beside them).

Hydrocephalus and juvenile hypoglycemia are both life-threatening conditions that must be attended to immediately. All Chihuahua owners should be on the lookout for these conditions and should be equipped and prepared to handle an emergency while on the way to the veterinarian for additional critical care.

Hydrocephalus

Hydrocephalus is commonly confused with the presence of a molera, or soft spot on the Chihuahua's head. The two are not related. Hydrocephalus is the collection of cerebrospinal fluid (the fluid in and around the puppy's brain). As fluid collects, more and more pressure is applied to the brain. In severe cases, the puppy dies within a matter of days. In moderate cases, the fluid collection may take months before symptoms begin to appear, and in very slight cases, the pup may not show any signs of the condition until much later in life.

Symptoms of hydrocephalus include the following:

- Domed skull that becomes more pronounced over time
- Failure to thrive
- Abnormal movements
- Odd behaviors
- Vision impairment
- Seizures
- Difficulties learning (impossible to housetrain, slow with obedience, and so on)

For most Chihuahuas, if the fluid pressure on the brain can be minimized quickly either through surgery (placement of a permanent drainage shunt) or medications (corticosteroids), the condition usually stabilizes by the age of two. These Chis, however, almost always suffer brain damage, and in some cases your veterinarian may recommend euthanasia.

Hypoglycemia

Puppies of all toy breeds can have difficulties maintaining a high enough level of sugar in their blood. The Chi's body's response to low blood sugar is very much like a diabetic suffering from the same condition: anxiety, dizziness, disorientation, trembling, a racing heart beat, seizures, and collapse.

 **Fact**

Adult Chihuahuas that are very tiny, as well as those that have recently suffered an illness or are currently ill, may also suffer from hypoglycemia.

To help prevent a pup from becoming hypoglycemic, feed your Chi many small meals throughout the day, and make sure that the puppy has actually eaten what you've given her. Additionally, keep a small container of honey in the home to rub on her gums if she appears to be suffering from low blood sugar. As always, seek advice from your veterinarian. The symptoms of hypoglycemia are similar to other diseases, and the problem may not be your puppy's diet at all.

A Case of Too Little or Too Much

Two other puppy problems include too many teeth and not enough private parts. Chihuahua puppies on occasion retain their deciduous or baby teeth. The adult teeth erupt and grow in, giving the Chi a sharkish appearance. In addition to looking a bit odd, it is important to have the baby teeth removed by your veterinarian. Retention of these teeth leads to trouble, not the least including food that gets caught between two sets of teeth and increases a Chi's chances of developing tooth and gum disease.

Cryptorchidism is the term given to undescended testicles. All male puppies begin with testicles in their body cavity, which usually descend by the time the puppy is six to eight weeks. This process can take up to twelve weeks in some cases. If a male Chi puppy has one or both testicles that refuse to descend, it is critical that you have the puppy neutered and the testicles removed. Male Chis with undescended testicles are at far greater risk for cancer. Since this trait is hereditary, these dogs should never be bred.

▲ If your Chi shows any signs of ill health, be sure to take them to the vet right away before it develops into something worse.

Adult Ailments

Two internal conditions that can plague Chis include bladder stones and pancreatitis. Bladder stones are hard, rock-like collections of minerals that have literally stuck together in the bladder. These stones can form due to bacteria (a bladder infection) or the presence of abnormal levels of these minerals due to the dog's diet and her inability to process the contents. Symptoms are the same as for a bladder infection, including straining when urinating, frequent need to urinate, blood in the urine, and expressions of pain while urinating. Bladder stones can be removed surgically or treated long-term with a specific diet.

Pancreatitis is the inflammation of the pancreas, the organ located to the left of the stomach that produces hormones, such as insulin, and digestive enzymes to aid with the metabolizing of food.

The inflammation stimulates a premature release of digestive enzymes, which are supposed to go into the stomach but instead remain in the pancreas and effectively eat away at this organ. Symptoms of pancreatitis include nausea and vomiting, fever, and diarrhea. A Chi's abdomen may be painful and sensitive to touch. In severe cases, the Chi can go into shock and even die. Seek veterinary help immediately.

Skin Issues

The Chihuahua suffers from several skin conditions at higher rates than many other breeds. Among these are demodicosis, pattern baldness, and color dilution alopecia.

Demodicosis

Demodicosis results in nasty, crusty infected lesions over the Chihuahua's head, legs, and body. The culprit is a mite that is usually present on the skin surface of all dogs; however, in some dogs, the population of this mite virtually explodes and wreaks havoc with a Chi's health. This condition is treatable, and even the most severe cases can generally be managed with medications.

Pattern Baldness

Pattern baldness usually begins with a thinning of hair underneath the dog's neck, in her temple area, and on the chest, stomach, and back of the thighs. The thinning continues until these areas are completely void of all hair. Over time, the skin in these areas may darken and become scaly. The good news is that the condition doesn't seem to bother the dog in any way; the bad news is that there's really nothing that can be done to prevent or regrow the dog's hair.

Color Dilution Alopecia

Color dilution alopecia is an inherited loss of coat that tends to affect Chihuahuas with fawn or blue (light to dark gray) coloring the most. A Chi with this disease usually has small outbreaks of infected hair follicles (which appear as little bumps) on her back. As the disease progresses, the Chi's coat continues to thin until the age of two to three years, at which time the Chi's coat is bald on all the light-colored areas of her body. The exposed skin is susceptible to sunburn (use sunscreen!) and can be scaly in appearance. There is no way to regrow the lost hair; however, as with pattern baldness, the condition does not seem to cause the Chi any discomfort.

The "C" Word

It's the word no one wants to hear; however, as the life spans of our beloved pets continue to lengthen, the risk of developing cancer increases, too. The Chihuahua is not at increased risk for any particular cancer. Still, it is always wise to recognize the ten warning signs of cancer and to seek veterinary medical attention immediately.

A trip is warranted to the veterinarian if your Chi shows one or more of these signs:

1. Abnormal swellings that persist or continue to grow
2. Sores that do not heal
3. Weight loss
4. Loss of appetite
5. Bleeding or discharge from any body opening
6. Offensive odor
7. Difficulty eating or swallowing
8. Hesitation to exercise or loss of stamina
9. Persistent lameness or stiffness
10. Difficulty breathing, urinating, or defecating

Reprinted courtesy of the American Veterinary Medical Association

Methods, modalities, medications, and treatments to help slow, halt or cure various cancers are becoming more available and many are very much within financial reach of even the cash-strapped pet owners.

If your Chihuahua is diagnosed with cancer, listen to your veterinarian, research your options, and make good, educated choices. Cancer no longer has to be a death sentence. However, it is important to place everything in perspective and choose the care plan that is most likely to maintain a high quality of life for your Chi.

CHAPTER  19

The Senior Chi

A healthy Chihuahua can live a very long time. Even the average lifespan of fourteen to sixteen years is nearly double that of many large- and giant-breed dogs. Along with longevity can come some aches and pains and perhaps a few special needs. Caring for an aging Chihuahua, however, is rarely a chore. Instead, it's a way for us to show our love by offering a little extra care and tenderness in sincere appreciation for all the years of joy we've received from our dogs.

Seniors and Geriatrics

Veterinarians label aging canines as either "senior" or "geriatric." A dog is considered to be a senior when she has lived two-thirds the average lifespan for her breed. The expected lifespan of a healthy Chihuahua is roughly fourteen to sixteen, so a Chi would become a senior at the age of ten.

The point at which a Chihuahua is old enough to be labeled a geriatric is when she is halfway through the final third of her expected lifespan. In other words, a Chi would be considered a geriatric when she's thirteen years old.

As your Chihuahua ages, she will undergo changes. These changes are generally subtle and often occur over a long period of time; however, they will affect your Chihuahua both physically as well as mentally. Anticipating these changes and knowing how to best address them will go far to extend the quality of your Chihuahua's final years with you.

 **Fact**

> The average life expectancy of a purebred dog decreases as the height and weight increases. It should be no surprise then that toys have a lifespan that is nearly twice that of many large- and giant-breed dogs.

Grooming

Paying attention to your Chihuahua's coat, skin and nails is just as important now as it was when your Chi was in her prime. Brushing or combing your Chihuahua daily makes you very familiar with your dog's normal body contours. By knowing what is "normal," you will quickly spot any suspicious lumps, bumps or tender areas on your Chi's body.

 **Alert!**

> Diseases of all kinds have the best potential outcome if they are caught in their earliest stages.

Senior dogs, particularly those that are overweight, frequently develop fatty tumors or lipomas. These are harmless, spongy tumors that can be found just under the skin. Even if you think the lump you've found is a lipoma, have your veterinarian check to confirm that the lump is not a more dangerous tumor, such as a mast cell tumor (MCT).

MCTs often appear on older dogs and vary in their appearance. Some MCTs are relatively benign in that they are slow to grow and don't seem intent on spreading. More aggressive forms of MCT metastasize or spread to the dog's lymph nodes, bone marrow, liver, and spleen.

Brushing

Another change you may notice as you brush your dog is the beginnings of a sore on his tail or paws. Often, older dogs become bored and will lick themselves as a response. The licking can become obsessive with the Chi actually licking away layers of skin to create sores. More involvement and activities with your Chi will help him in the long run. In the short term, seek veterinary advice on healing the sores and preventing more damage.

Daily brushing, of course, has many other benefits. Whether you have a shorthaired or longhaired Chihuahua, grooming your elderly Chi not only provides you with opportunities to spot disease in its early stages and gives her added quality time with you (reducing the boredom factor), it also increases blood flow to the skin. Increased blood circulation to the surface provides aging skin with much-needed nutrients.

Brushing also works to counter dry, flaky skin that is so often a problem with aging dogs. Brushing all the way to the skin (more difficult but exceedingly important with longhaired Chihuahuas) stimulates the secretion of oils, a natural lubricant that keeps the dog's skin from becoming dry and flaky. These oils, when spread evenly throughout the dog's coat (by brushing), also work to make dull, dry hair more lustrous and less brittle.

Toenails

You would think that age would slow the growth of a dog's toenails. In reality, many elderly dogs have issues with nails that are far too long. The reason for this is most often that the aging Chihuahua has become less active. Without her frequent, long walks around the neighborhood or in the city, her toenails aren't being naturally filed down every day by the concrete surfaces of sidewalks and streets.

 Essential

Don't forget to look between your Chi's toes. If she is longhaired and tends to grow hair between the pads of her feet, this can cause her to slip and slide on slick floors. Keep these areas neat and trimmed short so she can get as much traction as possible.

If a Chihuahua's toenails are too long, you will hear them clicking when she walks on a hard floor. This affects the Chi's mobility. Long toenails cause the foot to spread and shifts the dog's balance from a more forward position on the toes to the heel of the paw. Think of it as wearing stilettos, only backwards. Your Chihuahua is more likely to slip, become unbalanced, and even fall. And, if your Chi has any soreness at all in her joints, long toenails will seriously affect her ability to move and can cause lameness. Cut those toenails!

Nutrition

As your Chihuahua ages, her nutritional needs change, too. Obviously, if your Chi is less active than she once was, she won't need the calories she required as a youngster. You can reduce your Chihuahua's caloric intake by either decreasing the amount of food she is fed on a daily basis, or you can keep the portion size the same but provide her with a reduced-calorie food.

 Alert!

Obesity is a huge problem among less active, older dogs. Every extra ounce on a Chihuahua places additional stress on worn out joints, as well as the Chi's heart. And, research indicates that overweight dogs are twice as likely to suffer from cancer as their more slender counterparts.

But caloric needs are not the only changes that an aging Chihuahua experiences, and this is where meeting the Chihuahua's nutritional needs becomes more complex. Elderly dogs lose some of their ability to taste as well as their ability to metabolize food efficiently.

Addressing the Changing Palate

The commercial foods available today are made to be highly palatable or very appealing to dogs. In fact, many dogs find these foods so good that they overeat. With an older dog, however, the ability to taste what she is eating begins to dull. Suddenly the food she enjoyed eating previously isn't doing the trick for her anymore.

If you find that your Chihuahua is turning her nose up at what had been her favorite food, try revving up her appetite by increasing the smell of the food. Add a bit of something strong smelling and decidedly delectable, such as a little chicken broth or even a small amount of canned dog food.

Absorption Woes

Another change that senior dogs experience is decreased ability of their gastrointestinal tract to absorb important nutrients. Signs that your Chihuahua is not metabolizing her food well include increased stools, increased odor of stools, and weight loss. If your Chihuahua continues to eat a particular food that she can't metabolize, she can become malnourished.

If this is the case, talk to your veterinarian about alternative food choices. Some high-end, quality pet-food manufacturers have addressed this situation with foods specifically formulated for seniors. These foods contain higher concentrations of better quality nutrients in more easily digestible forms. Be sure to read labels carefully, as some foods packaged as senior products are actually weight-reduction formulas for seniors. Make sure you know what you are buying, as well as the quality and integrity of the manufacturer.

Exercise

An area in which many owners fail their aging Chihuahuas is in the exercise department. Older dogs may not spring to their feet and race to the door as they used to when they thought there was a chance of a walk. In fact, it may take a lot of convincing on your part to get the senior Chi to get off the couch and out the front door. Walks and other forms of exercise, however, are exceedingly important—not only in keeping your Chihuahua mobile but also mentally alert.

If your Chihuahua is already plagued with mobility problems, consider allowing her to swim for exercise. Because the Chihuahua is so small, you don't have to own your own pool for this. A large children's splash pool, if filled with enough water, can become a lap pool for your Chi.

 **Question?**

How much exercise should an older Chihuahua be getting?
The key to exercising an older Chihuahua is to let the Chi set the pace. She may not want to walk as far or as fast as she used to, for example, but she can walk the same amount of time. Or she may not be able to run after balls thrown across your backyard, but a ball tossed a few feet will give her a good chase. Follow her lead and know to stop when she tires.

In colder months, you can use a temperate spa to encourage your Chi to exercise—without any jets turned on, of course. Chihuahuas are not recognized as terrific swimmers, so make sure that you are always alongside your Chi when she is in the water, and take her introduction to water slowly. You might also consider purchasing her a doggie life jacket. These help greatly with a dog's ability to float.

Mental Stimulation

Dogs can suffer from decreased mental abilities just as aging humans can. Previously, dog owners thought there was nothing much they could do to counter this sad degeneration of the mind, but now we know much the opposite is true. You can have a direct influence on your aging Chihuahua's mental health.

The "use it or lose it" adage applies to aging dogs and their mental capacities. Research has shown that mentally stimulated elderly dogs retain their cognitive abilities at a significantly higher rate than those dogs that are not mentally stimulated. So, just how do you mentally stimulate a Chihuahua? In several ways!

A New Friend

If you've been dying to add a second Chihuahua to your household, veterinary behavior experts say this is the time to do it. A puppy will naturally create a myriad of new experiences for the older dog. The puppy will also interact with the older Chihuahua, whether she likes it or not. And, the puppy will breathe new life into a geriatric dog, often resurrecting the puppy in the old dog if just for brief moments at a time.

 **Fact**

Generally, senior dogs will readily accept puppies into their lives since the puppy is not seen as a direct threat. If, however, your older dog has issues and is dog-dog aggressive, it would be wiser not to introduce a puppy. Rather, mentally stimulate your older Chi in another way.

Exercise

If your Chihuahua is still mobile, take her out for walks. The sights, sounds, and smells are different every time you and your Chi go out. These kinds of experiences help to keep an elderly dog's mind alert and the dog more attentive. If your Chihuahua is *not* mobile, you can still offer her new experiences. Pack her up in your carry bag (with a good view of the world) and take her with you everywhere. Walk the neighborhood. Go for rides in the car (there are products available to elevate her carrier so she can see out the windows). Drive through the drive through. Create a carrier that fits in your bicycle basket and go for rides together. The more she sees, smells, and experiences, the more she'll be using her brain and stimulating those neurons!

Games

Old dogs *can* learn new tricks, and they can do so pretty well, thank you very much. One fun game to mentally stimulate your geriatric Chihuahua is "find the treat." Take a small bit of chicken or a hot dog and drag it a short distance across the floor. Have your Chihuahua start at the beginning of the trail and scent her way to the treat. Increase the length of the trail as your Chi catches on and shows interest in the game.

Continue to play the old games your Chihuahua has always loved, too. The key is in modifying these games, as needed, to meet your Chihuahua's current abilities. If your Chi is too frail to fetch a ball anymore but still loves the game, try rolling the ball a short distance and without too much speed. Does she like squeaky toys? What about a gentle little game of tug? Do whatever you can think of to keep your dog thinking. Get down on the floor and get silly; you might be surprised how perky your Chihuahua gets!

Time with You

And, finally, give your elderly Chihuahua lots of time with you. Stroke her. Cuddle with her. Talk to her. You are the center of her universe and have been for her entire life. Giving her a little extra TLC will be greatly appreciated, and this contact does work her gray matter. Every little bit helps to keep your Chi as sharp as she can be.

Veterinary Exams

As a dog ages, her need to see a veterinarian for regular wellness exams increases. This is not a ploy by the veterinary community to make more money. Rather, it is an effort to help spot illnesses quickly and find remedies or solutions to potentially lethal ailments. Here's why more regular exams are necessary. A twelve-year-old dog that weighs less than twenty pounds is roughly equivalent in age to a sixty-four-year-old man. At thirteen years of age, the Chihuahua is now the equivalent of a seventy-two-year-old man.

Now ask yourself, "If I were sixty-four years old, would I wait four years between visits to my doctor?" Of course not! But this is exactly what we are doing when we take our senior dogs to the veterinarian once a year. The recommendation to up your visits to twice a year with an elderly Chi is a minimum. Quarterly visits would be even better.

 Question?

Does my geriatric Chi still need vaccinations?
She will be required by law to continue receiving a rabies vaccination (yearly or every three years, depending on the state). However, because of the Chihuahua's higher risk of suffering a reaction to a vaccination, coupled with the fact that vaccinations temporarily lower a dog's immune system, your veterinarian may recommend to withhold booster shots if your Chihuahua is already in frail health.

Of course, your aging Chihuahuas first line of defense is you. If you are observant, you will be the first to notice if something is out of the ordinary. Even if you can't put your finger on it but know something is wrong with your Chi (for instance, a change in temperament or some more general malaise), call your veterinarian. It's always better to err on the side of being too safe than ignore a problem until the condition becomes serious.

Aging Ailments

Senior dogs of all breeds can suffer a variety of conditions that are primarily the results of years of living and parts simply beginning to wear out. For example, we've already touched on the Chihuahua's senses dulling with the geriatric's loss of taste and the effects it can have with appetite. In addition to taste, other senses diminish as well, as follows:

- **Hearing**—Does your Chi not turn her head when you call her name or hear the word "cookie" when whispered anymore? Chances are she's losing some of her hearing. You can help her with other aids to get her attention, such as a stomp on the floor (don't scare her!), or a very soft hum from an electric collar device made specifically for hearing-impaired or deaf dogs.
- **Vision**—Many pet owners don't realize their dogs have lost nearly all their vision because their canines adapt so well using their other senses. When a geriatric loses sight, however, she often doesn't have the other senses to rely upon. Don't rearrange the furniture or leave things lying about. Do use your voice to wake her before touching her, and do adapt games to keep her mentally stimulated with highly scented articles and close-up games such as tug.
- **Increased sensitivity**—Thunderstorms, in particular, seem to be more disturbing to some Chihuahuas as they age. Your Chihuahua may find some easing of anxieties with the holistic treatment, Rescue Remedy, or the synthetic hormone DAP. Your veterinarian may also be able to prescribe medications in extreme cases.

Temperature Control

Chihuahuas already have problems with maintaining body heat. As a breed, they have a tendency to get chilled easily. When the Chi ages, this tendency becomes increasingly pronounced.

Signs that your Chihuahua is cold include burrowing deeply into bedding in a tight, little ball (to conserve heat), and shivering.

To prevent your Chihuahua from becoming chilled, keep the thermostat a couple of degrees higher in the winter and in the summer. If this is cost-prohibitive or puts you in an uncomfortable climate, provide your aging Chihuahua with lots of warm, deep bedding that she can burrow down into to keep warm. Other solutions include placing her crate and bedding in warm, sunny spots around the house that do not have drafts; purchasing sweaters and other pullovers that can be worn on cold days in the house and cool days outdoors; and considering purchasing an electric heating pad if your Chihuahua can sleep on it without trying to shred the pad or chew the cord.

Mobility

Arthritis is a condition that affects all older pets. Arthritis, painful inflammation of the joints, is caused by the gradual wearing down of the natural cushioning (cartilage) between the bones of joints. Disease (for instance, luxating patellas) and/or trauma to joints can hasten this attrition, causing a Chihuahua to suffer pain at an earlier age. Symptoms of arthritis include the following:

- Inflammation
- Redness
- Tenderness to touch
- Heat in area
- Licking of joint
- Stiffness
- Limping
- Difficulties rising after lying down
- Reluctance to go up or down stairs
- Seeking out heat to lie on even on very hot days
- Aggression

Fortunately, there are many ways to help ease your Chihuahua's discomfort. First, however, you need to get a confirmation from your veterinarian that your Chi's mobility problems are truly due to arthritis. Some of these symptoms could indicate an entirely different condition or disease.

Nutritional supplements that are often added to senior dog foods to help halt or improve the degeneration of the joints are glucosamine and chondroiton sulfate. Nutritional supplements that are commonly prescribed to be added to a senior's diet may include polysulfated glycosaminoglycans (PSGAGs); selenium; vitamins C, E, and the B-complex; digestive enzymes; omega-3 fatty acids; superoxide dismutase (SOD); and green-lipped mussels. Shark cartilage was previously recommended; however, because of the over-fishing of this animal, it is no longer supported by environmentally conscious practitioners.

 **Alert!**

A new sufferer of arthritis (a year or less) or one that has periodic arthritic flare-ups benefits from cold packs on the ailing joint. A small pack of frozen peas is perfect for this job because they conform to the joint, and by the time it thaws, the treatment time is over. You can refreeze the pack of peas and use them again and again. Just be sure to label the pack so you don't eat them accidentally.

Holistic modalities used to treat arthritis and lessen a dog's pain include acupuncture, chiropractic, and massage therapy. These forms of care can be exceptionally helpful if the practitioner is skilled. Other therapies can include herbal remedies that include herbs such as buckbean, wild yam, valerian root, white willow bark, and alfalfa. Chinese herbal combinations containing multiple herbs in treating arthritis include Liu Wei di Huang Wan and Chin Koo Tieh Shang Wan. Consult your holistic practitioner for more information.

Heat is very comforting to the long-time, chronic sufferer of arthritis. The application of heat to the joint relieves pain, increases blood circulation to the joint and muscles, and relaxes muscle spasms. Use a light, small hot-water bottle wrapped in a hand towel.

Exercise is also important in maintaining joint mobility in the arthritic dog. Yes, it hurts when they first begin moving after a period of lying down; however, moderate and light exercise is beneficial in keeping the muscles surrounding the arthritic joint strong, which in turn provides the aching joint with more support—and less pressure to the joint.

▲ Age is nothing but a number to older Chis who are healthy and properly cared for.

Conventional veterinary care—in addition to using many of the complimentary treatments listed above—include the use of nonsteroidal anti-inflammatory drugs (NSAIDs), corticoid steroids (prednisone), and Rimadyl. These medications all have potentially serious side effects that your veterinarian will carefully weigh with the severity of your Chihuahua's arthritis and discomfort.

Incontinence

Your Chi has been perfect (or nearly perfect) all her life and then suddenly, she begins urinating more frequently or has an accident or two. What's going on? It is quite normal for older dogs to require more frequent opportunities to relieve themselves. As they age, they can't hold it for the long periods they could manage as younger dogs. Litter pans and doggie doors are extremely helpful because they allow the Chi to relieve herself whenever the need strikes.

If, however, you notice that your Chi is drinking enormous amounts of water, urinating repeatedly seconds after emptying her bladder, has blood in her urine, or wakes up in a pool of urine wondering what happened, you're dealing with something more than just an elderly dog's lessened ability to hold.

Your veterinarian will want to rule out illnesses such as diabetes, Cushing's disease, bladder stones, and urinary tract infection, among others. If the problem is incontinence, it could stem from lowered estrogen levels (in a female Chi) or a lack of the hormone naturally produced by both male and female dogs that limits the production of urine while the dog is sleeping. Medications are available to help lessen these conditions.

Heart to Heart

Older dogs of all breeds run a higher risk of developing an enlarged heart. This condition limits the dog's ability to efficiently pump blood through her body, making her tire more quickly, and cough as her heart enlarges against her lungs, among other symptoms. There is no cure for this form of heart disease, but there are several medications that are available that can greatly improve the quality of your Chi's life.

Making Life Easier

Our Chihuahuas can live a long, healthy life; however, they don't live forever. Perhaps the most important role we can play in our aging dogs' lives is to provide them all the care and attention they could possibly need—and then some. Be attentive to any changes that your Chihuahua displays that she didn't previously. And be creative when it comes to making your Chihuahua's life easier.

If mobility is an issue, place floor mats on slick floors that are difficult to navigate. If your Chi can't hop up into bed using a chair as a stepping stone, build her a ramp so that she can get up when she wants to on her own. A raised dog bowl can help an arthritic Chihuahua eat her meals more comfortably.

And, know when it's time to let go. Don't ignore what your Chihuahua (and your veterinarian) is telling you. Your Chi has been too wonderful of a companion to allow her to suffer for days, weeks, or even months with a debilitating, irreversible illness. Though she would be the first creature to forgive you for putting her through this agony, she will also be the most appreciative of your parting kindness of alleviating her pain. And worry not; she'll be patiently waiting for you at the Rainbow Bridge.

CHAPTER 20

Traveling with Your Chi

One of the beauties of owning a Chihuahua is that this compact breed is so easy to take traveling with you. Virtually anywhere a dog is allowed, your Chihuahua is welcome. If you've worked to socialize her and acclimate her to new surroundings, traveling with you will be a blast for your Chi, too.

The Benefits of a Small Dog

Weighing an average of four pounds has its advantages. The Chihuahua often can go where other dogs can't—in the cabin while jetting cross-country, in a designer bag worn over the shoulder at a tony boutique in Paris, overnight at exclusive hotels in New York City that pamper pooches, and seated outside at cafés sprinkled throughout the country. And, of course, there are the less elite locations (but great fun for the rest of us) that welcome small dogs: home improvement and hardware stores, the outdoor tables at a national coffee store that's everywhere but whose name will not be mentioned, pet supply shops, local parks (as well as many state and some federal parks), camp sites, and many roadside hotel and motels—and that's just to name a few.

As you can see, owning a toy breed has many advantages when it comes to travel. The toy breeds, particularly the Chihuahua, are almost always welcome in dog-friendly locations. Being small makes the Chi less intimidating to non-dog people, too, so people in not-so-dog-friendly locations are less likely to complain that a dog is present.

 **Fact**

In many countries, canines of all sizes are allowed on trains, buses, and other public transportation services, as well as in stores and restaurants. In the United States, canines are not allowed in indoor restaurants for health reasons unless the dog is certified as a service dog.

Weighing between a very tiny two pounds and up to six pounds, the Chihuahua is very portable by owners who don't have the strength to carry a larger toy breed. (Of course, there are the oversize Chis that tip the scale at ten pounds and require a bit of muscle for toting; however, that's not the norm.)

Carrier Types and Purposes

When purchasing a crate or carrier specifically for travel, you'll need to decide how the crate will be used the most. Will you be carrying it long distances, such as through a long terminal at the airport? Will you be flying with your Chihuahua, or will most of your travel, if not all, be by car? Where do you plan to stay when you are traveling, and is your Chihuahua destructive when left alone? Do you need a crate that can do it all, or are you in a position in which you could purchase more than one carrier?

Depending on how you answered these questions, one or more types of carriers could be suitable for your travel purposes. Within each type of carrier you'll also find a range of features, as well as prices.

Hard Plastic Shells

Crates that are made of hard plastic usually are quite inexpensive and break down into two large pieces for storage. This is the only type of crate that can be used for shipping dogs in the cargo hold of a plane. Hopefully, you'll never have to do this and will always travel in the cabin with your Chi. This crate is also approved to be placed under the seat in front of you when traveling by plane. (Check with the airlines for current limits on size and weight.) And, of course, it's a very safe and practical way to travel with your Chihuahua in the car.

 **Essential**

Look for carriers with a seat belt feature. Some crates have loops that are made for a seat belt to be threaded through and fastened. A dog in a crate is a good thing; a dog in a belted, secure crate is a better thing.

These crates are very light, but if you are walking any distance with them, the plastic crate is a bit cumbersome to carry. Even with a shoulder strap arrangement, this crate still isn't the easiest to carry. Of course, you can always put it on a luggage cart and wheel your dog around in airports, hotels, and such, but this isn't the crate you'll want if you're taking your dog with you into stores, shops, or for a latte.

Wire Crates

Wire crates come in a variety of styles. Some fold up to carry; others don't fold up as neatly. Wire crates are heavier than plastic, a bit more expensive, and are definitely not something you'd want to carry for any distance other than from the house to the car. They do provide the best air circulation, however, and a great view of the world when traveling in a car. These crates are not approved for air travel, whether in-cabin or in the cargo hold.

 **Alert!**

Be very aware of the difference in temperature in your vehicle. You may have the windows open and enjoying the fresh air while your Chihuahua is overheating in her crate in the back seat. Toy-breed dogs have died because their owners weren't aware that it was so much hotter in back. If necessary, attach a battery-operated fan in your Chi's crate to keep her cool.

Pup Tents

An extremely light, airy, breezy crate that provides shade on warm days and allows cooling breezes to pass through are the mesh, tentlike crates made of screening, nylon fabric, and PVC tubing. As you can imagine, these crates are very easy to stow while traveling and then to unfold and use as an in-room crate while staying at a hotel. The drawbacks to this marvelous invention are that it can't be used safely in the car and is not allowed in an airplane at all. If you have a Chi that suffers from separation anxiety, she will have this crate destroyed in minutes, too.

Soft-Sided Carriers

For many toy-breed owners, the soft-sided carrier is rapidly becoming the traveling crate of choice. Many different manufacturers are producing quality carriers that have a range of features. Most importantly, the best carriers are durable, allow for plenty of ventilation, are convenient to load and unload (with top-loading and front-door options), easy to clean, and are lightweight and comfortable to carry. There are no sharp corners or rigid plastic sides to bang against your legs as you walk.

Additionally, many soft-sided carriers are approved for in-cabin travel. These carriers are semi-collapsible with a flexible frame that crunches down slightly to fit under cabin seats and springs back to allow your Chi a bit more space when you're not airborne. Options can include extra pockets to carry travel necessities, including brushes, medications, and food; loops for securing the carrier with a seat belt; and retractable wheels and handle for transforming the carrier into a rolling carrier. There's also a myriad of fabrics, leathers, and other materials to choose from. Prices range from moderate and affordable to pricey and over the top.

Other Options

Your options don't stop at just carriers, however. Products that are also available for travel include a belted harness and booster seats. The belted harness is a very safe traveling option that allows your Chihuahua to stand up, turn around, and lie down or sit in a seat in the car.

Depending on the manufacturer, the seat belt either threads through the harness, or the harness has its own attachment for the seat. Adding a booster seat made especially for toy breeds (complete with water bottle that can be heated for a warm seat or cooled for a cool seat) allows your Chihuahua to have a great view from the car window.

Around Town

Just because your Chihuahua is easily carried, cute, and adored by all those who see her does not mean that owning a Chi gives you carte blanche when it comes to traveling. Before you take off for a day of shopping or to dine with a friend, find out whether the locations you are going to allow dogs. Be forewarned: Most do not. Those boutiques, stores, and cafés that do allow dogs are few and far between, but they are growing in popularity.

When taking your Chihuahua with you when you're running around town, here are some good rules to live by that will also serve to help keep dogs welcome:

- Don't think you can sneak your Chi in with you. If you get caught, and you will, the store has the right to prevent you from shopping there again—permanently. (It has happened.)
- Make sure your dog has good manners and is in control at all times.
- Know your dog's limits. If large crowds scare her, don't overwhelm her with a trip to a crowded park.
- Don't say "yes" when you mean "no." Control what kind of contact your Chihuahua has and who she has it with. People will want to pet the cute doggie, but if you know your Chi snaps, warn them off (nicely).
- Clean up after your Chihuahua. Don't run to the next aisle and pretend it wasn't your dog.
- Even if you plan on keeping your Chi in an over-the-shoulder pet carrier, always carry a leash with you.
- Bring a portable, foldable water bowl.
- Don't leave your Chihuahua alone in the car even for a second. You may be delayed while shopping, and the car will heat up much more quickly than you anticipated, making your beloved Chi suffer or die.
- Be careful how wide you crack the window if your Chi is loose in the car. A Chihuahua can escape from any vehicle if she can squeeze her head through the opening.

A lot of success in taking your Chihuahua with you on a daily basis hinges on your common sense and good manners—on both your part and your dog's. If your Chihuahua is well trained, well socialized, and comfortable in new surroundings, and if you are cognizant of being a good dog owner, cleaning up after your dog and not trying to break the rules by toting your Chi along, you and your dog will not only be a welcome sight, but you'll also enjoy your outings that much more.

Overnighting

Rules, rules, rules. To make your travels easier when you have your Chihuahua with you, it's important to know the rules. That pretty much determines how enjoyable your stay is when overnighting in a hotel, motel, or bed-and-breakfast. Okay, with this said, more and more hotels, motels, and even some B&Bs are becoming more open to traveling pets, especially those dogs that are as small as the Chihuahua.

Annual publications from AAA and independent publishers (both on the Internet and in book or magazine form) publish listings of all hotels—from national chains to privately owned hotels—that welcome pets. Some guides will even offer listings of dog-friendly outdoor restaurants, popular dog walks, and interesting canine boutiques in the area. Use these publications as a starting point, but always follow up with a telephone confirmation. Management changes and so do rules. Confirming the hotel's policies can avoid an unpleasant surprise.

 **Alert!**

Call ahead and make reservations. Confirm that the hotel allows dogs and is aware that you are bringing your Chihuahua. Expect to pay a surcharge for a dog in the room and/or a deposit for potential damages that will be reimbursed to you at the end of your stay—barring any damage.

Ground Rules

When staying at a hotel with your Chi, keep her on leash at all times. Walk her (for relief purposes) in less-traveled areas. In other words, don't walk your Chi right by the pool or on a path to the lobby. Many hotels have specific dog areas in which to take your Chi; however, these areas can be a breeding ground for all kinds of disease, not to mention worms and other parasites. If possible, walk your Chi in an out-of-the-way place and clean up after her. Always.

Crate your Chihuahua if you must leave your room for dinner or another activity. Hang the "Do Not Disturb" sign on the door, and alert the front desk that your dog is in the room and you would prefer maid service later. There are two reasons for doing these things. First, Chihuahuas are a popular breed that are sometimes stolen, and you don't want to lose your dog accidentally. Second, if your Chi is running loose in the room and maid service enters your room, chances are that your dog is going to zoom past this person and take flight. A Chihuahua lost in a strange city may never be found.

Identification

When traveling with your Chihuahua, take every precaution you can that if your Chihuahua gets loose, you have the best possible chances of recovering your Chi. Begin with a collar or halter that has a nametag. On the tag, put your name and your cell phone number with area code. When you're traveling, if you've put your home phone number on the tag, you might not hear the message that your dog was just down the street until you arrive home.

Next, have your Chihuahua permanently identified with either a tattoo, a microchip, or both. The tattoo is permanent and is placed on one thigh of the dog. (Tattooing is usually done under anesthesia; a good time to do this is when your Chihuahua is being altered.) Owners commonly use their Chihuahua's registration number and then register this tattoo with one or more national registries.

A microchip is roughly the size of a grain of sand and is inserted with a needle between the dog's shoulder blades. The microchip has a unique code that can be read by microchip readers used in veterinary offices, shelters, and pounds. A drawback to the microchip is that if someone finds your Chihuahua, he might not realize that the Chihuahua has any identification unless he takes the dog to the veterinarian or a shelter.

Usually, a combination of tags, tattoo and microchip will cover all the bases as best as possible. Additionally, carry with you a clear photograph of your Chihuahua. If she gets lost, you can quickly make posters and flyers and place ads in local papers.

▲ **When traveling with your Chi, make sure to bring some of the comforts of home, like certain toys and their bedding.**

Jetsetters

If you plan on traveling by air with your Chihuahua, always travel with your dog in the cabin of the plane. There is no reason for your Chi to risk the dangers of riding in the belly of the plane. When making travel arrangements, purchase a ticket for your Chi to ride in the cabin. This usually costs between $50 and $80 each way.

Before your Chihuahua will be allowed to travel, she will need a health certificate signed by your veterinarian no older than ten days prior to the departing flight date. You will need to show this certificate before you will be allowed to travel. Additionally, though fairly standard, each airline has its own limits as far as dimensions for your pet carrier and the carrier's total weight.

 Essential

Some airlines do not allow pets in cabin; other airlines will only allow a set amount of pets on a flight (usually one or two), so don't wait until you're at the ticket counter to purchase a ticket for your Chi. Make sure that any connecting flights are on planes that are large enough to allow dogs to travel in cabin. Not all are.

Most Chihuahuas in carriers will have no difficulties coming under this weight limit; however, if you use your carrier to cart along your dog's meds, supplies, food, and water, you could end up with have an overweight pet. Find out the exact weight limit for your airline, and weigh your Chi and carrier and all that you want to stuff in the carrier.

Preparations

When flying with your dog, it is usually helpful to withhold all food and snacks from your Chi for at least four hours prior to flight time. Water should be withdrawn about an hour before your flight. Walk your dog thoroughly as close to flight time as you can.

 Alert!

Be prepared to remove your Chihuahua from her carrier and carry her with you as you go through the metal detector at the security checkpoint. Do not run your carrier through the X-ray machine with your dog in it! This is extremely dangerous for your dog.

Line your Chi's crate with multiple layers of pee pads or a similar product. Then, if your Chi has an accident, you can slide the soiled pad out and throw it away. If travel really stresses your Chihuahua, consider using calming agents such as DAP and the flower essence Rescue Remedy to help. Your veterinarian will not give you sedatives for your Chihuahua's travel; these meds have been determined to be far more detrimental to your Chi than being nervous.

When Your Chihuahua Can't Come with You

There will be times when your Chihuahua cannot travel with you: business travel, trips to foreign countries (particularly those that require quarantine), or travel to Hawaii (the only state that requires a thirty-day minimum quarantine). You may also not want to travel with your Chihuahua if traveling is traumatic for your Chi.

If you find yourself in this position, you have several choices. You can count on family, friends, or neighbors. This is fine if you are fortunate enough to have extremely reliable people to count on. You must be able to trust that they will not only care for your Chihuahua but will recognize an illness or emergency and seek veterinary care immediately.

Most of us will find ourselves in a position in which we will need to pay for professional care. In addition to budgeting this option into the canine annual fund, finding a pet sitter or boarding kennel is not something that can be done at the last minute. Give yourself at least a month to interview and investigate sitter services and boarding facilities. Keep in mind, too, that holidays and summer are very busy times and book up quickly.

Pet Sitter

A pet sitter is an individual who comes to your home and feeds, plays with, and cares for your Chihuahua while you are gone. Remaining in the home around all that is familiar to her is much more comfortable and less traumatic than sending your Chi to a kennel filled with dogs. In addition to being a good alternative for your Chi, a pet sitter will water your plants, bring in the mail and newspaper, open and close blinds, turn lights on and off, and perform many other individualized duties as agreed upon prior to the visits.

It is important to find a pet sitter with whom both you and your Chihuahua are comfortable. The pet sitter should be bonded and able to explain her liabilities, your liabilities, and precisely what her contract spells out. Ask for references and call these people. Find out what this pet sitter is like and if she's honest and trustworthy and good with dogs.

Boarding Kennels

In order for your Chihuahua to be able to be boarded, she must have a current bordatella vaccine. She must also be at least fourteen to sixteen weeks old and fully vaccinated. A boarding kennel has the potential to transmit too many diseases to risk boarding a young puppy that hasn't built up her immunity to fatal illnesses.

Before making reservations to board your Chihuahua, request a tour of the kennel's facilities. They should be clean and without any strong odors. Look to see how the dogs are kept. Some kennels crate smaller dogs and allow them outside several times a day, while others provide an indoor pen and an outdoor run.

 Essential

Gather referrals from friends with dogs, your breeder, and your veterinarian as to suggestions for boarding kennels. Also, when visiting the kennel, ask the manager or owner for references. As always, call these people. Ask questions.

Find out how the dogs are exercised. Are they turned out in groups or exercised individually. What additional services do they offer? Boarding kennels vary from offering just the basic services all the way up to very posh, very expensive, full-service kennels. Trust your gut feelings when choosing a kennel. If something doesn't feel right or a person rubs you the wrong way, keep looking. Find the one that best fits your preferences, your Chihuahua's needs, and your budget.

Planning for the Unknown

No one can see the future. Accidents happen. Tragedies occur. And, as Americans now know all too well, terrorists strike. The best way to handle unforeseen events is to have a plan on how to handle the what-if situations.

Have a backup plan for if you don't come home to your dog one day. If you don't have a family member who would know that you are missing, can you count on a trusted friend or neighbor? You'll want this individual to know you have a dog and that you come home every day. You'll want him to have a key to your home to take care of your dog or at least have a number he can call if he thinks something has happened to you.

Post a sticker on your window saying that you have a dog. In case of fire, firefighters will know that they are also looking for a pet. Post a care plan or message that there is a care plan so that if you can't get into your home or apartment and only emergency personnel are in the building, they will know to look for an animal when they are making rounds of the building.

Finally, make arrangements for the care of your Chihuahua should you pass away. Remember that often friends or family may say they would always take your dog for you; in reality, this is often not the case. Don't think that you can will your dog to someone and leave the money in trust to your pet. A pet is not considered a person who has rights. They are chattel.

Ideally, you can make arrangements with a friend; however, back it up with alternative arrangements. Many owners have had good success with making arrangements for a trusted Chihuahua rescue to take the dog and rehome her if possible. If not, a set amount of money can be donated to the rescue specifically for the Chi's care for the remainder of her life.

 **Alert!**

Keep your Chi's medications in one place and make sure the care plan explains how these medications are to be given. Also note emergency numbers where you might be reached so that rescuers can tell you where your dog is.

We all hope that we outlive our Chihuahuas, but if this is not the case, make sure the little one who has given you so much love for so many years will be taken care of and that she won't be left alone, dumped, or disposed of. You owe it to her and, as they say, it will give you peace of mind that you've taken care of her. And then? You can forget about it and live life to the fullest with your enthusiastic canine companion.

Additional Resources

T he Chihuahua has so much more going for it than could ever be included in one volume, and you're bound to be interested in one or more specific aspects of the breed. In case your interest has been piqued in the breed's health issues, its history, or if you're just looking for more activities to participate in with your Chihuahua, many additional resources are included here to help you continue your Chi education.

Breed Clubs

Chihuahua Club of America
AKC Breeder Referral
      Representative
Josephine DeMenna
2 Maple Street
Wilton, CT 06897
ccgny@sbcglobal.net
www.chihuahuaclubofamerica.com

Chihuahua Club of Canada
2114 Dublin Street
New Westminster
Province, BC
Canada V3M 3A9
604-521-0922

The British Chihuahua Club
Mr. N. Farrugia
64 Kingham Close
Wandsworth
London
SW18 3BX
www.the-british-chihuahua-club.org.uk

All-Breed Registries

American Kennel Club
5880 Centerview Drive, Suite 200
Raleigh, NC 27606-3390
919-233-3600
www.akc.org

American Mixed-Breed Obedience Registry (AMBOR)
179 Niblick Road, #113
Paso Robles, CA 93446
805-226-9275
ambor@amborusa.org
www.amborusa.org

Canadian Kennel Club
89 Skyway Avenue, Suite 100
Etobicoke, Ontario
M9W 6R4 Canada
416-675-5511
www.ckc.ca

United Kennel Club
100 E. Kilgore Road
Kalamazoo, MI 49001-5598
616-343-9020
www.ukcdogs.com

Health and Behavior

Animal Behaviorists

Animal Behavior Society (certified animal behaviorists)
Indiana University
2611 East 10th Street, #170
Bloomington, IN 47408-2603
812-856-5541
aboffice@indiana.edu
www.animalbehavior.org

American College of Veterinary Behaviorists
Dr. Bonnie V. Beaver, Executive Director
Texas A&M University
Department of Small Animal
   Medicine & Surgery
4474 TAMU
College Station, TX 77843-4474
979-845-2351
bbeaver@cvm.tamu.edu

Disease Registries

Canine Eye Registration Foundation (CERF)
Purdue University
CERF/Lynn Hall
625 Harrison Street
W. Lafayette, IN 47907-2026
765-494-8179
canineeye@purdue.edu

VetCancer Registry
Dr. H. Steven Steinberg, Coordinator
The VetCancer Registry
P. O. Box 352, 168 West Main Street
New Market, MD 21774
info@vetcancerregistry.com
www.vetcancerregistry.com

Orthopedic Foundation for Animals (OFA)
2300 E. Nifong Boulevard
Columbia, MS 65201-3856
573-442-0418
ofa@offa.org
www.offa.org

Veterinarians

American Animal Hospital Association (AAHA)
P.O. Box 150899
Denver, CO 80215-0899
303-986-2800
info@aahanet.org
www.aahanet.org

American Veterinary Medical Association (AVMA)
1931 North Meacham Road, Suite 100
Schaumburg, IL 60173
847-925-8070
avmainfo@avma.org
www.avma.org

American Holistic Veterinary Medical Association (AHVMA)
Dr. Carvel G. Tiekert,
    Executive Director
2218 Old Emmorton Road
Bel Air, MD 21015
410-569-0795
office@ahvma.org
www.ahvma.org

Activities

Agility

American Kennel Club
(see All-Breed Registries)

United Kennel Club
(see All-Breed Registries)

American Mixed-Breed Obedience Registry (see All-Breed Registries)

Agility Association of Canada (AAC)
Membership: Arlene Lehmann
16648 Highway 48
Stoufille, ON, L4A 7X4 Canada
905-473-3473
alehmann@cherryhillarabs.on.com
www.aac.ca

North American Dog Agility Council (NADAC)
1152 South Highway 3
Cataldo, ID 83810
info@nadac.com
www.nadac.com

United States Dog Agility Association (USDAA)
P.O. Box 850955
Richardson, TX 75085-0955
972-487-2200
info@usdaa.com
www.usdaa.com

Animal-Assisted Therapy

Delta Society
580 Naches Avenue SW, Suite 101
Renton, WA 98055-2297
425-917-1114
DianneB@deltasociety.org.
www.deltasociety.org

Therapy Dogs International
88 Bartley Road
Flanders, NJ 07836
973-252-9800
tdi@gti.net
www.tdi-dog.org

Canine Good Citizen

American Kennel Club
(see All-Breed Registries)

Conformation

American Kennel Club
(see All-Breed Registries)

United Kennel Club
(see All-Breed Registries)

Freestyle Obedience

Canine Freestyle Federation, Inc.
Joan Tennille, President
4207 Minton Drive
Fairfax, VA 22032
president@canine-freestyle.org
www.canine-freestyle.org

**Musical Dog Sport Association
(MDSA)**
9211 West Road, Suite 143-238
Houston, TX 77064
MDSA@MusicalDogSport.org
www.MusicalDogSport.org

**World Canine Freestyle
Organization, Inc.**
P.O. Box 350122
Brooklyn, NY 11235-2525
718-332-8336
WCFODOGS@aol.com
www.worldcaninefreestyle.org

Obedience

American Kennel Club
(see All-Breed Registries)

United Kennel Club
(see All-Breed Registries)

American Mixed-Breed Obedience
Registry (see All-Breed Registries)

Rally-O

American Kennel Club
(see All-Breed Registries)

**Association of Pet Dog Trainers
(APDT)**
17000 Commerce Parkway, Suite C
Mt. Laurel, NJ 08054
1-800-PET-DOGS
information@apdt.com
www.apdt.com

Chihuahua Rescue

Breed rescues are the number one source for good adult Chihuahuas. If you can't adopt a Chi, please consider volunteering and/or making a donation to a local, regional, or national rescue. If you can drive dogs to the veterinarian, pick up donated food, collect dog-food coupons, or provide a specialized service, such as Web site design or legal services, your generous help will be greatly appreciated. Short on time? Think about stroking a check to your favorite rescue: Chihuahua rescues are always in need of cash to help defray veterinary bills, pay for food, and keep supplies on hand as dogs come in to their foster programs.

National Rescues

Keeping track of contact information for national, regional, and local rescues can be quite frustrating. Internet Web sites and e-mails frequently change, as does the ability of smaller rescues to continue providing such an outstanding service to the breed.

To make things a bit easier, however, the Chihuahua Club of America elects a breed rescue referral representative to help maintain a list of Chihuahua rescues with current contacts. To find current contact information for a Chihuahua rescue in your area, call or e-mail:

Chihuahua Club of America, Inc.
Breed Rescue Referral Representative
Lynnie Bunten
11489 S. Foster Road
San Antonio, TX 78218
210-633-2430
kachina@tgti.net

Chihuahua Rescue and Transport, Inc.
Information and donations:
3414 Pemberton Drive
Pearland, TX 77584
800-876-5504
www.chihuahua-rescue.org

Chihuahua—Toy Breed Rescue & Retirement (CTBRR)
Nick De Pompa, President
7111 SW 9 Street
Pembroke Pines, FL 33023
Chihuawa10@msn.com
www.crar.org

Regional and Local Rescues

Virtually every state and several regions of the country has dedicated Chihuahua fanciers working to rehome unwanted Chihuahuas. Even with these committed individuals working long, hard hours, the numbers of Chis needing homes are still staggering—as is the need for funds to help run these organizations. To find a rescue in your area, contact the CCA's breed rescue referral representative or do an Internet search for "Chihuahua rescue" in your home state. Be aware that Internet contact information can change frequently, so not all information you find will be up to date.

Rescues in Canada

Canadian Chihuahua Rescue & Transport (CCRT)

Canadian Chihuahua Rescue and Transport
Box 33040
Ottawa, Ontario
Canada K2C 3Y9
info@ccrt.net
www.ccrt.net

Index

The Everything® Breed-Specific Series

Trade Paperback, $12.95
ISBN: 1-59337-316-3

Trade Paperback, $12.95
ISBN: 1-59337-048-2

Trade Paperback, $12.95
ISBN: 1-59337-424-0

Trade Paperback, $12.95
ISBN: 1-59337-121-7

Available wherever books are sold!

The definitive, must-have guides for the most popular breeds!

Trade Paperback, $12.95
ISBN: 1-59337-314-7

Trade Paperback, $12.95
ISBN: 1-59337-047-4

Trade Paperback, $12.95
ISBN: 1-59337-423-2

Trade Paperback, $12.95
ISBN: 1-59337-122-5

To order, call 800-289-0963, or visit us at *www.everything.com*

The definitive, must-have guides for the most popular breeds!

Trade Paperback, $12.95
ISBN: 1-59337-527-1

Trade Paperback, $12.95
ISBN: 1-59337-526-3